Political Philosophy

Political Philosophy

From Plato to Mao

Second Edition

MARTIN COHEN

PLUTO PRESS
www.plutobooks.com

First published 2001 by Pluto Press
345 Archway Road, London N6 5AA

Second edition published 2008

www.plutobooks.com

British Library Cataloguing in Publication Data
A catalogue record for this book is available from the British Library

ISBN   978 0 7453 2471 5   Hardback
ISBN   978 0 7453 2470 8   Paperback

Library of Congress Cataloging in Publication Data applied for

10   9   8   7   6   5   4   3   2   1

Designed and produced for Pluto Press by
Chase Publishing Services Ltd, Fortescue, Sidmouth, EX10 9QG, England
Typeset from disk by Stanford DTP Services, Northampton
Printed and bound in the European Union by
CPI Antony Rowe, Chippenham and Eastbourne

To a respected Professor of Confusion Philosophy

Contents

Note to the Second Edition

This book is adapted from my earlier *Political Philosophy: From Plato to Mao* (Pluto Press, 2001). And if many elements are thus reproduced, which might seem a little like mere repetition, it is also an opportunity to build something new using a previously established foundation.

In the original book, I adopted a very subjective view of what is politically significant, and concentrated on that. And now, in the new edition, I have added new chapters, including ones on the Koran, on the Confucian *Analects*, and on Hitler's *Mein Kampf*. It is more evident than ever that treating works written with perhaps very different intentions than expounding political philosophy distorts the original texts. But then, the same is true of more conventional works in philosophy: much of the *Republic* (which is not, of course, solely a political work) has to be discarded to make it suitable for inclusion in a book such as this, and even then, as I explain here, Plato insists he intended the political discussion of the ideal society to be merely an illustration of a more important truth. The same editing and the same distortion must take place too with those keystone works of politics, Hobbes' *Leviathian* and Machiavelli's *The Prince* and *Discourses*. These again are not solely political works, but history, especially military history – and bad history at that.

In the latter portion of the book, the style is further changed of necessity, and rather than picking over the entrails of the ultimately rather unimportant works of Comte, Weber and Durkheim, nor yet Gentile and Mussolini, I opted here for providing a rather more conventional account of their 'ideas', albeit one with as much direct quotation and close paraphrase as is compatible with revealing their arguments. Always, as the aim, attempting to do so in an interesting, accessible and not too lengthy way. (For the same reason, occasionally some of the direct quotation was retranslated, for style or for flow.) Hegel does not, it is true, fit into the category of political philosopher very comfortably, nor yet Nietzsche. They would prefer the lofty heights of metaphysics to the dirty practicalities of politics. But the reader can decide in which realm their writing truly belongs. At the same time, I have also tried to fit these great political texts into a wider scheme, to discern a kind of unfolding pattern. But this is a path littered with traps and failed theories, Marxist or fascist – the folly, as Karl Popper puts it, of historicism.

For a crucial element in this book, as in all books, is that the reader not only may disagree with much in this book, but should do so. The written word appears dispassionate, authoritative, definitive. Yet any writer, much more the political philosopher, is only expressing one perspective, drawn from necessarily incomplete and unreliable information. Here at least, by offering such a wide selection of views, the reader is allowed a chance to judge the evidence and choose between approaches.

And finally, as they say, I would like to thank, once again, Anne Beech at Pluto, for shrewd advice and guidance, and Anthony Winder, copy-editor for both editions, for his professionalism, commitment and overriding desire to 'get it right'. This time, I think we're nearly there!

Introduction

This is the story of political society. It's not an evolutionary story, although some would have us think so. It's not the story of technological advance, far less of economic progress. It's the story of a few powerful ideas, which have been around for millennia, but reappear in different guises. It's a story told in the language of political philosophy, in the words of just a handful of writers.

This branch of philosophy is concerned with practical questions: about the organisation of social life, about the make-up of the government, the role and rights of the citizens, the duties and limitations of the state. But it is not to be unduly concerned with details, the nuts and bolts of particular ways of governing (although many of the great philosophers do like to dabble in these). What characterises political and social philosophy is an awareness and a commitment to answering – or at least raising – certain great questions:

What is happiness? (Human flourishing?)
What is justice?
What is freedom?

Only after the theoretical questions are settled do the practical issues arise:

How can happiness be maximised?
How can justice and equality best be achieved?
How can human rights be respected?

The origins of the word 'political' itself come, like so many others, from ancient Greece: *politikos*, pertaining to the running of the city, or *polis*. In this sense, political philosophy is concerned with the very practical matters of administration. For that reason, Plato's *Republic* discusses not only such obscure matters as the nature of goodness, but also the merits and demerits of various constitutional systems. Machiavelli writes not only of successful duplicity, but also of storming castles and military tactics, and Mill concerns himself not only with liberty, but with corn prices. But despite this practical purpose, 'political philosophy' remains a much wider and deeper subject, concerned with fundamental questions about equality, needs and interests, welfare, and human nature. This is the reason why politics is important – it is a fundamental part of us. As Durkheim later put it, through social rules and conventions, we define and create ourselves.

And, of the philosophers here, each offers a particular response to one or other of the key questions. Plato outlines, in his *Republic*, a solution (although many today will not rush to accept it) to the question of 'justice'; Confucius preaches a view of duty; Aristotle advocates a rationale for discrimination. Hobbes offers a particular view as to the nature of freedom – that it involves a sublimation of individual power into the collective whole; whilst Locke sets out an argument for 'inalienable' human rights.

This book, then, aims to serve as a kind of grand tour of the landscape of political science, not to mention economics, philosophy and sociology. On this journey, our maps will be the timeline sections preceding each chapter, locating each theory in its technical and social context.

On the way, we travel necessarily fast, clutching a comprehensive itinerary amounting almost to a history of civilisation. Starting in the Far East with Imperial China, before examining Greece with its city states, we move across the Tyrrhenian Sea to Machiavelli's Italy, north to the splintered war-torn England of Hobbes' *Leviathan* and Locke's civil rights, on through France, Germany and Russia, eventually to end up in the twentieth century with the most widely read political pamphlet of all time: Chairman Mao's little Red Book. But on this journey we are more than mere political tourists, collecting snapshots. When we pause, it is to thoroughly explore and closely examine what we find, taking out the magnifying glass and investigating in detail, so as not only to recognise the main characteristics of the texts, but also to understand how they were constructed – and why.

Similarly, incorporated into the chapters are short biographical notes on each philosopher, encouraging the reader to see them as individuals reflecting their particular circumstances and times. For the concerns, subject matter and even the methods of the philosophers depend on their epochs, and reflect both the ethical and 'epistemo-logical' assumptions of their contemporaries. In medieval Europe, for instance, the greatest political issue of the day was the battle for ultimate authority between church and state, a struggle eventually resolved in favour of the secular. In the sixteenth, seventeenth and eighteenth centuries, the primary issue became that of how the state should use this power, whether as absolutism or within the constraints of a limiting constitutional framework. By the nineteenth century, with increasing industrialisation, the emphasis had changed again to debates over social issues, a process carried forward into the last hundred years with a new language of human rights and international relations.

Speaking of which, my selection is itself idiosyncratic, even controversial, and certainly skewed towards the western realities of the writers it attempts to describe, but it aims not so much to impose any value judgements on history, as to reflect some of the hopes and ideas that (no doubt) inspired these political theorists.

At the end of each chapter, the various strands which have been teased apart in the process of both analysing the philosophers and occasionally, too, demolishing them, are drawn together in an equally idiosyncratic and controversial section – the key ideas. Even so, I have tried also to reflect the breadth of each philosopher's vision of human society, rather than impose on them a straitjacket of critical analysis.

The ancient oracle at Delphi is said to have advised seekers after wisdom, Socrates amongst them, that the key task was to 'know thyself'. Later, Pope said that the proper study of mankind was man. Now, apart from the obvious lack of political correctness in such a statement, there is another, more important ambiguity. Is it 'man' as an individual or 'man' as a collective noun – that 'great Leviathan', society itself – that is to be studied? In an age of rampant political and social individualism, yet also a time when the lives of individuals are only possible through an increasingly complex web of collective efforts, it is more important than ever to return to the fundamentals of political society.

Prologue:
The Story of Human Society

The idea that human society depends on the technologies and economic structures of the time, so emphatically reinvented by Marx and Engels, is a commonplace. Plato makes much the same point in his *Republic*, as do ancient Chinese and other commentators. Yet history is also about the spread of ideas, and changes in human consciousness. The *Communist Manifesto* itself recognised this (paradoxically) as its very presence was supposed to speed up the transition from capitalism to socialism by awakening in the workers their sense of exploitation and alienation.

The *Manifesto* was never read much, but the ideas certainly had a powerful resonance, spreading across the continents and toppling monarchies and regimes. Similarly with the liberal ideas of citizenship and equality espoused by the likes of John Locke and Thomas Paine, or indeed the elitism and authoritarianism of Hegel and Nietzsche.

In the alternative story of philosophy, the shape of society is determined less by economics than by ethics; less by technology than by psychology. And this is a point to be found in all the great political blueprints, from Plato to Machiavelli, to Weber and Durkheim.

But rather than opposing the two sides of the story of human society, it is better to run them together. And so I start each chapter here by recalling the 'key events' in the world as the philosophers started to write about it.

Most political science claims a historical authenticity, and so we should also take a long perspective, and start by briefly recalling the first chapter of the story of human society. Human beings have been around a long time – at least 2 million years, depending on how you classify being 'human' – but human society itself is comparatively new. Indeed, between about 1 million and 12,000 years ago, it seems to have scarcely existed, and what collective life there was changed very little. There were no rules, no traditions, no laws and no social structures. It seems it was really only with the end of the last Ice Age that social life began to evolve, in the various partially desirable, partially successful but also, all too often, partially dreadful forms that we have come to know.

After the ice finally retreated, about 12,000 years ago, with improved climate and growing conditions, perhaps along with changes in animal life, farming and the first static communities appeared like so many unexpected mushrooms on the fertile plains and in the ancient woods, along with new social demands. These earliest 'societies' were groups of perhaps 100 families, living in simple buildings grouped around a central, communal hall used for social and spiritual meetings. (Psychologists say we can only relate on a one-to-one basis within groups of fewer than 500 people.) Many of these societies seem also to have been feminine in character, worshipping not only fertility in nature, but fertility in the human form. Some of the oldest stone statuettes represent pregnant women. In some, the grandmother was head of the community, and the mother head of the family. There are still today large communities, notably in southern China, following this ancient model.

Fortune-telling played a large role, both in the cave paintings and other early forms of inscription and indeed in social organisation. The practice of making symbolic marks on pieces of bone, which are then burnt in a fire, with the results inspected for clues as to the intentions of the gods, has left evidence of some of the first words. Short phrases relating to hunting, religious ceremonies, and wars have also been discerned, all carved into the oracular bones by ancient diviners. And it is no coincidence that the first published political theory, and probably the oldest book in the world – the *I Ching* – developed by the Emperor Fu-Hsi in China's first dynasty nearly 5,000 years ago, is a mix not only of divination but also of practical wisdom. As much as any overtly political work, the *I Ching* was a guide for those in power. All decisions and situations are represented there in the form of 64 'hexagrams' made up of several smaller 'trigrams', in turn made up of 'strong' or 'yielding' lines. Over the centuries, sages such as King Wen and Confucius wrote full commentaries on the lines, presented as guidance for 'the superior man'.

Other fragments and scraps of the first written records, perhaps maps or stock records, etched on tablets of clay some 5,000 years ago by the Sumerians of Mesopotamia, reflect a separate linguistic tradition. These ancient people may well have had a sophisticated culture and considerable technical skill, as the Pyramids and remains of ancient towns like Kish, Lagash and Uruk suggest. Indeed, some anthropologists believe they had both telescopes and theodolites.

But these early words are evidence not only of the mental tools of writing and number, but of the key social tool of property, the tool identified not just by Marx, but also by Plato, Locke and Rousseau, as the key to understanding social life.

The Phoenicians were amongst the first people to set sail and begin to systematically develop trade (as opposed to just plunder). And it was around this time that they discovered in Spain a valuable source of the attractive and useful metal silver. But the practical uses of silver are not where its importance in the story of human society comes from. Rather it is the fact that the Phoenicians immediately began to fortify the trade routes to prevent others from joining in. These military outposts developed into towns, such as Carthage in North Africa, which, in due course, became social and indeed cultural centres in their own right. When the Greeks followed 250 years or so later, developing a string of colonies along the coast of the Aegean, a new Mediterranean society evolved, with a common written language and a sophisticated political culture.

These Greek city states were small and frequently fought wars with each other (and the rest of the Mediterranean). They would have had little long-term influence had it not been, paradoxically, for the military success of one of their enemies. The Roman Empire, with its unprecedentedly well-organised and efficient armies and navies, enabled many of the Greek political and social innovations to be adopted, adapted and, above all, spread.

So it was through the Romans that Greek thinkers shaped the new world. Even if their society was still based on an Iron Age economy and dependent on slavery for the production of goods, it was enough to support new intellectual and political elites, with their polished cultural and intellectual structures. Athens is a case in point. Lucky enough to find its own rich vein of silver at the mines of Laurion, it was able to grow to become a city of an unprecedented 35,000 people, making it then by far the world's largest city. Even after building the all-important warships, Athens still had money to spare, which it spent on making itself the most beautiful city in the world. But Athens spawned more than just magnificent buildings. It produced a sophisticated and politically active citizenry who delighted in poetry, music, theatre and, of course, philosophy. It is these intangible investments by the ancient Greeks that left a legacy of thought, first amongst them the writings of Plato, which has yet to be exhausted.

But if Athens was exceptional in supporting some tens of thousands of inhabitants, Rome went several steps further. By the reign of the Emperor Augustus, it was home to hundreds of thousands of citizens, all supported (in a system to make social conservatives today quail) for free by the Imperial government. One of the main responsibilities of the paternalistic Roman state, along with the provision of public entertainments, was the safe delivery of bread to the people. Grain was brought from the fertile Nile delta in Egypt in specially built freighters, and was stored in huge warehouses in the capital, ready to be baked and distributed. And in later years, the government added in free cooking oil and meat as well. But it is for the provision of free mass entertainment that ancient Rome is most notorious. This was likewise done on a massive scale. The Colosseum alone catered for 50,000 spectators (under a cunningly designed canvas roof intended to keep the hot Roman sun at bay). Ultimately, though, even such remarkable engineering feats were insufficient to sate social discontent. With such an enormous population located in such cramped conditions, Rome was too far ahead of its time, too big for its physical well-being – and too underemployed for its mental well-being. It slowly succumbed to both corruption and disease. Yet, for all that, here was the first truly 'cosmopolitan' society – of a type which is easily recognisable today, even across the ages.

Although the notion of 'natural law' is there in ancient Greece, it is Roman law that became the basis upon which European government attempted to justify itself. The statesman and philosopher Cicero summed up natural law as being the 'true law – namely, right reason – which is in accordance with nature, applies to all men, and is unchangeable and eternal'. True law is in fact moral law – to disobey it is to commit wrong, not just to break the law. Similarly, natural law is higher than any earthly legislature.

It was as a consequence of this point of view that the Romans established the notion that the ultimate source of all legitimate political authority in a state comes from somewhere other than the ruler. This theme is at the heart of medieval political thought. The medieval schoolmen considered the origin of natural law to be divine, since they tied natural law to God. Illustrative of this view is the statement of Thomas Aquinas in the *Summa Theologica* that man, as a 'rational creature ... has a share of the Eternal Reason ... and this participation of the eternal law in the rational creature is called the natural law'.

In medieval England, the nobles obliged the king to sign a document called *Magna Carta* (1215), mainly to guard their privileges and wealth, but in so doing asserting the supremacy of 'law' over individual rulers. The charter was confirmed by future kings of England 44 times between 1327 and 1422 and was very much in John Locke's mind when in 1690 he drafted his *Second Treatise of Civil Government*, which asserts that government is based on a social contract respecting natural law and in particular individual liberties.

After Rome's destruction by the northern barbarian hordes, Europe declined and produced little of consequence for the next thousand years. It became locked instead into a petty and credulous mindset in which the human spirit was ruled by a mixture of fear and force – the force of armies and the fear of damnation. This is also the context for that other social blueprint, the Koran. Not until after the year 1500 did the 'rise of science' (together with a period of benign climatic warming) begin to provide the conditions for the great thinkers of the Enlightenment to renew social progress. This is the backdrop to the writings of Niccolò Machiavelli and Thomas Hobbes.

Then, towards the end of the seventeenth century, economic, social and political life begins to change dramatically. If our selection here includes three British philosophers, this is not just parochialism – it reflects the peculiar historical facts of the time. In particular, London became the biggest city in the world. By the mid 1700s, its population had grown to nearly 700,000, outstripping its rival, Paris, by nearly a quarter of a million people. This growth, like that of Athens 2,000 years earlier, reflected the island's success as a centre for trade and its associated inflows of wealth, particularly from the new growth industry of banking. This is the time and context of Adam Smith's *Wealth of Nations*. Not that the wealth, any more than the city's size, did the Londoners much good. At this time, *three-quarters* of children born in the capital did not live to see the age of five. The inventions of the Industrial Revolution – the spinning jenny in the 1760s, the first waterwheel-powered cotton mills and the steam engine itself – brought in their wake both poverty and prosperity to the new industrial cities.

Politics remained an English affair in the last years of the eighteenth century, with Thomas Paine discussing the implications of the writings of John Locke in quiet, half-timbered Lewes, as the old political structures began to break up across the globe. In both America and France, new ideas meant that republics would displace monarchies. Of these, it is the American revolution that has proved the most successful. The care the Patriots took in drawing up a new constitution that would respect the new fundamental principles of 'liberty' and 'opportunity' (at least for the rich elites) ensured that their revolution would continue to have a profound effect both on the way people see the world and in the way they perceive their place in it.

On the other hand, the French government, left impoverished by its support for the American Revolution, was less successful in its attempts at finding a new constitution – a situation worsened by the pressing need to raise new taxes. On 14 July 1789, the mob stormed the Bastille and set in motion a chain of events that would culminate in mass executions, each drop of the guillotine like the tick of a metronome marking out the progress of the purges of class enemies. First to the scaffold were the royal family and the aristocracy (inherited power), followed by the clergy (divine power, in the form of priests and nuns both), finally finishing up (as it usually does) with the political 'reformists'. France thus pioneered a new form of socialist anarchy which would continue for several years until its antithesis, the military dictatorship, arrived – led by a young officer by the name of Napoleon Bonaparte. But his military prowess was no cure, for he had no solution to the social illness.

So, after the fall of the Napoleonic Empire, Europe had to stagger through another tumultuous period of political and social revolution. Between 1815 and 1848, the year in which the *Communist Manifesto* claimed that the history of all previous society was the history of class struggle, the French alone got through three kings, whilst in Germany, Italy and Austria, rioters took to the streets demanding new political rights and institutions. All over Europe the call was for social justice, a demand aggravated both by the sight of the wealth of the capitalists and by a new nationalist awareness. One activist, claiming to speak for the poor, wrote of the new English industrial towns:

The cottages are old, dirty and of the smallest sort, the streets uneven, fallen into ruts and in part without drains or pavement; masses of refuse, offal and sickening filth lie among standing pools in all directions; the atmosphere is poisoned by the effluvia from these, and laden and darkened by the smoke of a dozen tall factory chimneys.

The writer was the son of a rich German mill owner, sent to Manchester, who had become concerned at the condition of the mill workers in his charge. He was to become well-known later to the world as the infamous co-author of the *Communist Manifesto* – Friedrich Engels.

The *Communist Manifesto* marked a particular moment in time – a time when it seemed that society was rapidly moving towards the resolution of its final crisis, and that the new industries, which perpetually lurched between overproduction and glut, underproduction and recession, *must* yield to a new socialist order.

Yet the moment passed. Capitalism proved more adept at resolving its contradictions than Marx and Engels had expected, and the workers they urged to unite proved less conscious of their collective interests than the two revolutionaries had hoped. Instead of political change bringing about a radical redistribution of wealth and power, reform in the modern states simply created ever more complex mechanisms designed to protect and placate individuals and enable the huge new industrial cities to continue to expand, function and develop.

And develop they did. In not much more than two generations, Europe transformed itself from a poor agrarian region to a wealthy industrialised zone. The first working internal combustion engine (using gas) came in 1859; at the end of the century the engine was successfully adapted to run on petrol and oil, and Benz and Daimler then applied the technology to the task of making a 'horseless carriage'. The invention of the motor car, symbol as it would become of modern society, was only the tangible aspect of a more fundamental technological breakthrough – the new production methods and 'white-collar' skills of 'Fordism' itself. Henry Ford's dream of a mass-produced car for the new class of consumers had introduced two new 'tools' to the art of making things: time-and-motion studies and the production line. The first Model Ts were towed around the Detroit works by two men with a rope, each car taking twelve hours to assemble, for an output of 100 vehicles a day. By the end of the first year, with the assembly line completed, production time per car was down to just an hour and a half, and the factory was turning out 5,000 cars a week.

For the United States especially (with Europe still distracted by the legacy of the futile nationalism of the First World War) the 1920s was the decade of consumer durables – not just cars, but radios, electrical appliances for the home, and new leisure products: jazz music, dances, the movies and, for the first time, organised consumer credit. In 1929 President Hoover announced that the end of poverty was in sight, and promised a new era of prosperity for all. The announcement was made only just in time, however, for a year later the poverty and mass unemployment of the Slump and the Great Depression arrived.

Expansion, it turned out, had been fed on a diet rich in loans and expected future profits – a spiral of credit both within countries and between them. When things began to go wrong, as they inevitably did, the end was swift. In three years, production halved in America. The motor-car market plummeted to a paltry one-tenth of its 1929 level. At a time when not to work meant not to eat, one in four workers lost their jobs. As no one could afford to buy anything, prices fell, and in doing so, made yet more businesses collapse. When F. D. Roosevelt was elected president, he inherited an economy that had effectively imploded. Even his dramatic 'interventionist' emergency economics could barely stem the decline. Nevertheless, the 'New Deal' seemed to offer hope, indeed, the only hope, and his combination of public works and organised poor relief enabled the political structures of the world's largest democracy to struggle on in search of better times. In Europe, similar economic problems spawned instead a new creed, fascism, which began taking hold in Italy, in Spain – and in Germany.

Fascism is a political throwback, a powerful but ultimately self-defeating creed, simply because, like communism, it fails to respect human beings as ends in themselves, treating them instead only as a means to an end. Perhaps more importantly, from the point of view of the impersonal forces of history, it also fails to respect economic realities and the reality of human nature.

Only in China would there arise one totalitarian model, a new form of communism, which for a while at least would manage to combine both of these things. Maoism, although often regarded (particularly by the western transnational companies that dallied so disastrously with Japanese nationalism) as just another form of Marxism, and a demon to be exorcised, needs to be understood as a doctrine in its own right. Maoism was the necessary embodiment of peasant power, in a society that had never before accorded this colossal force any recognition. In much of the world today, the land is, likewise, still the social key.

Under Chairman Mao (as in conventional notions of legal justice), the *welfare of the people* was to be the measure of the success of the system. For 20 years, until the Cultural Revolution, on this criterion it succeeded. The Chinese masses were raised from national weakness and individual poverty to become collectively an economic and military superpower. But today it seems likely that although Maoism, and to some extent Russian communism, can raise people above subsistence, neither form can for long hold back from the economic reforms stipulated by the likes of Adam Smith, reforms which have resulted in such prodigious gains in efficiency and productivity – and ultimately wealth – for the nations that have embraced them.

For that reason, the end of the twentieth century has seen a convergence of all societies around a capitalist model that was foreseen much earlier.

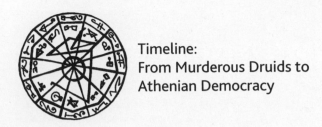

Timeline:
From Murderous Druids to
Athenian Democracy

ABOUT 3400 BCE
Construction of Stonehenge, actually originally made of wood, begun in ancient Britain. Mysterious and elaborate rituals involving mass executions or suicides supervised by Druids.

ABOUT 750 BCE
The first true alphabet, with separate signs for consonants and vowels, developed by the Greeks, who, together with the Lydians, become the first people to use coins. (The first banknotes have to wait until the middle of the seventeenth century, 1658 CE, when they are issued in Stockholm.)

ABOUT 420 BCE
Another early use for writing is for the cataloguing of doctrine, which yields powerful religious works. The *Ramayana* becomes the main text of Hinduism. The first five books of the Christian Bible, the Hebrew *Torah*, traditionally ascribed to Moses, are written at this time.

399 BCE
Socrates, Plato's teacher and inspiration, is executed by the first Athenian democracy, for heretical views.

1

Plato's Vegetarian Republic

It has been said that all subsequent philosophy is merely a footnote to Plato, and this is certainly true of political philosophy. But much of Plato is in fact a retelling of Pythagoras, who founded a mysterious cult of vegetarian mathematicians. With this in mind, much of Plato's Republic *makes more sense. The origins of society, it suggests, are in practical self-interest. But although the pursuit of wealth motivates all, it must not motivate the rulers – the Guardians. Plato sees two main threats to society, either* external *– requiring a military response, or* internal *– requiring a political response. Internal threats are minimised by ensuring the ruling class are there solely on merit, and receive no rewards other than satisfaction from performing their duty and achieving a well-ordered society.*

THE CONTEXT

The origins of human society may be, as they say, obscured in the mists of antiquity, but they certainly lie outside Europe, probably with the ancient African cultures. The first theorising that left written records only seems to have been about 5,000 years ago. But these early cultures and records are by no means primitive. In China, the great sages Confucius and Lao Tzu were teaching the virtues of the well-ordered, harmonious society, whilst in the south-west coastal strip of what is now modern Turkey, the trading ports that would later grow into the city states of Asia Minor were founded, and with them an unparalleled period of innovation in art, literature, architecture, politics – and philosophy.

It was here, in the fifth century BCE, that Democritus described the shadows cast by the mountains on the moon, and realised that the pool of celestial light in the night sky – the Milky Way – was in fact made up of thousands upon thousands of stars. And it was here too that Democritus observed that 'one should think it of greater moment than anything else that the affairs of state are conducted well', neither being 'contentious beyond what is proper' nor 'allotting strength to oneself beyond the common good'. For a state which is conducted well is the best means to success: 'everything depends on this, and if this is preserved, everything is preserved and if this is destroyed everything is destroyed'.

It was whilst Democritus was devising a theory of atoms in Mesopotamia that Socrates, in Athens, was holding the philosophical discussions that, through the *Republic*, and many other writings of Plato, have come not merely to influence but to determine much of western culture, education and society. Socrates' position in European thought, it has been said, is like that of a religious leader, who, although he himself wrote nothing, has had the kind of influence normally reserved only for messiahs, spread through the accounts of his followers, of whom Plato is only the most immediate and direct. And the style of Plato's political philosophy is also religious in tone, set out in the form of dialogues in the *Republic*. Socrates is portrayed there as the wise one, extolling the need to come to know the 'Good', or to be precise 'the Form of the Good'. This some see as indistinguishable from 'God', and it certainly has many similarities.

Plato was born about 40 years after Socrates, and knew him only in his last years. He grew up during the Peloponnesian wars, which ended in 401 BCE with the defeat of Athens and was followed by a putsch by a small group of aristocrats. After only eight months, this degenerated into a tyranny, counting in due course among its victims Socrates himself, on charges of 'impiety' and 'corrupting the young'.

Plato writes as a member of a highly distinguished family, and had both the means and the inclination to be a member of the governing elite. That he never did govern, in fact, having to content himself with setting out his blueprint for society in the *Republic*, was due, he felt, to his inability to find others with whom to share the burden of government. Like the British prime minister, Margaret Thatcher, who is reported to have once said that she needed just six men, good and true, to govern the United Kingdom, but could never find them all at the same time, Plato found human capital to be the critical factor lacking, and decided instead that education was the key to society. Rulers, in particular, would need special training, if there were ever to be enough of them.

On the other hand, in addition to Socrates himself, there were many others around to influence Plato in the design of his 'republic'. As well as Democritus, there was Parmenides, advising that 'truth must be eternal and unchanging', and Heraclitus, who had conversely concluded (it is said after standing in the river) that 'all is flux' – the two views being reconciled and reflected in a tradition in which the earthly, visible world was seen as being illusory and impermanent, whilst the world of the intellect and truth was eternal and timeless. For Plato, it followed that the ideal state would be designed not to continually adapt and evolve, but rather to have a fixed and unalterable structure controlling and directing changes.

But it is Pythagoras who evidently cast the longest shadow over Plato's dialogues. For example, at a time when such thoughts were rare, Pythagoras insisted that men and women were equal, that property should be held in common, and that his followers should live and eat communally. All of this reappears in the *Republic* as Plato's recommended lifestyle for the Guardians, alongside the Pythagorean doctrines of the heavenly forms and the split between the world of knowledge and the world of matter (of which last, philosophers must remain aloof).

In addition:

- In the *Meno*, Pythagoras' view of how learning is really recollection appears, as the 'slave boy' recalls the geometrical theorem that bears Pythagoras' name.
- In the *Gorgias*, there is the Pythagorean doctrine that the better one knows something, the more one becomes like it.
- The *Timaeus* is a Pythagorean description of the universe in terms of (musical) harmonies and matter, which is revealed mystically here as being made up of geometrical shapes, notably triangles.
- In the *Phaedo* is the Pythagorean view that philosophy is a preparation for death and immortality.

But perhaps the most distinctive thing that Plato takes from Pythagoras is the need for his Guardians to have strict rules and to live by them. And for Pythagoras' followers, the first rule was silence. 'He, Pythagoras, says it' was the only thing they needed to know in their search for wisdom. Similarly, the citizens of Plato's ideal state are not required to participate in decisions.

The *Republic* then is a serious bid to sketch out the ideal society, an effort which partly reflects Plato's frustration at being unable to play a significant political role in his own society. Its main recommendation, coming from a philosopher, is that philosophers should be in charge of governments. The rule of philosophers had already been tried in other city states, and it was common practice to employ a sage to draw up laws. Plato would certainly have agreed with Marx, in believing that the point is not only to understand the world – but to change it.

His writings are in the form of conversations, or dialogues, between historical characters, the most important of whom is Socrates. The title is misleading – the *Republic* is really about any form of political organisation that a community the size of a Greek city could take. Similarly, Plato's preoccupation with 'justice' – *dikaiosyne* in the Greek – is not so much with the administration of the law, with seeing that criminals get their just deserts, but with the right way to behave. It is justice in a moral, not a legal sense, and is closely linked to the idea of wisdom. Justice is to Plato the 'correct ordering' of the organism.

THE TEXT

Plato starts by making the equation, strange to modern eyes, of justice in the workings of the state with justice observed in the behaviour of the human individual. Indeed, Plato believes that because it is easier to see justice at work in the larger organism, we should look at the ordering of society in order to find the answer to the question of how to live ourselves.

We think of justice as a quality that may exist in a whole community as well as in an individual, and the community is the bigger of the two. Possibly, then, we may find justice there in larger proportions, easier to make out.

In this way, Plato's politics is based on the philosophical and ethical question, 'What should I do?' His concern at the deterioration of morals in Greek society is the wellspring of the *Republic*, and strengthens his conviction that there can be no escape from injustice and the many ills of society until it is guided by those who have come to a knowledge of the 'Good'.

Plato, like Marx, is actually a materialist in this, saying that a state comes into existence because no individual is self-sufficient. We all have many needs – for food and shelter, for heat and tools, for roads and paths, and for protection from attack. We call on one another's help to satisfy our various requests and when we have collected a number of others together to live in one place, helping and supporting each other, we call that settlement a state, he says. It is here that we find the origin of society, in the free exchange of goods and services between people. But this coming together of people is not a social contract, nor even an enlightened act. For 'one man gives a share of his produce to another, if he does, or accepts a share of the other's produce, thinking it is better for himself to do so'. Economic need and self-interest comes first; this is the defining feature of Plato's society.

Let us build our imaginary state from the beginning. Apparently, it will owe its existence to our needs, the first and greatest need being the provision of food to keep us alive. Next we shall want a house; and thirdly, such things as clothing.

How can the state supply this? Plato suggests, through the division of labour. 'We shall need at least one man to be a farmer, another a builder, and a third a weaver.' In fact, as Socrates and his audience then apparently realise, at least two more will be useful: namely a shoemaker and someone to provide for 'personal' wants, the like of which are not specified. This 'minimum state' works best when each member of it is making only the things for which he or she is best suited (Plato is very egalitarian, giving women the same employment opportunities as men, because, after all, the only important part of human beings, the soul, is neither male nor female). And that means specialisation. 'The work goes easier and is better done when everyone is set free from all other occupations to do, at the right time, the one thing for which they are naturally fitted.'

As Socrates goes on to say (at least according to Plato's dialogues), a bigger organisation, encompassing carpenters and blacksmiths, shepherds and weavers, builders and masons, is in fact more efficient and successful still. Indeed, Socrates even suggests a middle class of sorts, composed of shopkeepers and bankers, managing and selling goods. After all, as his companion puts it, perhaps rather unkindly: 'In well-ordered communities there are generally men not strong enough to be of use in any other occupation.' These middle classes stay in the marketplace, whilst the farmers are out farming and the craftsmen crafting, to take money from those who wish to buy, and to purchase goods from those who wish to sell.

Both Plato and his pupil Aristotle, who would later categorise the natural world, rather obsessively, into the various species and genera that we still use today, saw social life as a means to enable individuals with particular skills to achieve their proper 'function': the businessman to produce wealth, the doctor, health and the soldier, victory. The ruler's art of 'politics' is in turn fulfilled when the state is in balance and human happiness and the 'Good' are maximised. When, on the other hand, a ruler believes the nation should concentrate on generating wealth to the detriment of this, or tries to pursue power and military adventure, then the political art is perverted.

It has to be remembered here, as elsewhere, that in the *Republic* there is always that slight, but vital, distinction to be drawn between the views of its main character, Socrates, and its author, Plato. For the historical Socrates, the only sort of happiness that counts is that which comes through wisdom – specifically, the realisation that the only thing worthwhile is knowledge of the 'Good'. It could quite easily be suffering that brings about this discovery and illumination. However, for Plato himself, the 'Good' is a slightly broader notion, rooted in the social and political context, although still not solely the materialist concept it is often taken for today.

Let us begin, then, with a picture of our citizens' manner of life, with the provision that we have made for them. They will be producing corn and wine, and making clothes and shoes. When they have built their houses, they will mostly work without their coats or shoes in summer, and in winter be well shod and clothed. For their food, they will prepare flour and barley-meal for kneading and baking, and set out a grand spread of loaves and cakes on rushes or fresh leaves. They will lie on beds of myrtle-boughs and bryony and make merry with their children, drinking their wine after the feast with garlands on their heads and singing the praises of the gods. So they will live pleasantly together and a prudent fear of poverty or war will keep them from begetting children beyond their means.

If we recognise the material impulse, Plato argues that we must also recognise that, 'in time, the desire for a life of idle luxury will inevitably lead to conflict', and the land which was once large enough to support the original inhabitants will now be too small.

If we are to have enough pasture and plough land, we shall have to cut off a slice of our neighbour's territory; and if they too are not content with necessities, but give themselves up to getting unlimited wealth, they will want a slice of ours.

This will mean a considerable addition to the community – a whole army – 'to go out to battle with any invader, in defence of all this property and of the citizens we have been describing'. For as Plato records in another dialogue, the *Phaedo*, 'All wars are made for the sake of getting money.'

By now the state has become unable to manage itself. Who will run the new society? Who will be in charge? A small group of philosophers known as the 'Guardians' are Plato's (self-serving) choice. The Guardians are appointed primarily to protect the state, and are specialists in the arts of war, but are also skilled in the arts of ruling, and in management. They must be 'gentle to their own people yet dangerous to others', like a well-trained guard dog. Dogs, says Plato, extending the metaphor (presumably humorously), are philosophical creatures. They distinguish friend from enemy by the simple test of deciding whether they know the person or not. The dog, like the philosopher, likes only that which he knows.

In Plato's republic, the bringing up of the 'guard dogs' is the key to sound government. The young are selected for aptitude, and brought up in a tightly controlled environment by older Guardians. It is a community of Spartan simplicity, free of the distractions of family ties and bonds. Goods are held in common, unlike the situation for the lowly industrious classes of the republic, who are allowed to accumulate private property. But the Guardians will step in to prevent extremes of either great wealth or great poverty from occurring, as such extremes set rich against poor, disturbing the equilibrium of society. For unity is all important, and the Guardians must further protect it by ensuring that the state does not grow too large, and by preserving the principle of promotion only on merit – there must be no hereditary governing class. Generally the balance of the state is akin to the balance needed in the individual.

When a man surrenders himself to music, allowing his soul to be flooded through the channels of his ears with those sweet and soft and mournful airs we spoke of, and gives up all his time to the delights of song and melody, then at first he tempers the high-spirited part of his nature, like iron whose brittleness is softened to make it serviceable; but if he persists in subduing to such an incantation, he will end by melting away altogether.

He will have 'cut the sinews of his soul'. Likewise, if there is no attempt to cultivate the mind, but an overemphasis on training the body, it leads to a soul that is blind and deaf, because 'the darkness that clouds perception is never cleared away' and the man becomes a dull beast 'in a stupor of ignorance without harmony or grace'. Balance, says Socrates, mirroring the conclusions of the Eastern philosophers and mystics, is the key for the individual, and equally, for the state.

In many ways, Plato is more progressive than he gets credit for. Plato believes that, at least in relation to education and philosophy, men and women are equal. He says that they must share the same education and practise the same occupations 'both in peace and war', and that they should be governed by 'those of their number who are best'. Since, at the time, women in Athens lived in seclusion and took no part in politics or most of social life, Plato's suggestion that they should have equal opportunities to become Guardians was quite revolutionary. However, it made sense for Plato, as he believed the physical person was not important (as mentioned above), that it was the soul in which morality resided; and souls have no gender.

Of course, this might cause some practical problems, as the *Republic* notes in one of its regular whimsical asides.

'Possibly, if these proposals were carried out, they might be ridiculed as involving a good many breaches of custom.'

'Indeed, Socrates, they might.'

'The most ridiculous being the notion of women exercising naked along with the men in the wrestling schools; some of them elderly women too, like the old men who still have a passion for exercise when they are wrinkled and not very agreeable to look at ...'

Only relevant differences, such as the slighter build of women, should be allowed to influence their treatment.

However, far from being considered a progressive, Plato is often accused of being an early advocate of totalitarianism, particularly censured for his approach to the arts and education, with children being brought up by the state rather than by parents.

Actually, the abolition of private property for the Guardians also includes the breaking of parental bonds with children, as part of the general scheme. Offspring were instead to be reared collectively by everyone, using the guiding principles of eugenics to sort the good from the not-so-promising. By destroying family ties, Plato believed it would be possible to create a more united governing class, and to avoid the dangers of rivalry and oligarchy. Inferior children would be demoted to the appropriate class. In the perfect state, women too would be 'held in common', producing the children for the state, and there would be no permanent marriage or pair-bonding. As for the upbringing of the children, his aim is primarily to get people to think for themselves, rather than to put thoughts into their heads. Education is in any case too important to be left to parents, and so all children must essentially be brought up by the state. The child is not to be passive, but active in the learning process. Education is not indoctrination, Plato imagines; rather, the teacher will only try to show the 'source of the light'. After all, as Plato says at one point: 'A free man ought not to learn anything under duress. Compulsory physical exercise does no harm to the body, but compulsory learning never sticks in the mind.' And he advises: 'Don't use compulsion, but let your children's lessons take the appearance of play.'

However, Plato is insistent on the need to control the influences on developing minds, and does advocate strict censorship of poetry and literature.

Our first business is to supervise the production of stories and choose only those we think suitable and reject the rest ... Nor shall any young audience be told that anyone who commits horrible crimes, or punishes his father unmercifully is doing nothing our of the ordinary but merely what the first and greatest of the gods have done before.

Because, as Socrates explains, 'Children cannot distinguish between what is allegory and what is not', and opinions formed at that age are usually difficult to eradicate or change. It is therefore of the utmost importance that the first stories they hear aim at producing 'the right moral effect'. In general,

ugliness of form and disharmony are akin to bad art and bad character, and their opposites are akin to and represent good character and discipline ... Our artists and craftsmen must be capable of perceiving the real nature of what is beautiful, and then our young men, living as it were in a good climate, will benefit because all the works of art they see and hear influence them for the good, like the breezes from some healthy country, insensibly moulding them into sympathy and conformity with what is rational and right.

This is a striking passage, both for a message which is becoming more, not less, relevant with the creation of high-tech, densely populated societies, with weakened family structures and bonds, and stronger media and peer-group ones, and for its more sinister, totalitarian undertones.

It is not just bad theatre and poetry that corrupt. Indeed, Plato holds that 'wealth and poverty have a bad effect on the quality of work and on the workman himself'. Wealth produces 'luxury and idleness and a passion for novelty', whilst poverty produces 'meanness and bad workmanship and revolution into the bargain'. That is why the upbringing of the ruling class, the Guardians, has to be so closely prescribed and detailed.

All Guardians follow the same basic education, and undertake years of military training. At this point, some will become just 'auxiliaries', charged with defending the state, whilst a minority progress to studying philosophy and take on the burden of actually ruling.

The rest of the citizenry are also sorted into their correct, humbler but perhaps more lucrative, roles. Physicians look after physically sound citizens, physically unsound ones are left to die – although not actually killed. That is reserved for 'those who are incurably corrupt in mind'. Killing these, all agree, is the 'best thing for them [!] as well as the community'.

In due course (Plato suggests at about the age of 50) the Guardians are ready for public office and taking up their burden of guiding the community. Their lives must be as simple as possible, with their only pleasures being the pursuit of philosophy, although, perhaps, they can be allowed some pleasure from serving the community. Property, certainly, is forbidden. 'They shall eat together in messes and live together like soldiers in camp. They must be told that they have no need of moral and material gold and silver as they have in their hearts the heavenly gold and silver.'

If this can be done, then Plato's republic, the justly ordered state, will exemplify the following virtues:

- wisdom – in the manner of its ruling;
- courage – in the manner of its defending;
- temperance – in the acceptance of all of the system of government.

Wisdom, we have seen, stems from the Guardians themselves. 'Courage' is passed over quickly by Plato, but assumed to be the key ingredient of a professional army. But 'temperance' is more subtle, and comes about only by ensuring that there is a balance between the various parts of the state – the governing part or rulers, the administering part or executive, and the productive part or the working classes.

Critics of Plato have seen a parallel in modern times between Plato's political approach and that which, for over half a century, was being applied in the Soviet Union. (Karl Popper, for example, has done so, of which more in the concluding chapters.) The Soviet approach was certainly 'neo-Platonism', in the key respects that there was a governing elite – the Communist Party – rigorous attention to education and moral influences, equality of the sexes and weakening of family ties, and, last but not least, a general disapproval of private property and wealth. However, the system failed to produce the wise and beneficent society that Plato imagined.

But Plato not only described the ideal state, where justice flourishes: he also tried to show how such a state could decline, examining the various forms of the degenerate state – unjust societies where evil permeates throughout. Curiously, or perhaps presciently, Plato attributes the decline to diet, and in particular a taste for meat over the more ecological lifestyles of vegetarians. After describing so rosily the merits of the simple life, he is challenged by his interlocutor, Glaucon, who complains that he has not given the people 'a relish to their meal'. It seems a simple enough question, and Socrates replies in kind:

SOCRATES: True, I had forgotten; of course they must have a relish – salt, and olives, and cheese, and they will boil roots and herbs such as country people prepare; for a dessert we shall give them figs, and peas, and beans; and they will roast myrtle-berries and acorns at the fire, drinking in moderation. And with such a diet they may be expected to live in peace and health to a good old age, and bequeath a similar life to their children after them.

But Socrates has missed the point entirely. Figs and peas indeed! Glaucon's objection runs much deeper. 'Yes, Socrates,' he now says with sarcasm, 'and if you were providing for a city of pigs, what else would you feed the beasts?'

SOCRATES: But what would you have, Glaucon?
GLAUCON: Why, you should give them the ordinary conveniences of life. People who are to be comfortable are accustomed to lie on sofas, and dine off tables, and they should have sauces and sweets in the modern style.
SOCRATES: Yes, now I understand. The question which you would have me consider is, not only how a State, but how a luxurious State is created; and possibly there is no harm in this, for in such a State we shall be more likely to see how justice and injustice originate. In my opinion the true and healthy constitution of the State is the one which I have described. But if you wish also to see a State affected by fever heat, I have no objection. For I suspect that many will not be satisfied with the simpler way of life. They will be for adding sofas, and tables, and other furniture; also dainties, and perfumes, and incense, and courtesans, and cakes, all these not of one sort only, but in every variety.

For the *Republic is not ideal at all*. It is stated quite plainly: in fact, it is the *Luxurious State*. It is a response to Glaucon's demand for a few of the 'ordinary conveniences' of life, or as he apologetically puts it, 'a relish to the meal'.

SOCRATES: So, we must go beyond the necessaries of which I was at first speaking, such as houses, and clothes, and shoes: the arts of the painter and the embroiderer will have to be set in motion, and gold and ivory and all sorts of materials must be procured.

GLAUCON: True.

SOCRATES: Then we must enlarge our borders; for the original healthy State is no longer sufficient. Now will the city have to fill and swell with a multitude of callings which are not required by any natural want; such as the whole tribe of hunters and actors, of whom one large class have to do with forms and colours; another will be the votaries of music – poets and their attendant train of rhapsodists, players, dancers, contractors; also makers of divers kinds of articles, including women's dresses. And we shall want more servants. Will not tutors be also in request, and nurses wet and dry, and barbers, as well as confectioners and cooks; and swineherds, too, who were not needed and therefore had no place in the former edition of our State, but are needed now? They must not be forgotten: and there will be animals of many other kinds, if people eat them.

GLAUCON: Certainly.

SOCRATES: And living in this way we shall have much greater need of physicians than before?

GLAUCON: Much greater.

SOCRATES: And the country which was enough to support the original inhabitants will be too small now, and not enough?

GLAUCON: Quite true.

SOCRATES: Then a slice of our neighbours' land will be wanted by us for pasture and tillage, and they will want a slice of ours, if, like ourselves, they exceed the limit of necessity, and give themselves up to the unlimited accumulation of wealth?

GLAUCON: That, Socrates, will be inevitable.

SOCRATES: And so we shall go to war, Glaucon. Shall we not?

GLAUCON: Most certainly.

SOCRATES: Then without determining as yet whether war does good or harm, thus much we may affirm, that now we have discovered war to be derived from causes which are also the causes of almost all the evils in States, private as well as public.

GLAUCON: Indubitably.

It is only greed and materialism that require not only the division of labour generally, but class distinctions, an army, and the creation of a ruling elite – the famous Platonic Guardians. It is no longer a 'Utopia' but merely the best solution available to any society where the basest elements of human nature are allowed to predominate and warp the whole. And Plato warns of the alternative paths societies take in their decline. First, Plato describes the 'timocratic state' (Greek *timé*: honour), where ambition has become the motivating force of the rulers. In Plato's republic, the danger is that of a divided ruling class of Guardians beginning to compete amongst each other. (Timocracy was often an element in the competition amongst the aristocracy in the Middle Ages in Europe, for example.)

Once civil strife is born, the competing parties will begin to pull different ways: the breed of iron and brass towards moneymaking and the possession of house and land, silver and gold; while their rivals, wanting no other wealth than the gold and silver in the composition of their souls, try to draw them towards virtue and the ancient ways. But the violence of their contention ends in a compromise: they agree to distribute land and houses for private ownership; they enslave their own people who formerly lived as free men under their guardianship and gave them maintenance; and holding them as serfs and menials, devote themselves to war and to keeping these subjects under watch and ward.

Plato specifically suggests that the usurpers will fear merit and tend towards authoritarianism. They will become greedy, avaricious and secretive, 'cultivating the body in preference to the mind and saving nothing for the spirit'.

In time, an elite emerges, defined by wealth. This is 'oligarchy', or the rule of a clique.

As the rich rise in esteem, the virtuous sink ... the competitive spirit of ambition in these people turns into mere passion for gain; they despise the poor and promote the rich, who win all the prizes and receive all the adulation.

Oligarchy, by making wealth the sole purpose of life and at the same time ensuring that only a few have that wealth, sows the seeds of its own destruction in the masses' eventual demand for more. Here, Plato influences Hegel and Marx. However, the resolution of this, for Plato, is democracy. Not that he thinks very much of it, considering it a close relation of anarchy.

'What is the character of this new regime? Obviously the way they govern themselves will throw light on the democratic type of man.'

'No doubt, Socrates.'

'First of all, they are free. Liberty and free speech are rife everywhere; anyone is allowed to do what he likes ... every man will arrange his manner of life to suit his own pleasure.'

The kind of democracy the city states practised was significantly different from more recent versions. Decisions were not delegated to representatives, who would, we might like to suppose, have special expertise and training, but were decided upon at mass meetings of all citizens, that is citizens with no particular knowledge or claim to qualification.

So democracy was, in this sense, 'an agreeable form of anarchy with plenty of variety', liberty 'its noblest possession'. But, worse still, the democratic state was vulnerable to sinking into tyranny. This at least was Plato's objection to democracy, and it has a certain plausibility, even piquancy, being presented in the dialogues as coming from Socrates, who was one of that system's first victims. Because it is almost anarchic in form, the democratic state must gradually settle into three classes: the capitalists (not that Plato uses the term), gradually accumulating wealth; the common people, uninterested in politics but just working steadily away; and the sharks and demagogues, perpetually looking for ways to usurp the system for quick personal gain. Inevitably, one such will succeed and seize control, which he can then only maintain by despotism. Although, in the early days, the tyrant

has a smile and a greeting for everyone he meets; disclaims any absolute power; makes large promises to his friends and to the public; sets about the relief of debtors and the distribution of land to the people and to his supporters; and assumes a mild and gracious air ...

– this does not last for long. Soon the demagogue will be provoking wars and conflict as a means of ensuring power at home, and purging his followers as well as his enemies.

THE SUBTEXT

Plato's aversion to tyranny was shared by Aristotle, for 20 years one of his pupils in the Greek forums, and one of three candidates for Plato's post as head of the Academy. However, like many job candidates since, he was to be disappointed – the job went to Plato's nephew, Speusippus. Aristotle left Athens after this, but, writing later, in his description of the rule of the tyrant he seems to speak of a very modern age: 'the forbidding of common meals, clubs, education and anything of a like character ... the adoption of every means for making every subject as much of a stranger as possible to every other'.

All citizens, Aristotle warned, would be constantly on view, and a secret police, 'like the female spies employed at Syracuse, or the eavesdroppers sent by the tyrant Hiero to all social gatherings', would be employed to sow fear and distrust. For these are the essential and characteristic hallmarks of tyrants.

Aristotle was more of a scientist than Socrates and Plato, and had a resolutely practical – 'rational' – approach to most matters, which served well in the fields of logic, biology and so on, albeit less so in ethics and psychology. As part of his practical bent, he was particularly concerned at the fractious nature of the Greek city states in his time (the fourth century BCE). The states were small, but that did not stop them continually splitting into factions that fought amongst themselves. A whole book of Aristotle's political theory is devoted to this problem. But that is Aristotle's story, not Plato's.

And not only was it Plato's version of the origins of political society that became Marx's 'materialist conception of history', but his picture of self-interest governing economic relations is also both Hobbes' social contract and Smith's hidden hand, while there is a plea for liberalism in his strategy of mitigating the effects of either extreme wealth or extreme poverty. There is even an early type of utilitarianism at work in ascribing to the ruler the task of maximising happiness.

But Plato's most important influence comes from the suggestion that the natural and most 'efficient' form of social organisation is one in which individuals and classes have different roles and specialisations. Plato justifies using this to create both an educational and a social hierarchy. That hierachy is the factor that, above all others, determines the practical reality of society.

Can the ideal state ever be brought into existence? Plato certainly thought so. The first stage would be to put a philosopher into power. This has happened, but it has not been particularly successful. Plato himself had a spell at advising the new king of Syracuse, in Sicily – a tyrant called Dionysius II, who considered himself also to be a philosopher, but otherwise had little in common with Plato. The two soon fell out and Plato only just managed to escape to Athens.

At other times philosophers have established small-scale radical communities, most of which seem to have been highly unpleasant. After the Berlin Wall came down at the end of the twentieth century, the modern Czechoslovakian state was even able to have a professional philosopher, Václav Havel, take over – for a while. But Plato has in mind the philosophical virtues – commitment to truth, justice and beauty – rather than any more formal training or qualification. And even if his ideal can never be achieved, and must remain just theory, the example it offers may still be valuable, informing the actions of earthly rulers in the light of what might be.

In a letter written from prison, Plato describes Socrates awaiting execution at the hands of the Athenian democracy. Plato recalls him saying:

I came to the conclusion that all existing states were badly governed, and that their constitutions were incapable of reform without drastic treatment and a great deal of good luck. I was forced, in fact, to the belief that the only hope of finding justice for society or for the individual lay in true philosophy, and that mankind will have no respite from trouble until either real philosophers gain political power or politicians become by some miracle true philosophers.

This is the theme of the *Republic*.

KEY IDEAS

- People come together naturally and start to specialise.
- The state is like an individual – with a head, a heart and a body. It is most successful when the parts can fulfil their different functions.

KEY TEXT

Plato's *Republic*

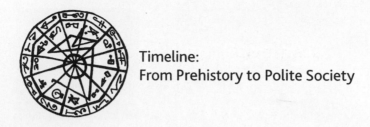

Timeline:
From Prehistory to Polite Society

ABOUT 6,000–7,000 YEARS AGO
Neolithic pottery fragments provide first clues as to early writing and social life.

ABOUT 3000 BCE
Menes, king of Upper Egyptian region, conquers the Nile Delta and becomes pharaoh, in a world previously grouped only by tribes or cities, of the first nation state. Egypt, at this time, was made up essentially of villages. The first written records on papyrus date from this period.

2500 BCE
The first pyramid constructed. Not smooth but stepped like a ziggurat, to conduct the pharaoh Zoser into the next world.

1700 BCE
In China, an early use for writing is for fortune-telling by burning bones with names and symbols scratched on them. In the Middle East, another early use is for issuing laws to the general public, greatly increasing the efficiency and effectiveness of the law-making process. The 'Eye for an Eye' code is published by Hammurabi, setting out precise penalties for all types of wrongdoing.

ABOUT 1500 BCE
The first writing systems using alphabets, that is with symbols for combinations of consonants and vowels, are developed in the Middle East.

ABOUT 500 BCE
In China, Confucius teaches the five virtues of humanity, courtesy, honesty, moral wisdom and steadfastness.

2
Confucius' Polite Society

The Analects are hard to make sense of today as a political text, especially for those from outside China. Historically, they are part of a debate over the succession to the Western Zhou dynasty, whose 300 years of power (1066–771 BCE) are counted as a period of great success. The dynasty used a series of ritual rules to create an attitude of 'human centredness' in the people, both those with political power and those required only to obey it, and this indeed is also at the heart of the Confucian political philosophy. Yet even at the time he was teaching, alternative strategies were competing for influence.

Confucius' response to these criticisms was to say that the problem was not the traditions and rituals themselves, but the attitude of the people adopting them. Rites were not important in themselves, but only in bringing individuals into harmony with each other, with Confucius thinking here not only of the present but also of past and future generations. He claims that human nature is calm and quiet but is easily disturbed by the outside world, buffeted by ambitions and desires. Here lie the origins of conflict in society. So, for Confucius, the 'taming of the desires' is a primary aim. In this sense, Confucius is, to paraphrase Marx, a kind of opiate for the people.

THE CONTEXT

Master Kongfuzi, or Confucius as he is rather better known, was born in Qufu in the state of Lu, what is now part of Shandong province in modern China. As a child, he is said to have liked arranging vases on the table as part of traditional ritual observance. Like other political philosophers, he was a minor civil servant. His first role was as an administrative manager in the state of Lu but he soon rose to the position of justice minister charged with ensuring rules were respected. He acquired a reputation for fairness, politeness and love of learning. It is said that he studied ritual with the Daoist master Lao Dan, music with Chang Hong, and the lute with music master Xiang. In fact, Confucius became a skilled 'qin' (or zither) player) and he always valued music very highly, seeing it as a way of calming the mind and allowing spiritual harmony. As he puts it: 'A man who does not have humanity, what can he have to do with music?' Confucius considered music the most effective way for governments to regulate public morality and ensure good order.

At about the age of 50, seeing no way to improve the government, least of all through zither playing, he gave up his political career in Lu, and began a twelve-year journey around China, seeking the 'way' and trying unsuccessfully to convince many different rulers of his political beliefs and to put them into reality.

Around his sixtieth year, Confucius returned home and spent the remainder of his life teaching and editing the ancient classics. Sometimes called the 'throneless king', he now tried to share his experiences with his disciples and to transmit the old wisdom to the later generations. 'I am a transmitter, rather than an original thinker', says Confucius, in one of the *Analects*. 'I trust and enjoy the teachings of the ancients. In my heart I compare myself to old P'eng.' He added, 'I was not born with wisdom. I love the ancient teachings and have worked hard to attain to their level.'

The wisdom he attained is summed up in his famous, and quite possibly his only work (although many are attributed to him), the *Analects*. This is a series of aphorisms or moral maxims, which superficially are obsessed with the question of the proper observation of ancient ritual. But their philosophical and social scope is much broader, and the *Analects* became the basis of educational theory, political and social science in China.

THE TEXT

For Plato, the central purpose in describing his 'Republic' is that of illustrating and identifying the nature of 'justice'. Plato says it is easier to see 'justice' in the large case of the state than in the small case of the individual. In the *Analects*, however, it seems that Confucius takes the opposite view, deciding to focus on domestic rituals and the model of the 'superior man' instead.

Naturally, much of the *Analects* is offering advice on the importance of following traditions and rituals. One section starts by reminding us that Confucius, speaking about an aristocratic family of the time, warned: 'He has eight rows of dancers in his court. If he does this, what will he not do?'

By which he meant that those who adopt pretensions beyond their proper status in domestic matters will be excessive in more important relations too. 'Eight rows of dancers' was the number allowable to only the most important nobles. Later, when Lin Fang asks the master about the fundamentals of ritual, Confucius' reply is, 'What an excellent question! In ritual, it is better to be frugal than extravagant; in funerals deep sorrow is better than ease.'

Confucius' descriptions of the 'superior man' are a little like Aristotle's later account of his character model the 'great souled' or 'magnanimous' man. Magnanimous man offers great banquets for fear of being considered stingy, but Confucius tell us in *Analects* 1:14 that 'When the Superior Man eats he does not try to stuff himself' while at rest he does not 'seek perfect comfort' and in general that he is diligent in his work and careful in speech. 'He avails himself to people of the *Tao* and thereby corrects himself. This is the kind of person of whom you can say, "He loves learning."'

And in a following passage, we are reminded that when Tzu Kung asked Confucius: 'What do you think of a poor man who doesn't grovel or a rich man who isn't proud?' the Master said, 'They are good, but not as good as a poor man who is satisfied and a rich man who loves propriety.'

'The Superior Man takes Rightness as the essence', Confucius says. 'He actualises it through propriety, demonstrates it in humility, develops it by truthfulness. This is the Superior Man!' And Confucius explains: 'The Superior Man stands in awe of three things:'

- He is in awe of the decree of Heaven.
- He is in awe of great men.
- He is in awe of the words of the sages.

The inferior man does not know the decree of Heaven; he takes great men lightly; and he laughs at the words of the sages. The superior man concerns himself with the fundamentals. Once the fundamentals are established, the proper way (*tao*) appears. This figure, the 'superior man', appears throughout Chinese philosophy, and the literal translation, from the Chinese, is 'son of a prince'. But for Confucius and the Taoists, like Chuang Tzu, it means one who was skilled in finding the 'way'. And what is the 'way'? Ah, now that truly is mysterious.

The ancient text of the *I Ching* (circa 900 BCE), or *Book of Changes*, is essentially an investigation of the *tao*, and how to understand the world. Jung wrote of the *I Ching* that 'this is a book for lovers of wisdom', and so it is; but it is foremost a guide to action, a guide to achieving the best outcome in the circumstances. It has been used as a practical manual for 3,000 years, consulted by farmers and generals as much as by emperors and sages. Chinese philosophy regards thinking and acting as two aspects of one activity – two sides of the same coin – and *T'ai Chi* – ultimate reality – is a combination of mind (*li*) and matter (*chi*). So what is the *tao*? *Tao* is empty. Lao Tzu, Confucius' contemporary, wrote in the fourth chapter of the *Tao Te Ching:* (350–250 BCE)

like a bowl, it may be used, but is never emptied, it is bottomless, the ancestor of all things, it blunts sharpness, it unties knots, it softens the light, it becomes one with the dusty world – deep and still, it exists for ever.

Scarcely surprising then that the superior man also makes mistakes. The difference between him and other people is that he 'rectifies', or corrects, his errors as soon as he becomes aware of them. The Master says:

If the Superior Man is not 'heavy,' then he will not inspire awe in others. If he is not learned, then he will not be on firm ground. He takes loyalty and good faith to be of primary importance, and has no friends who are not of equal (moral) calibre. When he makes a mistake, he doesn't hesitate to correct it.

It is partly because of this human fallibility that Confucius considers traditions and rituals to be so important.

Confucius continues: 'If you would govern a state of a thousand chariots [by which he means a small-to-middle-size state], you must pay strict attention to business, be true to your word, be economical in expenditure and love the people. You should use them according to the seasons.' And similarly the next section advises that

A young man should serve his parents at home and be respectful to elders outside his home. He should be earnest and truthful, loving all, but become intimate with humaneness. After doing this, if he has energy to spare, he can study literature and the arts.

It may seem strange that a text should rush from the commonplace to the grand, but then Confucius' focus is not on acts, but on motives. Like Plato, he is concerned with the state only as a way of illustrating how everyone should conduct their lives.

Confucius counsels: 'While your parents are alive, it is better not to travel far away. If you do travel, you should have a precise destination.' Furthermore he specifies: 'When your father is alive, observe his will'; and 'When your father is dead observe his former actions. If, for three years you do not change from the ways of your father, you can be called a "real son".'

But interspersed with the homilies for children are the guidelines for rulers. For Confucius, it is not just the same attitude that is needed by both ministers and parents, it is the activity that is one and the same. One analect recalls that someone asked Confucius: 'Why are you not involved in government?' The Master replied, 'What does the Book of History say about filial piety? "Just by being a good son and friendly to one's brothers and sisters you can have an effect on government." Since this is also "doing government", why do I need to *do* "doing government"?'

The *Analects'* first overt statement on government comes at the start of the second section. Confucius says: 'If you govern with the power of your virtue, you will be like the North Star. It just stays in its place while all the other stars position themselves around it.' This is a significant point, as the contemporary Confucian philosopher, Charles Muller, has put it, because of the often claimed radical distinction between Confucian 'authoritative' government and Taoist 'laissez-faire' government. Here, as elsewhere in the *Analects*, Confucius is indicating that governing by example and by gentle attunement with an inner principle of goodness, without unnecessary external action, is better than following programmes of action.

On the same theme, Confucius continues:

If you govern the people legalistically and control them by punishment, they will avoid crime, but have no personal sense of shame. If you govern them by means of virtue and control them with propriety, they will gain their own sense of shame, and thus correct themselves.

And he adds: 'How sublime was the manner in which Shun and Yu handled the empire, without lifting a finger!'

When Tzu Kung asked about government, the Master said: 'Enough food, enough weapons and the confidence of the people.' Tzu Kung said, 'Suppose you had no alternative but to give up one of these three, which one would be let go of first?' Confucius replied, 'Weapons.' Tzu Kung said: 'What if you had to give up one of the remaining two, which one would it be?' Confucius replied again: 'Food. From ancient times, death has come to all men, but a people without confidence in its rulers will not stand.'

Chi K'ang Tzu too is recorded asking Confucius about government, saying: 'Suppose I were to kill the unjust, in order to advance the just. Would that be all right?' To this, Confucius replied:

In doing government, what is the need of killing? If you desire good, the people will be good. The nature of the Superior Man is like the wind, the nature of the Inferior Man is like the grass. When the wind blows over the grass, it always bends.

On another occasion, Chung Kung, who was then serving as prime minister to the head of the Chi family, also asked about government. Confucius advised him: 'First get some officers; then grant pardon for all the petty offences and then put virtuous and able men into positions of responsibility.' He asked, 'How am I going to find these virtuous and able men to get them into these positions?' The Master said, 'Select from those you know. Will the people let you ignore the ones you don't know of?'

When Tzu Lu said: 'The ruler of Wei is anticipating your assistance in the administration of his state. What will be your top priority?' Confucius replied: 'There must be a correction of terminology.' Tzu Lu said, 'Are you serious? Why is this so important?' Confucius said, 'You are being simple, aren't you? A Superior Man is cautious about jumping to conclusions about that which he does not know.' He then goes on:

If terminology is not corrected, then what is said cannot be followed. If what is said cannot be followed, then work cannot be accomplished. If work cannot be accomplished, then ritual and music cannot be developed. If ritual and music cannot be developed, then criminal punishments will not be appropriate. If criminal punishments are not appropriate, the people cannot make a move. Therefore, the Superior Man needs to have his terminology applicable to real language, and his speech must accord with his actions. The speech of the Superior Man cannot be indefinite.

Nonetheless, Confucius' philosophy is often enigmatic, if not actually 'indefinite'. Like Plato, for instance, he venerates the art of 'knowing what you do not know', saying: 'Yu, shall I teach you about knowledge? What you know, you know, what you don't know, you don't know. This is knowledge.'

One analect recalls that when Confucius entered the Grand Temple, he asked about everything. Someone commented, 'Who said Confucius is a master of ritual? He enters the Grand Temple and asks about everything!' Confucius, hearing this, said, 'This is the ritual.' And sometimes, in line with admitting the limits of his knowledge, Confucius simply admits not knowing. Another analect recalls that when someone asked for an explanation of 'the Great

Sacrifice', Confucius said, 'I don't know.' He then pointed to the palm of his hand and added 'If there were someone who knew this, he could see the whole world as if it were this.'

On another occasion Confucius notes: 'I have spent a whole day without eating and a whole night without sleeping in order to think, but I got nothing out of it. Thinking cannot compare with studying.'

One of the last of the analects recalls that Tzu Kung asked the Master: 'Is there a single concept that we can take as a guide for the actions of our whole life?' Confucius said, 'What about "fairness"? What you don't like done to yourself, don't do to others.' This is sometimes credited by moral philosophers as 'the golden rule'. But as to that other great question, 'What is justice?' the *Analects* records what happened when the Duke of Sheh told Confucius: 'In my land, there are Just men. If a father steals a sheep, the son will testify against him', Confucius then said, 'The Just men in my land are different from this. The father conceals the wrongs of his son, and the son conceals the wrongs of his father. This is Rightness!'

Yet on another occasion, when he was asked 'What do you think of the saying: "Repay harm with virtue"?' Confucius replied, 'Then how will you repay virtue? Repay harm with Justice and repay virtue with virtue.' If this seems contradictory, it is here that the example of the 'superior man' is needed. 'When you see a good person, think of becoming like her/him. When you see someone not so good, reflect on your own weak points.' Indeed, Confucius values mistakes, saying that 'It is by observing a person's mistakes that you can know their goodness.' This is because 'People err according to their own level.' It is only when you are really committed to humanity, Confucius says, that you will have no evil in you. The *Analects* explains that there were four things the Master had eliminated from himself: imposing his will, arbitrariness, stubbornness and egotism.

If today education is often claimed as a worthy political goal, it is for Confucius not education in itself that is the purpose, but changing people's attitudes and behaviour. One analect relates that Confucius asked: 'Is anyone incapable of following words giving correct instruction? But it is self-transformation according to it that is important. Is anyone incapable of enjoying words of gentle advice? But it is inquiring deeply into their meaning that is important. If I enjoy without inquiring deeply, and follow without changing myself, how can I say that I have understood them?'

One time when the Master was extremely ill, Tzu Lu wanted the disciples to become Confucius' 'ministers'. During a remission in his illness, Confucius said, 'Ah, Yu has been deceitful for a long time. Though I don't have ministers, you would make it appear that I have them? Who would I be fooling? Heaven? I would much rather die in the hands of my disciples than in the hands of ministers. And I would prefer dying in the streets to a pompous funeral!'

But more often, the Master is simply enigmatic. Explaining how the quality of becoming 'humane' is part of the philosophical character of the sage, Confucius says: 'The wise enjoy the sea, the humane enjoy the mountains. The wise are busy, the humane are tranquil. The wise are happy, the humane are eternal.' When Tzu Lu asked if it was a good idea to immediately put a teaching into practice when he first heard it, Confucius replied: 'You have a father and an older brother to consult. Why do you need to be so quick to practise it?' Yet when Zan Yu asked the same question, Confucius said: 'You should practise it immediately.' Kung Hsi Hua then said, 'When Yu asked you, you told him he should consult his father and elder brother first. When Ch'iu (Zan Yu) asked you, you told him to practise it immediately. May I ask why?' Confucius' response was, 'Ch'iu has a tendency to give up easily, so I push him. Yu (Tzu Lu) has a tendency to jump the gun, so I restrain him.'

A similar thing happened, we learn, when Meng Wu Po asked Confucius whether Tzu Lu was a humane man. Confucius said, 'I don't know.' Meng Wu Po asked again. Confucius said this time, 'Yu could direct the public works forces in a state of 1,000 chariots, but I don't know if I would call him a humane man.' Meng again asked: 'What about Ch'iu?' And Confucius said, 'Ch'iu could be the governor of a city of 1,000 families, or of a clan of 100 chariots, but I don't know if he is a humane man.' Finally, Meng asked: 'What about Ch'ih?' The Master said, 'Dressed up with his sash, placed in the middle of the court, he could make conversation with the guests, but I don't know if he is a humane man.'

On the other hand, of himself , Confucius says: 'I can live with coarse rice to eat, water for drink and my arm as a pillow and still be happy. Wealth and honours that one possesses in the midst of injustice are like floating clouds.' As to pleasures, he advises that

There are three kinds of enjoyment which are beneficial and three kinds of enjoyment which are harmful. The enjoyment of cultivation in music and ritual, the enjoyment of speaking of the goodness of others and the enjoyment of being surrounded by friends of good character are all beneficial. The enjoyment of arrogance, the enjoyment of dissipation and the enjoyment of comfort are all harmful.

The key to Confucian philosophy, as to society itself, is the concept of balance. When Tzu Kung asked who was the most worthy between Shih and Shang, the Master said, 'Shih goes too far, Shang does not go far enough.' 'Then is Shih superior?' The Master said, 'Going too far is the same as not going far enough.'

Balance is so important that it takes precedence even over avoiding suffering or achieving greatness. One key analect explains that

Riches and honours are what all men desire. But if they cannot be attained in accordance with the *Tao* they should not be kept. Poverty and low status are what all men hate. But if they cannot be avoided while staying in accordance with the *Tao*, you should not avoid them. If a Superior Man departs from humanity, how can he be worthy of that name? A Superior Man never leaves humanity for even the time of a single meal. In moments of haste he acts according to it. In times of difficulty or confusion he acts according to it.

The simple life of Yu affords Confucius an inspiring example. He says:

Yu was flawless in character. Surviving on the simplest food and drink, yet perfect in his piety to the ancestral spirits. Normally wearing coarse clothing, he looked magnificent in his ceremonial cap and gown. Living in a humble abode, he exhausted himself in the excavation of drainage ways and canals. I cannot find a flaw in his character!

This is made even more explicit later, when we are reminded that Confucius said:

The Superior Man indulges in the *Tao* and does not indulge in his stomach. Doesn't agriculture have the avoidance of starvation as its motivating factor, and study have enrichment as its motivating factor? The Superior Man is concerned about following the *Tao*, and is not concerned about avoiding poverty.

After all, Confucius warns: 'Luxury leads to laxity, frugality leads to firmness. It is better to be firm than to be lax.' And Confucius emphasises the importance of the human spirit, in even the humblest of simple farmers. Confucius said: 'You can snatch away the general of a large army, but you cannot snatch away the will of even the lowliest of men.'

On one occasion, Chung Kung asked about the meaning of humaneness. The Master replied:

Go out of your home as if you were receiving an important guest. Employ the people as if you were assisting at a great ceremony. What you don't want done to yourself, don't do to others. Live in your town without stirring up resentments, and live in your household without stirring up resentments.

Chung Kung said, 'Although I am not so smart, I will apply myself to this teaching.'

On another occasion, when Duke Ting asked if there were a single phrase which could uplift a country, Confucius replied:

Words in themselves cannot have such an effect. Nonetheless, there is a proverb which says, 'Being a ruler is difficult, and being a minister is not easy.' If you really understand the difficulties of rulership, might this not be enough to uplift a country?

The Duke asked further: 'Is there a single phrase which could ruin a country?' Confucius answered:

Again, words in themselves cannot have such an effect, but the people also have a proverb which says: 'I do not enjoy ruling; I only enjoy people not disagreeing with me.' Now if you are a good man and no one disagrees with you, it is fine. But if you are evil, and no one disagrees with you, perhaps you could destroy the country with a single utterance.

Towards the end of the *Analects*, and of his life, Confucius says: 'I wish I could avoid talking.' At this, Tzu Kung replies, 'Master, if you didn't speak, what would we disciples have to pass on?' And Confucius then says: 'Does Heaven speak? Yet the four seasons continue to change, and all things are born.'

THE SUBTEXT

During his lifetime, Confucius was considered a great 'teacher', but his teachings themselves were not accepted. Nonetheless, 3,000 'disciples' came to study under him, and so, several generations after his death, his ideas had spread and found widespread acceptance throughout China. Indeed, by the second century CE they had become the official ideology of the Chinese state, under the Han dynasty. Confucianism then spread to other Asian countries, such as Japan, Korea and Singapore. And although Marxism claims that feudal ideologies like Confucianism can have no useful lessons for industrial or post-industrial societies, Mao himself was careful to incorporate, some would say appropriate, many elements of Confucianism into his supposedly 'new' philosophy.

Confucius' key idea was that a particular kind of humanism, loosely translated as 'human-heartedness' (ren, pronounced 'jen'; the word has the same sound in Chinese as 'people') is the key to a harmonious society and is the highest state that individuals can achieve. 'If you lead the people with political force and restrict them with law and punishment', one central analect warns, they will respect the letter of the law, but 'have no sense of honour or shame'. On the other hand, if you guide the people towards an understanding of morality, then 'they will do good of their own accord'. In fact, the promotion of human-heartedness is the central task of the state. It is education, traditions and rituals that are the tools available to the public authorities in creating and encouraging ren, the social cement. For Confucius, in order for society to be just, each individual member of it must be brought to behave justly, and the best way to achieve that was to promote mutual respect through respecting 'traditions'. It is then not necessary that individuals understand the finer points of morality.

Yet at the same time Confucius was a social conservative who entrenched divisions in Chinese society, condemning the vast majority of the population to lives of grinding poverty and political irrelevance. His harmonious society was created at the cost of both social justice and change. He was disparaged by the Mozi and the Mohists, who saw ritual as 'inefficient' and a distraction, as well as by the Taoists, such as Lao Tzu, who saw ritual as empty and false, 'a superficial expression of loyalty and faithfulness, and the beginning of disorder'. And, perhaps most resonant today, there were the views of the 'Legalists', who saw the proper aim of politics as the creation of a wealthy and powerful nation. The Legalists saw the traditions as holding back progress and perceived ethics itself as an obstacle to good law. To all of this, Confucianism takes lofty refuge in its obscurity.

On one occasion, Confucius was asked his opinion of a dispute between the Duke of Ai and Tsai Wo about the correct way to plant out sacred temple grounds. Tsai Wo pointed out that the Hsia emperor had planted them with pine trees; the Hsiang people had planted them with cypress and the Chou people had planted them with chestnut, all hoping to cause people to be in awe of their trees. Confucius' response on hearing this was characteristically unhelpful: 'Don't bother explaining that which has already been done; don't bother criticising that which is already gone; don't bother blaming that which is already past.'

KEY IDEAS

* People are not of equal importance, nor need they be treated as such. Instead, they should be adapted to their allotted roles.
* Society cannot be regulated solely by force, but requires the cultivation of the virtue of its citizens, to be achieved through respecting rituals and tradition.

KEY TEXT

The Analects of Confucius

SOURCE

I have relied upon the translation of Charles Muller, Tokyo Gakuen University, formerly to be found at http://www.hm.tyg.jp/~acmuller/contao/analects.htm. Over time, this has become unavailable (although, strictly speaking, all pages are archived on the Internet and remain there 'for ever'). A broadly equivalent text can be found at http://classics.mit.edu/Confucius/analects.html.

Timeline:
From Sacred Duties to Church Homilies

ABOUT 300 BCE
The ancient Indian philosopher Kautilya produces the *Arthasatra*, a ruthless political work sometimes compared to *The Prince*. Kautilya describes a system in which the king is just one amongst seven powers, all charged with the sacred duty of safeguarding the welfare of the people.

ABOUT 150 BCE
The Chinese use written examinations to select civil servants – but the process becomes tainted by the practice of training the applicants in the correct responses, a problem no examination system has yet overcome.

115 BCE
High point of the Roman Empire – in 122 BCE Emperor Hadrian builds Hadrian's Wall in Britain to defend the civilised areas from the barbarians. In 212 CE citizenship is conferred on all free adults in the Empire.

FOURTH CENTURY
The Indians create the 'empty circle', or 'zero', to stand in for 'nothing', and with it make possible modern mathematics.

EARLY FIFTH CENTURY
After Rome falls to the 'barbarians', a collection of Aristotle's manuscripts find their way to Persia, where they are preserved by the Arabs throughout the 'Dark Ages' in Europe.

AROUND 1100–1300
A reformed Christian church, anxious to combat heresies, regains Aristotle's manuscripts from the 'infidel'. Catholic monks, who regarded his views as possessing an almost divine authority, carefully

translate the books into Latin during the twelfth and thirteenth centuries. It is only now that Aristotle begins to supplant Plato as 'the Philosopher'. Indeed, in his heyday, according to Brother Giles of Rome, there were churches in Reformation Germany in which Aristotle's *Ethics* was read every Sunday morning to the people instead of the Gospel.

3
Aristotle and the Hierarchy of Nature

There is a suitably grand oil painting depicting the 'two great' Greek philosophers in the Academy surrounded by the other Greek illuminati. The 'School of Athens', painted by the Renaissance artist Raphael in the sixteenth century (when such things were back in vogue), shows Plato, remembered for teaching the virtues of the mysterious world of the Forms, gesticulating with his hand directed upwards as if saying: 'Look to the perfection of the heavens for truth.' Aristotle, by contrast, whose philosophy is supposed to start with observation of earthly phenomena, is pointing downwards, as if to say: 'Look around you at what is if you would know the truth.'

That's an idealised picture of course. In fact, Aristotle's reputation during his lifetime, and for a long period afterwards, was nowhere near as elevated as that of Plato. Yet it is Aristotle's politics that came to have the greater influence on the development of western society. This is partly because of the historical accident by which Plato's writings were largely unknown, and Aristotle's were carefully guarded and later spread by the religious authorities.

THE CONTEXT

As a small boy, Aristotle was introduced to the mysteries of the natural world by his father, who was a minor aristocrat, being the official doctor and herbalist for the Macedonian king. Alas, this time was cut short by the early deaths of both his parents, and instead Aristotle found himself the ward of one Proxenus, the husband of his sister, Arimneste and, it seems, a friend of Plato. For whatever reason, in 367, at the age of 17, Aristotle left home to become a student of Plato at the renowned Academy at Athens. And if he arrived intending to learn simply how to practise medicine, he soon became caught up instead with all the other debates there at the time, concerning mathematics, astronomy, laws and politics. But not too caught up. For Aristotle the aristocrat proclaims that 'the first principle of any action is leisure' (*Politics*, Book 8), adding approvingly that 'the proverb says, "there is no leisure for slaves"'.

So he should not have been too disappointed when, following Plato's death in 347 BCE, it was Speusippus, Plato's nephew, who was named head of the Academy. Shortly afterwards Aristotle left mainland Greece, with his friend Xenocrates, to set up a mini-academy of his own in the city of Assos in what is today north-western Turkey and was then a mini-statelet ruled by Hermias, a dictator if not a tyrant.

At this time Aristotle concentrated on the 'sciences', notably biology. Forever fascinated by the huge variety of animal life, he was always working on arranging them into hierarchies and in fact, about a quarter of all his writing is concerned with categorising nature, including the different forms the soul takes in different creatures. He was best at classifying sea life and even observed that since the dolphin gave birth in the manner of certain land animals, it belonged with the mammals, not with the other fish. However, away from the sea his observations led him astray as often as not. He declared wrongly that plants reproduced only asexually, and that for humans the heart was the centre of consciousness, and indeed that it beat only in men's breasts. He thought that the left side of the body was colder than the right, and that the brain was there merely to cool the blood, although there was an 'empty space' in the back of every man's head, for the soul. Thus he denied women souls, as indeed he did plants and animals. In fact, Aristotle denies the power of thought to all three groups, maintaining that they are capable only of sensation and appetite, and that they need the rule of men in order to survive.

When Aristotle describes the nature of space and time, his cosmology is always conservative. On Earth all things are changeable and corrupt, while in the heavens all is permanent and unchanging, He thought that the 'heavenly spheres' of Ptolemy were not just meta-phorically but literally crystal spheres, and then went on to calculate that for the heavens to function properly, there must be a few more of them, arriving eventually at the inelegant total of 54 spheres.

As the Earth was the centre of the universe, everything was arranged around it in layers. Water was above earth, air above water, and fire highest of all. That this was so was born out by observation: an object composed largely of earth, such as a rock, would, if suspended in air, fall downward; droplets of water fall as rain; bubbles of air trapped under water rise upwards, as do flames in a fire.

It also seemed obvious to Aristotle that the heavier an object was, the faster it would fall. Simple practical experiment can prove this is false, but instead this error blocked progress in physics until Galileo and Newton managed to demonstrate it was a logical and not just an empirical impossibility. Likewise, Aristotle considered but rejected Democritus' theory that things were made up of atoms, thereby holding up chemistry for 2,000 years. By a queer symmetry, as one commentator has observed, it almost seemed as though his statements were most accepted when they were most incorrect.

Fortunately perhaps for progress, Aristotle's studies were interrupted by a royal injunction to return to Macedonia to help educate Alexander the Great, the heir to the Macedonian throne. His main activity seems to have been preparing and copying out a special version of the *Iliad* for the young warrior. But if Alexander enjoyed this ripping yarn, he seems not have shared any of Aristotle's other interests.

Returning at last to Athens, Aristotle set up the new college which became known as the 'peripatetic school', after the Greek for 'walk about', because Aristotle, it was said, used to walk about whilst giving his lectures in the open air. Whether he did this or not, Aristotle seems to have made sure that all his thoughts were committed to paper, and this in time, if rather unfairly, would ensure his pre-eminence amongst the ancient Greek thinkers.

THE TEXT

Aristotle's politics are scattered throughout his writings, but conventionally his thoughts are gathered together in the eight 'books' (we should say essays more accurately) of the *Politics*. Here, Aristotle offers his alternative vision of society, in opposition to the *Republic* of Plato. Like Plato, he starts by describing the origins of the state.

The family is the association established by nature for the supply of men's everyday wants, and the members of it are called by Charondas, 'companions of the cupboard,' and by Epimenides the Cretan, 'companions of the manger.' But when several families are united, and the association aims at something more than the supply of daily needs, the first society to be formed is the village. And the most natural form of the village appears to be that of a colony from the family, composed of the children and grandchildren, who are said to be suckled 'with the same milk.'

Aristotle, unlike Plato, likes to back up all his assertions with 'evidence', either in the form of observations or with endorsements by ancient authorities. In this case, his chosen source is Homer, who he reminds us agrees that 'Each one gives law to his children and to his wives.' However, a village is yet too small to be a 'society', so it is only when several villages 'are united in a single complete community, large enough to be nearly or quite self-sufficing', that the state comes into existence, 'originating in the bare needs of life, and continuing in existence for the sake of a good life'.

Aristotle deduces that this process is natural – a key concept for him – and hence, that man too must be 'by nature a political animal'. He goes on:

Now, that man is more of a political animal than bees or any other gregarious animals is evident. Nature, as we often say, makes nothing in vain, and man is the only animal whom she has endowed with the gift of speech. And whereas mere voice is but an indication of pleasure or pain, and is therefore found in other animals (for their nature attains to the perception of pleasure and pain and the intimation of them to one another, and no further), the power of speech is intended to set forth the expedient and inexpedient, and therefore likewise the just and the unjust. And it is a characteristic of man that he alone has any sense of good and evil, of just and unjust, and the like, and the association of living beings who have this sense makes a family and a state.

And of course, there is the proof, as he puts it, that society is natural, and indeed, 'prior to the individual', and that is the fact that whenever an individual is obliged to live on their own, they find it difficult to survive. For that reason, the 'social instinct is implanted in all men by nature'. This instinct is characterised by the need for justice, an instinct which can exist only in the context of social relations. For if man, at his best, is 'the best of animals', once separated from law and justice, he becomes the worst of all, 'the most unholy and the most savage of animals, and the most full of lust and gluttony'. Justice is the bond that protects man from himself.

Yet Aristotle's sense of justice, we must always recall, is not everyone's. He insists that some men are created superior to others, and many are intended by nature to be slaves. Of men and women, 'the male is by nature superior, and the female inferior; and the one rules, and the other is ruled; this principle, of necessity, extends to all mankind'. Plenty of people then thought this, indeed still think it, but Aristotle's significance has been to offer a theoretical justification that, weak as it was, would nonetheless ensure that the prejudice would dominate the western world during the Middle Ages and leave many traces to today, especially in conservative Islam. Not that Aristotle is completely oblivious to women's abilities. He adds later, generously, that 'All classes must be deemed to have their special attributes; as the poet says of women: "Silence is a woman's glory."'

In similar spirit, Aristotle theorises that whole races must be inferior to the Greeks, and just as animals exist for the sake of man, inferior races existed only for the sake of the superior races. For this reason, 'the art of war' is a natural art of acquisition; 'for the art of acquisition includes hunting, an art which we ought to practise against wild beasts, and against men who, though intended by nature to be governed, will not submit; for war of such a kind is naturally just'.

Aristotle has concerns though even about some of the routine activities of the superior races. 'The laziest are shepherds', he writes, those 'who lead an idle life, and get their subsistence without trouble from tame animals', but not much better are those who indulge in the retail trade. He objects that a shopkeeper who 'gives a shoe in exchange for money or food to him who wants one, does indeed use the shoe as a shoe, but this is not its proper or primary purpose, for a shoe is not made to be an object of barter'. The same may be said of all possessions, for 'the retail trade is not a natural part of the art of getting wealth; had it been so, men would have ceased to exchange when they had enough'.

Contrariwise, trade in 'necessities' between countries is natural, and occasions, also 'necessarily', the use of money. This is because 'the various necessaries of life are not easily carried about', and hence men were obliged to exchange instead something which was 'intrinsically useful and easily applicable to the purposes of life', for example, he suggests, iron, silver, and the like. 'Of this the value was at first measured simply by size and weight, but in process of time they put a stamp upon it, to save the trouble of weighing and to mark the value.'

Alas, inventing coins also created the pursuit of wealth. 'Indeed, riches is assumed by many to be only a quantity of coin.' But how can it be, asks Aristotle rhetorically, that a man like Midas in the fable (the king whose wish that everything set before him be turned to gold disastrously came true) may have wealth in great abundance and yet perish with hunger? Dislike of shopkeepers was reflected for centuries by Christian societies, while Aristotle's prohibition of usury or moneylending lives on to the present day amongst the Islamic societies that adopted and transmitted his thoughts from ancient Greece to the modern world.

There are two sorts of wealth-getting, as I have said; one is a part of household management, the other is retail trade: the former necessary and honourable, while that which consists in exchange is justly censured; for it is unnatural, and a mode by which men gain from one another. The most hated sort, and with the greatest reason, is usury, which makes a gain out of money itself, and not from the natural object of it. For money was intended to be used in exchange, but not to increase at interest. And this term interest, which means the birth of money from money, is applied to the breeding of money because the offspring resembles the parent. Wherefore, of all modes of obtaining wealth, this is the most *unnatural*.

In Book 2 of his 'Politics', Aristotle turns more directly to consideration of Plato's vision of the citizens of a new republic living communally and sharing all possessions, including children. Aristotle is sceptical, saying:

That all persons call the same thing 'mine' in the sense in which each does so may be a fine thing, but it is impracticable; or if the words are taken in the other sense, such a unity in no way conduces to harmony. And there is another objection to the proposal. For that which is common to the greatest number has the least care bestowed upon it. Every one thinks chiefly of his own, hardly at all of the common interest; and only when he is himself concerned as an individual. For besides other considerations, everybody is more inclined to neglect the duty which he expects another to fulfil; as in families many attendants are often less useful than a few. Each citizen will have a thousand sons who will not be his sons individually but anybody will be equally the son of anybody, and will therefore be neglected by all alike.

In fact, he says, if self-sufficiency is to be desired, 'the lesser degree of unity is more desirable than the greater'. He has other criticisms too – of the danger of incest if no one knows who are their relatives in a small community, of the difficulty of transferring children born into the lower ranks to the rank of Guardians, and vice versa, not to forget the general problem that arises when everyone lives in close proximity together, which is that people 'generally fall out over everyday matters and quarrel about any trifle which turns up'. So it is with servants, he adds. We are most apt to take offence at those with whom we most frequently come into contact in daily life.

Aristotle takes issue with Plato over the question of property too. It should, he thinks, as a general rule, be private. After all, when everyone has a distinct interest, every one will be too busy attending to his own business to create discord. In any case, Aristotle remarks, the great pleasure of doing a kindness or service to friends or guests 'can only be rendered when a man has private property'.

The trouble is that Plato 'makes the Guardians into a mere occupying garrison', while the husbandmen and artisans and the rest are made into the citizens! He even deprives the Guardians of happiness, saying instead that legislators will be content to make the whole state happy. Yet, if the Guardians are not happy, who will be? 'Surely not the artisans, or the common people.' However, Aristotle thinks that Plato's greatest error is not his focus on property, but his neglect of population control. Like an early-day Malthusian, Aristotle the biologist is preoccupied with the population bomb.

One would have thought that it was even more necessary to limit population than property; and that the limit should be fixed by calculating the chances of mortality in the children, and of sterility in married persons. The neglect of this subject, which in existing states is so common, is a never-failing cause of poverty among the citizens; and poverty is the parent of revolution and crime.

He continues, in commonsense style, to say that 'the legislator who fixes the amount of property should also fix the number of children'. Otherwise, that old bogey of revolution soon threatens. Plato, by focusing on the need for equality of property, has missed the point: 'want is not the sole incentive to crime; men also wish to enjoy themselves and not to be in a state of desire – they wish to cure some desire, going beyond the necessities of life, which preys upon them'. The greatest crimes are caused by excess and not by necessity. Men, Aristotle points out, do not become tyrants in order that they may not suffer cold. In any case, if the 'equalisation of property' is intended to prevent the citizens from quarrelling, the strategy is mistaken:

For the nobles will be dissatisfied because they think themselves worthy of more than an equal share of honours; and this is often found to be a cause of sedition and revolution. And the avarice of mankind is insatiable; at one time two *obols* was pay enough; but now, when this sum has become customary, men always want more and more without end; for it is of the nature of desire not to be satisfied, and most men live only for the gratification of it. The beginning of reform is not so much to equalise property as to train the nobler sort of natures not to desire more, and to prevent the lower from getting more; that is to say, they must be kept down, but not ill-treated.

Having thus despatched Plato's republic, Aristotle outlines in its place his own one. Instead of an elite supervising the masses, in Aristotle's ideal state it is essential that each citizen actively participate. However, the superficial contrast diminishes immediately when one recalls that Aristotle counts as citizens not the bulk of the population, but only the male aristocrats. However, even noting this, it is significant that Aristotle makes political power the defining characteristic of being a citizen. Citizens are different in each kind of state, but 'the citizen whom we are seeking to define is a citizen in the strictest sense, against whom no such exception can be taken, and his special characteristic is that he shares in the administration of justice, and in offices'.

Aristotle then touches upon the problems of people holding power over others, saying that in politics,

when the state is framed upon the principle of equality and likeness, the citizens think that they ought to hold office by turns. Formerly, as is natural, every one would take his turn of service; and then again, somebody else would look after his interest, just as he, while in office, had looked after theirs. But nowadays, for the sake of the advantage which is to be gained from the public revenues and from office, men want to be always in office. One might imagine that the rulers, being sickly, were only kept in health while they continued in office; in that case we may be sure that they would be hunting after places. The conclusion is evident: that governments which have a regard to the common interest are constituted in accordance with strict principles of justice, and are therefore true forms; but those which regard only the interest of the rulers are all defective and perverted forms, for they are despotic, whereas a state is a community of freemen.

In a perhaps surprising aside, Aristotle adds that the real difference between democracy and oligarchy is poverty and wealth. 'Wherever men rule by reason of their wealth, whether they be few or many, that is an oligarchy, and where the poor rule, that is a democracy. But as a fact the rich are few and the poor many.' Because of this, there is a doubt as to what should be the supreme power in the state: Should it be the many? Or the wealthy? Or the good? Or the one best man? Or the strongest? Any of these alternatives, Aristotle says, seems to involve disagreeable consequences. The poor, for example, because they are more in number, will try to divide among themselves the property of the rich – is not this unjust, he asks? 'No, by heaven (will be the reply), for the supreme authority justly willed it. But if this is not injustice, pray what is?'

Nonetheless, the 'principle that the multitude ought to be supreme rather than the few best is one that is maintained, and, though not free from difficulty, yet seems to contain an element of truth'. Aristotle offers the comforting comparison with a feast to explain why: a banquet to which many people contribute is bound to be better than a dinner provided out of a single purse. Similarly, in politics, each individual among the many has a share of virtue and prudence, and when they meet together, 'they become in a manner one man, who has many feet, and hands, and senses; that is a figure of their mind and disposition'. Hence, he says, the many are better judges than a single man of music and poetry; for some understand one part, and some another, and among them they understand the whole.

There is a similar combination of qualities in good men, who differ from any individual of the many, as the beautiful are said to differ from those who are not beautiful, and works of art from realities, because in them the scattered elements are combined, although, if taken separately, the eye of one person or some other feature in another person would be fairer than in the picture.

What is more, the low-grade common people mingling with the higher kind can actually improve the state, 'just as impure food when mixed with what is pure sometimes makes the entire mass more wholesome than a small quantity of the pure would be'.

This seems very enlightened, coming from Aristotle the aristocrat, but he hastens to add that as legislation is necessarily concerned only with those who are equal in birth and in capacity, for men 'of pre-eminent virtue there is no law – they are themselves a law'. And he adds that anyone who attempted to make laws for them would look ridiculous: 'they would probably retort what, in the fable of Antisthenes, the lions said to the hares, when in the council of the beasts the latter began haranguing and claiming equality for all'. It is for this reason that democratic states have instituted ostracism, Aristotle complains, as equality is above all things their aim, and therefore they wish to banish from the city any who seem to predominate too much 'through their wealth, or the number of their friends, or through any other political influence'.

Thinking of the fate of the elite reminds Aristotle of the evolution of human society. He says that the first governments were kingships, 'probably for this reason, because of old, when cities were small, men of eminent virtue were few'. These men of 'eminent virtue' were made kings, he asserts groundlessly, 'because they were benefactors, and benefits can only be bestowed by good men'. The problem arose that as many persons equal in merit arose, the pre-eminence of one became unendurable and so the aristocrats desired to have a commonwealth, and set up a constitution. However, the ruling class so formed 'soon deteriorated and enriched themselves out of the public treasury; riches became the path to honour', and so oligarchies swiftly passed into tyrannies. The end of the decline is democracy, for the love of gain in the ruling classes always tends to diminish their number, 'and so to strengthen the masses, who in the end set upon their masters'.

Aristotle thinks that democratic government is almost inevitable, once a city state reaches a certain size. If royal rule is the best, and tyranny the worst, democracy is at least 'the most tolerable' of the three forms of government. Because democracies have a middle class, which is more numerous and has a greater share in the government, they are safer and more permanent than oligarchies. Where there is no middle class, and the elite are outnumbered greatly by the poor, troubles soon arise, and the state quickly comes to an end. 'Inferiors revolt in order that they may be equal, and equals that they may be superior. Such is the state of mind which creates revolutions.'

In fact, the city which is composed of middle-class citizens

is necessarily best constituted in respect of the elements of which we say the fabric of the state naturally consists. And this is the class of citizens which is most secure in a state, for they do not, like the poor, covet their neighbours' goods; nor do others covet theirs, as the poor covet the goods of the rich; and as they neither plot against others, nor are themselves plotted against, they pass through life safely.

Aristotle even proposes a redistribution of wealth to encourage the middle classes, suggesting that the proceeds of the public revenues should be accumulated and distributed amongst the poor, 'if possible, in such quantities as may enable them to purchase a little farm, or, at any rate, make a beginning in trade or husbandry'.

Aristotle, like Plato before him, then steps dogmatically through all the possible permutations of government, but this time additionally enumerating various arrangements for distributing offices and for administering justice and arriving at new laws. Above all things, he explains, every state should be so administered and so regulated by law that its magistrates cannot possibly make money. In oligarchies special precautions should be taken to ward off this evil. For the people do not take any great offence at being kept out of the government – indeed they are rather pleased to have more leisure for their private business – but what irritates them is to think that their rulers are stealing the public money. Then they will be doubly annoyed; for they lose both honour and profit. If office brought no profit, Aristotle adds wisely, 'then and then only could democracy and aristocracy be combined; for both notables and people might have their wishes gratified'.

Thus the law makers are governed. As for those to whom they give the laws, in all 'properly balanced governments' there is 'nothing which should be more jealously maintained than the spirit of obedience to law', and this most especially in small matters; 'for transgression creeps in unperceived and at last ruins the state, just as the constant recurrence of small expenses in time eats up a fortune'. Aristotle also warns that

the habit of lightly changing the laws is an evil, and, when the advantage is small, some errors both of lawgivers and rulers had better be left; the citizen will not gain so much by making the change as he will lose by the habit of disobedience.

Disobedience is the corollary of too much freedom:

in democracies of the more extreme type there has arisen a false idea of freedom which is contradictory to the true interests of the state. For two principles are characteristic of democracy, the government of the majority and freedom. Men think that what is just is equal; and that equality is the supremacy of the popular will; and that freedom means the doing what a man likes. In such democracies every one lives as he pleases, or in the words of Euripides, 'according to his fancy.' But this is all wrong; men should not think it slavery to live according to the rule of the constitution; for it is their salvation.

Not that Aristotle is against what he calls 'liberty':

The basis of a democratic state is liberty; which, according to the common opinion of men, can only be enjoyed in such a state; this they affirm to be the great end of every democracy. One principle of liberty is for all to rule and be ruled in turn, and indeed democratic justice is the application of numerical not proportionate equality; whence it follows that the majority must be supreme, and that whatever the majority approve must be the end and the just. Every citizen, it is said, must have equality, and therefore in a democracy the poor have more power than the rich, because there are more of them, and the will of the majority is supreme. This, then, is one note of liberty which all democrats affirm to be the principle of their state. Another is that a man should live as he likes. This, they say, is the privilege of a freeman, since, on the other hand, not to live as a man likes is the mark of a slave.

But it would be unwise retrospectively to interpret Aristotle as an early 'liberal'. As he explains with regard to the democratic tendencies of tyrants,

the measures which are taken by tyrants appear all of them to be democratic; such, for instance, as the license permitted to slaves (which may be to a certain extent advantageous) and also that of women and children, and the allowing everybody to live as he likes. Such a government will have many supporters, for most persons would rather live in a disorderly than in a sober manner.

This is because 'in the last and worst form of democracy the citizens are very numerous, and can hardly be made to assemble unless they are paid, and to pay them when there are no revenues presses hardly upon the notables'. Aristotle's solution is that the government should hold few assemblies, and the law courts should consist of many persons, but sit for a few days only.

This system has two advantages: first, the rich do not fear the expense, even although they are unpaid themselves when the poor are paid; and secondly, causes are better tried, for wealthy persons, although they do not like to be long absent from their own affairs, do not mind going for a few days to the law-courts.

For, practical thinker as he is, Aristotle recognises, and indeed is preoccupied by, the cost of running the state. The functions of a state, he tries to cut down to just half a dozen.

First, there must be food; secondly, arts, for life requires many instruments; thirdly, there must be arms, for the members of a community have need of them, and in their own hands, too, in order to maintain authority both against disobedient subjects and against external assailants; fourthly, there must be a certain amount of revenue, both for internal needs, and for the purposes of war; fifthly, or rather first, there must be a care of religion which is commonly called worship; sixthly, and most necessary of all there must be a power of deciding what is for the public interest, and what is just in men's dealings with one another.

Similarly, he delimits the necessary, indeed the unavoidable 'offices' as follows:

- offices concerned with matters of religion, with war, with the revenue and expenditure, with the market, with the city, with the harbours, with the country;

- offices concerned with the courts of law, with the records of contracts, with execution of sentences, with custody of prisoners, with audits and scrutiny and accounts of magistrates;
- offices presiding over the public deliberations of the state;
- lesser offices such as those guardians of women, guardians of the law, guardians of children, and directors of gymnastics; and finally,
- superintendents of gymnastic and Dionysiac contests, and of other similar spectacles.

Curiously, priests must be recruited from the ranks of retired warriors and councillors, as 'it is seemly that the worship of the Gods should be duly performed, and also a rest provided in their service for those who from age have given up active life'.

Practical matters dealt with (including such things as communal meals, city walls and so on), Aristotle then, perhaps rather belatedly, returns to the consideration of 'virtue', agreeing to assume for the moment that 'the best life, both for individuals and states, is the life of virtue'. He notes that some think that a very moderate amount of virtue is enough, but set no limit to their desires of wealth, property, power, reputation, and the like.

To whom we reply by an appeal to facts, which easily prove that mankind does not acquire or preserve virtue by the help of external goods, but external goods by the help of virtue, and that happiness, whether consisting in pleasure or virtue, or both, is more often found with those who are most highly cultivated in their mind and in their character, and have only a moderate share of external goods.

Nor is there much to be praised in military virtues – though in some nations there are even laws tending to stimulate the warlike virtues, 'as at Carthage'. He continues:

There was once a law in Macedonia that he who had not killed an enemy should wear a halter, and among the Scythians no one who had not slain his man was allowed to drink out of the cup which was handed round at a certain feast. Among the Iberians, a warlike nation, the number of enemies whom a man has slain is indicated by the number of obelisks which are fixed in the earth round his tomb; and there are numerous practices among other nations of a like kind, some of them established by law and others by custom. Yet to a reflecting mind it must appear very strange that the statesman should be always considering how he can dominate and tyrannise over others, whether they will or not.

Rather, it is the task of the state to care for each citizen's 'character'.

This is a subject which can be easily understood by any one who casts his eye on the more celebrated states of Hellas, and generally on the distribution of races in the habitable world. Those who live in a cold climate and in Europe are full of spirit, but wanting in intelligence and skill; and therefore they retain comparative freedom, but have no political organisation, and are incapable of ruling over others. Whereas the natives of Asia are intelligent and inventive, but they are wanting in spirit, and therefore they are always in a state of subjection and slavery. But the Hellenic race, which is situated between them, is likewise intermediate in character, being high-spirited and also intelligent. Hence it continues free, and is the best-governed of any nation, and, if it could be formed into one state, would be able to rule the world.

Aristotle adds that 'the citizens must not lead the life of mechanics or tradesmen', for such a life is 'ignoble, and inimical to virtue'. Neither must they be husbandmen, since leisure is necessary both for the development of virtue and the performance of political duties. The creation of good citizens, as Plato saw, must start young – indeed, Aristotle says, in the womb. Commenting now with his biologist's hat on, Aristotle explains that:

The union of male and female when too young is bad for the procreation of children; in all other animals the offspring of the young are small and undeveloped, and with a tendency to produce female children, and therefore also in man, as is proved by the fact that in those cities in which men and women are accustomed to marry young, the people are small and weak ... for women who marry early are apt to be wanton; and in men too the bodily frame is stunted if they marry while the seed is growing (for there is a time when the growth of the seed, also, ceases, or continues to but a slight extent). Women should marry when they are about eighteen years of age, and men at seven and thirty; then they are in the prime of life, and the decline in the powers of both will coincide.

Similarly, Aristotle advises that women who are with child should be careful of themselves:

they should take exercise and have a nourishing diet. The first of these prescriptions the legislator will easily carry into effect by requiring that they shall take a walk daily to some temple, where they can worship the gods who preside over birth. Their minds, however, unlike their bodies, they ought to keep quiet, for the offspring derive their natures from their mothers as plants do from the earth.

As to the exposure and rearing of children, he recommends that there be a law that 'no deformed child shall live', but that, on the other hand, couples with children in excess, should be prevented from committing infanticide but must instead seek abortion 'before sense and life have begun'.

Aristotle has strong views on childcare too, saying that after the children have been born, 'the manner of rearing them may be supposed to have a great effect on their bodily strength'. He continues:

It would appear from the example of animals, and of those nations who desire to create the military habit, that the food which has most milk in it is best suited to human beings; but the less wine the better, if they would escape diseases. Also all the motions to which children can be subjected at their early age are very useful. But in order to preserve their tender limbs from distortion, some nations have had recourse to mechanical appliances which straighten their bodies. To accustom children to the cold from their earliest years is also an excellent practice, which greatly conduces to health, and hardens them for military service. Hence many barbarians have a custom of plunging their children at birth into a cold stream; others, like the Celts, clothe them in a light wrapper only. For human nature should be early habituated to endure all which by habit it can be made to endure; but the process must be gradual. And children, from their natural warmth, may be easily trained to bear cold. Such care should attend them in the first stage of life.

From ages nought to five, a child is to be treated relatively gently, spared both study and labour 'lest its growth be impeded'; but there should be 'sufficient motion to prevent the limbs from being inactive'. This can be secured, among other ways, by amusement, but the amusement should not be vulgar or tiring or effeminate. The 'Directors of Education', Aristotle goes on, should be careful as to which tales or stories the children hear, 'for all such things are designed to prepare the way for the business of later life, and should be for the most part imitations of the occupations which they will hereafter pursue in earnest'.

Aristotle says that of all the things affecting good government and the survival of the constitutions, the most important, as Plato had said too, is education. Or more precisely, adaptation of education to the form of government. Yet, 'in our own day, this principle is universally neglected', Aristotle exclaims! The best laws, though sanctioned by every citizen of the state, 'will be of no avail unless the young are trained by habit and education in the spirit of the constitution'. And like Plato, Aristotle is concerned about what influences children are exposed to. The 'Directors of Education' in particular 'should take care that children are left as little as possible with slaves'. Indecency of speech must be prevented 'for the light utterance of shameful words leads soon to shameful actions'. The young especially should never be allowed to repeat or hear anything of this sort. Legislators should not allow youth to be spectators of *iambi* or of comedy 'until they are of an age to sit at the public tables and to drink strong wine; by that time education will have armed them against the evil influences of such representations'.

Aristotle considers too the question of how young people should be educated, noting that there is much disagreement about the subject – in particular, about the things to be taught, and whether to promote virtue or to concentrate on the best life (the two evidently being in conflict, he thinks). Leaving that unresolved, he thinks it is uncontroversial to define the customary branches of education as the following:

(1)   reading and writing,
(2)   gymnastic exercises,
(3)   music,

and, although it seems rather less often,

(4)   drawing.

Music, although neither 'necessary' nor 'useful', is included for intellectual enjoyment in leisure, even though 'obviously youths are not to be instructed with a view to their amusement, for learning is no amusement, but is accompanied with pain'. Music is there because 'nothing is more absolutely necessary than to provide that the highest class, not only when in office, but when out of office, should have leisure and not disgrace themselves in any way'.

THE SUBTEXT

Aristotle's views on science have slowly been dethroned, despite the church's support, but his views on morality, set out in the *Nicomachean* and the *Eudaemian Ethics*, are still considered to be the finest moral philosophy. He starts with a survey of popular opinions on the subject of 'right and wrong', to find out how the terms are used, in the manner of a social anthropologist. Plato makes very clear his contempt for such an approach. The *Nicomachean Ethics* includes accounts of what the Greeks considered to be the great virtues, exemplified by Aristotle's 'great souled', or 'magnanimous' man, the human being who, we are told, will speak with a deep voice and level utterance, and not be unduly modest either. The main idea is that the proper end of mankind (or rather aristocrats) is the pursuit of *eudaimonia* which is Greek for a very particular kind of 'happiness'. This pursuit has three aspects: as well as mere pleasure, there is political honour, and the rewards of contemplation. Quintessentially, of course, philosophical (though it might also include making lists of animals).

Aristotle's method was to observe the world around him and explain what he saw from how things seemed to be arranged. When Aristotle turned his attention towards social life, he immediately saw that women were treated much worse than men. This, he then deduced, must be because 'Women are defective by nature'; and this, he thought, was best explained by the fact that they cannot produce the male fluid (semen). The Greeks thought this contained little seeds which, when planted in the woman, in time grew into full human beings. During sex, the man supplies the substance of a human being, the soul, which is to say, 'the form', while the woman can only provide, and that later, the nourishment, that is to say, 'the matter'.

This all made sense to Aristotle since the world of 'matter', as Plato had taught, is generally inferior to the world of Forms. (Aristotle frequently attempts to differentiate himself from Plato, usually by unkind criticism; but in reality, Aristotle is Plato revisited.) And so, he realised, the gods had wisely split humanity into two halves, in order to leave the man untainted.

Greek society followed the same principle. Women were confined within the parental home until a husband was chosen for them – at which time they would be in their mid teens. The wife would then be transferred to the home of her husband, where she was expected to fulfil her principal function, of bearing and rearing children – or to be more precise, boys. Usually, only one daughter, at most, would be wanted. Surplus girl children might even be left on the hillside to die. Athenian men had plenty of other ways to satisfy their sexual drive than with wives. There were courtesans or *hetairai*, prostitutes or their own slave women, not to mention of course plenty of boys and other men. The wife's function was primarily that of bringing up a son.

Naturally, the wife could not socialise with her husband and his friends. Social gatherings, even if held in her own home, were strictly off limits. Well-off women were not permitted to leave the house to go to the marketplace or communal well; these were activities reserved for men or for women slaves. Actually, women slaves had in some ways more rights than their mistresses, as slaves were considered as being so low in any case that the distinction between men and women ceased to matter.

In the *Republic*, Plato controversially foresees an upper class of 'Guardians' among whom the chattel status of women is abolished (i.e. she is no longer owned by her husband) and in which women were to receive an education equal to that of men. Even so, in the *Timaeus*, he says that 'it is only males who are created directly by the gods and are given souls', and adds that while men who live rightly return to the stars, those who are 'cowards or lead unrighteous lives may with reason be supposed to have changed into the nature of women in the second generation'.

Aristotle follows the latter, misogynist approach, adding that a man needs to take charge over woman, because he has superior intelligence. Mind you, this arrangement will of course also profit women. Aristotle explicitly compares the relationship between men and women to that between human beings and domesticated animals:

It is the best for all tame animals to be ruled by human beings. For this is how they are kept alive. In the same way, the relationship between the male and the female is by nature such that the male is higher, the female lower, that the male rules and the female is ruled.

Slavery is a similar case, benefiting both slaves and masters. It is best and natural because some people are 'by nature' intended to be slaves. Most foreigners are like this, although, like wild animals, they will need to be conquered first. Among barbarians, remarks Aristotle, showing his cosmopolitanism, no distinction is made between women and slaves, because there is no natural ruler among them: they are a community of slaves, male and female. 'That is why the poets say: "It is correct that Greeks rule barbarians", he notes, 'for by nature what is barbarian and what is slave are the same.'

Then, in one of his occasional contrary thrusts, Aristotle also asks, 'But is there any one thus intended by nature to be a slave?' Are there really those for whom 'such a condition is expedient and right', or rather, is not 'all slavery a violation of nature?' Fortunately, he finds there is 'no difficulty' in answering this question, on grounds of both reason and fact. For 'that some should rule and others be ruled is a thing not only necessary, but expedient: from the hour of their birth, some are marked out for subjection, others for rule'. And he goes on:

That person is by nature a slave who can belong to another person and who only takes part in thinking by recognising it, but not by possessing it. Other living beings (animals) cannot recognise thinking; they just obey feelings. However, there is little difference between using slaves and using tame animals: both provide bodily help to do necessary things.

Slaves should be looked after properly – for economic reasons. But like women, they have no right to leisure, no free time. They can own nothing and should not be allowed to take decisions. They are not members of the community.

Indeed the use made of slaves and of tame animals is not very different; for both with their bodies minister to the needs of life. Nature would like to distinguish between the bodies of freemen and slaves, making the one strong for servile labour, the other upright, and although useless for such services, useful for political life in the arts both of war and peace. But the opposite often happens – that some have the souls and others have the bodies of freemen. And doubtless if men differed from one another in the mere forms of their bodies as much as the statues of the Gods do from men, all would acknowledge that the inferior class should be slaves of the superior. And if this is true of the body, how much more just that a similar distinction should exist in the soul? But the beauty of the body is seen, whereas the beauty of the soul is not seen. It is clear, then, that some men are by nature free, and others slaves, and that for these latter slavery is both expedient and right.

Certainly that is how most of his fellow aristocrats in Greece at the time thought, if not perhaps the slaves too. A possible weakness with this theory, Aristotle soon realised, is that the right kind of souls and bodies do not necessarily go together. So, potentially, one could have the soul of a slave and the body of a freeman, or vice versa. Otherwise, he was very satisfied with his analysis; and what is rather more unfortunate, so have been subsequent generations of political and religious authorities.

KEY IDEAS

Society should be constructed around higher and lower forms of human being. The most important distinctions are:

- Women are inferior to men.
- Barbarians ('foreigners') are inferior to the civilised races.
- Slaves are inferior to everyone.

KEY TEXT

Aristotle's *Politics*

SOURCES

The quotations in the chapter are based on Benjamin Jowett's translation of the *Politics*.

Timeline:
A New Religion Spreads Across
Three Continents

BETWEEN 600 AND 1300 CE

During the Dark Ages in Europe, social life continued to flourish elsewhere in the world. For the period of the Tang dynasty in China (between 618 and 907), Changan is believed to have been the world's largest city, home to more than a million people. The prize of being not only the world's largest metropolis, but also the dominant cultural and artistic centre, then went to the Middle East and Baghdad, followed by Fez and, by the end of the twelfth century, by Polonnaruwa in Sri Lanka. Today, this great city is little more than picturesque ruins.

AROUND 570

Mohammed is born in Mecca and later marries into the Quraysh, a wealthy family responsible for the city's most holy shrine, the Kabah.

AROUND 610

Mohammed announces to pilgrims at the shrine that they are wasting their time as the images there are false. Instead, he reveals that he has heard a voice telling him to take on the role of God's messenger.

622

After encountering oppositon, Mohammed and his supporters relocate to Medina, a town to the north of Mecca, where they formalise an alternative religion – backed by its own army. They return in force to Mecca, destroy the 'false idols' of the Kabah and oblige all the people of Arabia to conform to the new rules.

632

Mohammed dies.

636

Damascus falls to the army of Islam and the Roman army sent to relieve the city is similarly vanquished, leading to the retreat of the Christian forces from Syria and Palestine. Iraq soon follows.

640

The Romans are again defeated, this time at Heliopolis in Egypt, allowing the spread of Islam through Libya and Persia (modern-day Iran).

AROUND 700–730

The Army of Islam sweeps westward through North Africa to Spain and southern France, and eastward to Pakistan and Russian Turkestan. One century after the prophet's death, his successors rule an empire of 30 million subjects, spread out across half the Old World.

4

Mohammed's Message of Doom

The Koran is a work of political philosophy. Some may say it is the work of God, but in that case it is God's work of political philosophy. Whatever. Today, over a billion people accept its guidance on matters of social, economic and cultural life. As a blueprint for daily living it is far more accurately followed than those drawn up by Plato and Aristotle. And the reason is not so hard to find – where philosophers are conventionally bound to back up their political claims and positions with some sort of argument, even at the cost of diluting the message, Mohammed simply claims the contents of the Koran to have been communicated to him directly by God and outlaws differences of opinion. In place of reason, he offers stark pronouncements and dire warnings of the 'consequences' of ignoring his message.

THE CONTEXT

There is a 'culture gap', to say the least, between those who accept the possibility of divine revelations and those who don't – even if, today, many of the latter group are inclined to allow all sorts of concessions to the former, in the manner of a kindly psychiatrist to a confused patient. Muslims may have a prayer room for midday. Jews may erect poles around the city centre. Catholics may withdraw their children from classes where the theory of evolution is taught and request fish on Friday. All this is offered by secular societies to their religious minorities. But naturally, the 'lunatics' are not particularly grateful.

Yet the difference between believers and non-believers can be overstated. Moral values are just that – values. And values, like mathematical axioms, rest on nothing other than their own inherent plausibility. And equally, no one, no matter how rational, can *disprove* the existence of God, because a negative can never be demonstrated. Clinging to the non-existence of God is as irrational as insisting on any other religious doctrine.

But in order to cope with the claims of politico-religious systems, atheists will do their best to allow the existence of God, at least temporarily, 'as a possibility', and then see what would rationally follow. If there is a God, then it is possible, if still rather unlikely, that God might take an interest in the conduct of human affairs and might have delivered His view of the correct political system for mankind to follow, first to Moses and then to Mohammed. Perhaps then, yes, there is an obligation, indeed, a strong personal interest, in following the guidance.

On the other hand, it would also be reasonable to suppose that the mere mortals who receive such systems might make mistakes in transcribing the system. (Orthodox Islam admits that no less than 225 of the verses in the Koran are 'cancelled' by other, later ones.) Then of course there are the manifold errors introduced by the later copies, later versions, later translations. This alone makes the status of any religious injunction doubtful, leaving aside the more philosophical questions, such as whether God necessarily intended the instructions to apply for all time, or intended His document to evolve. Or perhaps, even, God wanted differences of opinion to trigger some sort of internecine human conflict in the time-honoured manner, summed up by the dismal Bible stories of Job and Lazarus, of testing and separating out the strong goats from the weak sheep.

So how should we treat the Koran nowadays? Indeed, even within Islam, there is considerable debate. Today, the world's most populous Muslim country, Indonesia, is progressive on women's rights and is even led by a woman president, while Mohammed's home country, Saudi Arabia, insists on a complete segregation of the two sexes, even to the extent of having 'male' and 'female' supermarket aisles. Saudi Muslims (the term 'Muslim' signifies one who surrenders or resigns himself to God) say that being the word of God, the Koran is timeless and immutable, and that therefore injunctions against usury and dispensation, or to cut off the hands of thieves, or to marry (at least) four wives, apply just as much today as they did to the tribes of Arabia in the fifth century CE. These people take literally Mohammed's claims to have had little or no knowledge of ancient scriptures, of the stories of Abraham and Noah, of Satan and of hell, but merely to have had them 'revealed' to him by God in the process of dreams and visions. For them, the evidence of the truth of the Koran is clear and beyond challenge. The work is a miracle, for how else could Mohammed have come to know so many of the ancient stories in so much detail? The historical figure who mixed and debated with religious scholars (many of them Jews) is of no interest to such as these.

And then there is the more modest claim of some that the Koran was indeed 'revealed' to Mohammed, but that there have been errors and misinterpretations in the transmission ever since. These allow that, furthermore, God's intentions were not necessarily limited once and for all to a series of rules for mankind, but were intended to direct the growth of human society as part of an organic and developing system. In support for this approach, they can point to the 'corrections' and retractions to the holy text made by the Prophet himself, as evidence of the fallibility of the process of transmission of divine will via human agent. They can also, simply by returning to the original text, challenge the 'interpretations' of the Koran made by the various competing religious authorities and sects today, such as restrictions on the activities of women, both in employment and in their personal lives, epitomised by the obligation to worship separately and to wear the veil in the presence of men. Other Muslims nowadays try to represent these restrictions as intended to protect or benefit women. But there is little enough support in the text for such an interpretation. Instead, the tone is unwaveringly patriarchal, as were the times.

For, indisputably, the style in which the Koran is written is that of the ancient Hebrew prophets in the Old Testament. Consider Mohammed's warning that 'every man's fate have we fastened about his neck: and on the day of resurrection will we bring forth to him a book which shall be proffered to him wide open', which is straight out of the Book of Revelations; or the rhetorical question, 'And since Noah, how many nations have we exterminated!' which draws on one of the Old Testament's most celebrated tales.

Frequent, indeed repetitious mentions of heaven, hell, judgement, apostles, alms, prayer, etc., pervade the Koran. If this comes as a surprise to some readers, it should not do so. Judaism was part of medieval Arabia, as was Christianity, although to a lesser extent. Even today, one of the world's largest (and most healthy) Jewish communities is in strictly Islamic Iran. Sceptics find it easier to believe that Mohammed learnt of the ancient stories from the people he mixed with at the time, notably many Jewish scholars, than by having had them revealed to him by God. They point to Mohammed's frequent turn of Scriptural phrase, probably drawn partly from popular legends, partly from personal contact with Jews and Christians. In fact, they consider it a dishonest tactic of Mohammed's, aimed at self-aggrandisement, to have denied the earthly origins of his political text in preference to the more impressive divine explanation.

But whether or not we wish to accept the authority of Mohammed to pronounce on the nature of truth, we still need to start by recalling what the Koran has to say. Or rather, to 'announce', for that is what the term signifies. In the following, I have relied upon the most poetic of all the English translations, produced 150 years ago by the Reverend J. M. Rodwell, who is credited with (or alternatively blamed for) inventing the so-called chronological sura order of the verses. According to him, the contrast between the earlier, middle, and later suras is very striking and interesting. Rodwell thinks this reflects the development of the prophet's mind 'as he gradually advanced from the early flush of inspiration to the less spiritual and more equivocal role of warrior, politician, and founder of an empire'. The style varies from that with a poetical element, a 'deep appreciation of the beauty of natural objects, brief fragmentary and impassioned utterances, denunciations of woe and punishment, expressed for the most part in lines of extreme brevity', to a more prosaic and a more didactic style, even if throughout the ornament of rhyme is preserved. 'We gradually lose the Poet in the missionary aiming to convert', suggests Rodwell. 'He who at Mecca is the admonisher and persuader, at Medina is the legislator and the warrior, who dictates obedience, and uses other weapons than the pen of the Poet and the Scribe.'

Rodwell, not only a Christian but a rector (of St Ethelberga's, London), is without doubt a sceptic when it comes to Mohammed's claims to speak for God. Within the Muslim intellectual community, the translation is not popular, not least on account of the numerous 'insulting' explanatory notes Rodwell offers, often belittling the claims the Prophet made, sometimes directly contradicting them. Be that as it may, it remains one of the finest translations, in terms of its respect for the style and aesthetic of the original. The Christian preacher's translation at least conveys some of the power of the verses – for the Koran is more akin to an epic poem than a conventional political text – and thereby helps better both to communicate its message and to explain why it has been for so many so powerful and so persuasive.

This much at least is uncontroversial. Mohammed himself was born at Mecca in 567 or 569 CE. His flight, or *hijra*, to Medina, which marks the beginning of the Mohammedan era, took place on 16 June 622 and he died there ten years later. The text of the Koran consists of scattered fragments of Mohammed's teachings, which were originally collected up by his successors, perhaps a year after the Prophet's death. Their concern was to prevent the knowledge from being lost as one by one Mohammed's followers died (often in the process of waging 'holy war'). These fragments were 'gathered together' from every quarter, 'from date leaves and tablets of white stone, and from the breasts of men'. Various copies were made, which soon led to various different versions circulating, and inevitably to disputes between the faithful. So it was then decided to interpose a standard text, 'to stop the people, before they should differ regarding their scriptures, as did the Jews and Christians'. Carefully transcribed copies of this text were forwarded to the key military strongholds of the new Mohammedan empire, and all other copies were destroyed.

Alas, as Rodwell remarks, the scattered fragments appear to have been put together 'just as they came to hand, and often with entire disregard to continuity of subject and uniformity of style'. The text became 'a most unreadable and incongruous patchwork', he complains. Yet, even so:

There is a unity of thought, a directness and simplicity of purpose, a peculiar and laboured style, a uniformity of diction, coupled with a certain deficiency of imaginative power, which proves the ayats (signs or verses) of the Koran at least to be the product of a single pen. The longer narratives were, probably, elaborated in his leisure hours, while the shorter verses, each claiming to be a sign or miracle, were promulgated as occasion required them. And, whatever Muhammad may himself profess in the Koran as to his ignorance, even of reading and writing, and however strongly modern Muhammadans may insist upon the same point ... there can be no doubt that to assimilate and work up his materials, to fashion them into elaborate Suras, to fit them for public recital, must have been a work requiring much time, study, and meditation.

And, Rodwell adds, Mohammed had 'that influence over the faith, morals, and whole earthly life of their fellow-men, which none but a really great man ever did, or can, exercise'. But let us now turn to the Koran itself.

THE TEXT

The word 'Koran' means to address or recite; to call, cry aloud or proclaim (analogous to the Rabbinic *mikra*). And the Koran is a special kind of announcement – it is a warning. The sura (verse, or chapter) entitled 'The Enwrapped', explains.

In their gardens shall ask of the wicked; –
'What hath cast you into Hell-fire?'
They will say, 'We were not of those who prayed,
And we were not of those who fed the poor,

And we plunged into vain disputes with vain disputers,
And we rejected as a lie, the day of reckoning,
Till the certainty came upon us' –
And intercession of the interceders shall not avail them.
Then what hath come to them that they turn aside from the Warning
As if they were affrighted asses fleeing from a lion?
And every one of them would fain have open pages given to him out of
Heaven.
It shall not be. They fear not the life to come.
It shall not be. For this Koran is warning enough. And who so will, it warneth
him.

Only a few passages offer a gentler, more 'Christian' picture, such as
the verses entitled 'The Brightness' (Sura 93), which promises that
by the noonday brightness,

And by the night when it darkeneth!
Thy Lord hath not forsaken thee, neither hath he been displeased.
And surely the Future shall be better for thee than the Past,
And in the end shall thy Lord be bounteous to thee and thou be satisfied.
Did he not find thee an orphan and gave thee a home?
And found thee erring and guided thee,
And found thee needy and enriched thee.
As to the orphan therefore wrong him not;
And as to him that asketh of thee, chide him not away;
And as for the favours of thy Lord tell them abroad.

If Christians today like to describe their message as one of good news,
Mohammed is more preoccupied with warnings of bad news, and
descriptions of the Day of Judgement become very frequent. Sura
104, 'The Backbiter', reveals,

Woe to every BACKBITER, Defamer!
Who amasseth wealth and storeth it against the future!
He thinketh surely that his wealth shall be with him for ever.
Nay! for verily he shall be flung into the Crushing Fire;
And who shall teach thee what the Crushing Fire is?
It is God's kindled fire,
Which shall mount above the hearts of the damned;
It shall verily rise over them like a vault,
On outstretched columns.

The verse entitled 'He Frowned' (Sura 80), rises to yet greater poetic heights, worth recalling at length to provide a sense of the overall impression given by the text, particularly when delivered theatrically by priests.

> Nay! but it (the Koran) is a warning;
> (And who so is willing beareth it in mind)
> Written on honoured pages,
> Exalted, purified,
> By the hands of Scribes, honoured, righteous.
> Cursed be man! What hath made him unbelieving?
> Of what thing did God create him?
> Out of moist germs.
>
> He created him and fashioned him,
> Then made him an easy passage from the womb,
> Then causeth him to die and burieth him;
> Then, when he pleaseth, will raise him again to life.
> Aye! but man hath not yet fulfilled the bidding of his Lord.
> Let man look at his food:
> It was We who rained down the copious rains,
> Then cleft the earth with clefts,
> And caused the upgrowth of the grain,
> And grapes and healing herbs,
> And the olive and the palm,
> And enclosed gardens thick with trees,
> And fruits and herbage,
> For the service of yourselves and of your cattle.
> But when the stunning trumpet-blast shall arrive,
> On that day shall a man fly from his brother,
> And his mother and his father,
> And his wife and his children;
> For every man of them on that day his own concerns shall be enough.
> There shall be faces on that day radiant,
> Laughing and joyous:
> And faces on that day with dust upon them:
> Blackness shall cover them!
> These are the Infidels, the Impure.

A similar dividing of the flock is outlined in Sura 29, entitled 'The Blow'.

What is the Blow?
Who shall teach thee what the Blow is?
The Day when men shall be like scattered moths,
And the mountains shall be like flocks of carded wool,
Then as to him whose balances are heavy, his shall be a life that shall please
    him well:
And as to him whose balances are light, his dwelling-place shall be the pit.
And who shall teach thee what the pit (El-Hawiya) is?
A raging fire!

Another sura, Rodwell's number 131, 'The Folded-Up', continues
firmly:

> When the sun shall be FOLDED UP,
> And when the stars shall fall,
> And when the mountains shall be set in motion,
> And when the she-camels shall be abandoned,
> And when the wild beasts shall be gathered together,
> And when the seas shall boil,
> And when souls shall be paired with their bodies,
> And when the female child that had been buried alive shall be asked
> For what crime she was put to death,
> And when the leaves of the Book shall be unrolled,
> And when the Heaven shall be stripped away,
> And when Hell shall be made to blaze,
> And when Paradise shall be brought near,
> Every soul shall know what it hath produced.
> It needs not that I swear by the stars of retrograde motions.

And Sura 78, 'The News', continues the tale of woe, but now offers
a glimpse too of Paradise.

Lo! the day of Severance is fixed;
The day when there shall be a blast on the trumpet, and ye shall come in
    crowds,
And the heaven shall be opened and be full of portals,
And the mountains shall be set in motion, and melt into thin vapour.
Hell truly shall be a place of snares,
The home of transgressors,
To abide therein ages;
No coolness shall they taste therein nor any drink,
Save boiling water and running sores;
Meet recompense!

For they looked not forward to their account;
And they gave the lie to our signs, charging them with falsehood;
But we noted and wrote down all:
'Taste this then: and we will give you increase of nought but torment.'
But, for the God-fearing is a blissful abode,
Enclosed gardens and vineyards;
And damsels with swelling breasts, their peers in age,
And a full cup:
There shall they hear no vain discourse nor any falsehood:
A recompense from thy Lord's sufficing gift!

These references to 'damsels with swelling breasts' may seem curious in view of the earthy injunction to Muslims to avoid such displays. In fact (as Rodwell notes) promises of the 'Houris of Paradise' are almost exclusively to be found in suras written at a time when Mohammed had but a single wife of 60 years of age, and that women are only rarely mentioned as part of the reward of the faithful. Actually, even if in some verses virgins (that ancient patriachal concern) seem to await in Paradise, in several suras, the proper wives of the faithful are spoken of as accompanying their husbands into the gardens of bliss. Strange too, is that Muslims are told that 'Choice sealed wine shall be given them to quaff' in Paradise, although on Earth it is, of course, a sin to consume alcohol.

Sura 83, 'Those Who Stint', introduces the restrictions on various personal pleasures, praising 'the prayerful'

Who are ever constant at their prayers,
...
And who control their desires,
(Save with their wives or the slaves whom their right hands have won, for there
    they shall be blameless;
But whoever indulge their desires beyond this are transgressors).

Abstinence is the primary message of the Koran, suitable for a community of monks if not so obviously a winner elsewhere. And the second injunction in the Koran, if rather a circular one, is that against confusing or criticising the Koran itself.

Shall I tell you on whom Satan descend?
They descend on every lying, wicked person:
They impart what they have heard; but most of them are liars.
It is the POETS whom the erring follow ...

Here Mohammed refers to the ridicule and satire of other poets, whose productions were recited at the great annual fair held at Okatz, the Olympus of the Hejaz. The poems which were judged the best were written up in letters of gold in the Kabah. These poetical contests were subsequently suppressed by Mohammed, as offering openings for discussions and challenges which might challenge his own claims.

> We have already given thee the seven verses of repetition and the glorious Koran.
> Strain not thine eyes after the good things we have bestowed on some of the unbelievers: afflict not thyself on their account, and lower thy wing to the faithful.
> And SAY: I am the only plain-spoken warner.
> We will punish those who foster divisions,
> Who break up the Koran into parts ...

In other words, the Jews and Christians, who receive part of the Scriptures and reject part. Curiously, Mohammed raises himself above such poets. The sura entitled 'Ya Sin' even explains: 'We have not taught him (Muhammad) poetry, nor would it beseem him. This Book is no other than a warning and a clear Koran, To warn whoever liveth; and, that against the Infidels sentence may be justly given.' And the self-reference then continues:

> And the infidels say, 'This Koran is a mere fraud of his own devising, and others have helped him with it, who had come hither by outrage and lie.'
> And they say, 'Tales of the ancients that he hath put in writing! and they were dictated to him morn and even.'
> SAY: He hath sent it down who knoweth the secrets of the Heavens and of the Earth. He truly is the Gracious, the Merciful.
> And they say, 'What sort of apostle is this? He eateth food and he walketh the streets! Unless an angel be sent down and take part in his warnings,
> Or a treasure be thrown down to him, or he have a garden that supplieth him with food . . .' and those unjust persons say, 'Ye follow but a man enchanted.'
> And the infidels say, 'Unless the Koran be sent down to him all at once. . . .'
> But in this way would we stablish thy heart by it; in parcels have we parcelled it out to thee;
> Nor shall they come to thee with puzzling questions, but we will come to thee with the truth, and their best solution.

Following this, as though rising to his full rhetorical height, Mohammed continues:

And we said, 'Go ye to the people who treat our signs as lies.' And them destroyed
we with utter destruction.

And as to the people of Noah! when they treated their Apostles as impostors, we
drowned them; and we made them a sign to mankind: A grievous chastisement
have we prepared for the wicked!

And Ad and Themoud, and the men of Rass, and divers generations between
them:

Unto each of them did we set forth parables for warnings, and each of them
did we utterly exterminate.

But enough. The listeners by now should surely accept the
importance of following Mohammed's rules. But what are they?
Moses listed his as the Ten Commandments. The Koran includes no
such useful list. However, we might try to draw up one of our own
using the verses of the Koran as the source.

THE RULES

1. Killing

Kill not your children for fear of want: for them and for you will we provide.
Verily, the killing them is a great wickedness. ...

Neither slay any one whom God hath forbidden you to slay, unless for a
just cause: and whosoever shall be slain wrongfully, to his heir have we given
powers; but let him not outstep bounds in putting the manslayer to death, for
he too, in his turn, will be assisted and avenged. ...

A believer killeth not a believer but by mischance: and whoso killeth a
believer by mischance shall be bound to free a believer from slavery; and the
blood-money shall be paid to the family of the slain, unless they convert it
into alms ...

But whoever shall kill a believer of set purpose, his recompense shall be hell;
for ever shall he abide in it; God shall be wrathful with him, and shall curse him,
and shall get ready for him a great torment.

2. Adultery

Have nought to do with adultery; for it is a foul thing and an evil way.

3. Fair Dealing in Business

And give full measure when you measure, and weigh with just balance. This will
be better, and fairest for settlement.

4. Wealth

Consume not your wealth among yourselves in vain things, nor present it to judges that ye may consume a part of other men's wealth unjustly, while ye know the sin which ye commit.

(However, contrariwise, the Koran also promises believers that 'Into the gardens of Eden shall they enter: with bracelets of gold and pearl shall they be decked therein, and therein shall their raiment be of silk.')

5. Inheritance

It is prescribed to you, when any one of you is at the point of death, if he leave goods, that he bequeath equitably to his parents and kindred. This is binding on those who fear God. But as for him who after he hath heard the bequest shall change it, surely the wrong of this shall be on those who change it: verily, God Heareth, Knoweth.

They will also ask thee concerning orphans. SAY: Fair dealing with them is best; And such of you as shall die and leave wives, shall bequeath their wives a year's maintenance without causing them to quit their homes; but if they quit them of their own accord, then no blame shall attach to you for any disposition they may make of themselves in a fair way

And if ye are apprehensive that ye shall not deal fairly with orphans, then, of other women who seem good in your eyes, marry but two, or three, or four... [Mohammed assumed to himself the privilege of having a yet greater number of wives.]

With regard to your children, God commandeth you to give the male the portion of two females ... This is the law of God. Verily, God is Knowing, Wise!

6. Religious Tolerance

Woe, on that day, to those who treated our signs as lies,
    Who treated the day of judgement as a lie!
    None treat it as a lie, save the transgressor, the criminal,
    Who, when our signs are rehearsed to him, saith, 'Tales of the Ancients!'
    O Believers! take not the Jews or Christians as friends. They are but one another's friends. If any one of you taketh them for his friends, he surely is one of them! God will not guide the evil doers. ...
    The Jews say, 'Ezra (Ozair) is a son of God' and the Christians say, 'The Messiah is a son of God.' Such the sayings in their mouths! They resemble the saying of the Infidels of old! God do battle with them! How are they misguided!

(The Mohammedan tradition is that Ezra was raised to life after he had been 100 years dead, and dictated from memory the whole Jewish law, which had been lost during the captivity, to the scribes. That the Jews regarded Ezra as a son of God, Rodwell points out, is entirely Mohammed's own invention.)

7. No Discussions

Dispute not, unless in kindly sort, with the people of the Book; save with such of them as have dealt wrongfully with you: And say ye, 'We believe in what hath been sent down to us and hath been sent down to you. Our God and your God is one, and to him are we self-surrendered' (Muslims).

As to those who split up their religion and become sects, have thou nothing to do with them: their affair is with God only. Hereafter shall he tell them what they have done.

8. Personal Demeanour

And walk not proudly on the earth, for thou canst not cleave the earth, neither shalt thou reach to the mountains in height:

All this is evil; odious to thy Lord.

9. Wine and Gambling

They will ask thee concerning wine and games of chance. SAY: In both is great sin, and advantage also, to men; but their sin is greater than their advantage. They will ask thee also what they shall bestow in alms ...

O believers! surely wine and games of chance, and statues, and the divining arrows, are an abomination of Satan's work! Avoid them, that ye may prosper.

10. Prayers and Devotion

Recite the portions of the Book which have been revealed to thee and discharge the duty of prayer: for prayer restraineth from the filthy and the blame-worthy. And the gravest duty is the remembrance of God; and God knoweth what ye do ... Accomplish the Pilgrimage and the Visitation of the holy places in honour of God ...

Let the Pilgrimage be made in the months already known: whoever therefore undertaketh the Pilgrimage therein, let him not know a woman, nor transgress, nor wrangle in the Pilgrimage. The good which ye do, God knoweth it. And provide for your journey; but the best provision is the fear of God.

O believers! a Fast is prescribed to you as it was prescribed to those before you, that ye may fear God ...

As to the month Ramadhan in which the Koran was sent down to be man's guidance, and an explanation of that guidance, and of that illumination, as soon as any one of you observeth the moon, let him set about the fast; but he who is sick, or upon a journey, shall fast a like number of other days. God wisheth you ease, but wisheth not your discomfort, and that you fulfil the number of days, and that you glorify God for his guidance, and that you be thankful.

10. Parents

Thy Lord hath ordained that ye worship none but him; and, kindness to your parents, whether one or both of them attain to old age with thee: and say not to them, 'Fie!' neither reproach them; but speak to them both with respectful speech;

And defer humbly to them out of tenderness; and say, 'Lord, have compassion on them both, even as they reared me when I was little.'

11. Women

Men are superior to women on account of the qualities with which God hath gifted the one above the other, and on account of the outlay they make from their substance for them. Virtuous women are obedient, careful, during the husband's absence, because God hath of them been careful. But chide those for whose refractoriness ye have cause to fear; remove them into beds apart, and scourge them: but if they are obedient to you, then seek not occasion against them: verily, God is High, Great!

And if ye fear a breach between man and wife, then send a judge chosen from his family, and a judge chosen from her family: if they are desirous of agreement, God will effect a reconciliation between them; verily, God is knowing, apprised of all! ...

God knoweth the burden of every female, and how much their wombs lessen and enlarge: with Him everything is by measure ...

(Women are at the heart of the Koran's political philosophy, as is shown by the numerous passages referring to them. Not all are unsympathetic, but collectively they attempt to institutionalise the subservient and secondary status of women. In this, as in much else, Mohammed follows Aristotle, as he does in the following 'biological' reference to women. He sees them, as did Aristotle, as a kind of field in which men plant their babies.)

You are allowed on the night of the fast to approach your wives: they are your garment and ye are their garment. God knoweth that ye defraud yourselves therein, so He turneth unto you and forgiveth you! Now, therefore, go in unto them with full desire for that which God hath ordained for you; and eat and drink until ye can discern a white thread from a black thread by the daybreak: then fast strictly till night, and go not in unto them, but rather pass the time in the Mosques. These are the bounds set up by God: therefore come not near them. Thus God maketh his signs clear to men that they may fear Him.

They will also question thee as to the courses of women. SAY: They are a pollution. Separate yourselves therefore from women and approach them not, until they be cleansed. But when they are cleansed, go in unto them as God hath ordained for you. Verily God loveth those who turn to Him, and loveth those who seek to be clean.

Your wives are your field: go in, therefore, to your field as ye will; but do first some act for your souls' good: and fear ye God, and know that ye must meet Him; and bear these good tidings to the faithful. ... And it is for the women to act as they (the husbands) act by them, in all fairness; but the men are a step above them. God is Mighty, Wise.

Ye may divorce your wives twice: Keep them honourably, or put them away with kindness. ... But if the husband divorce her a third time, it is not lawful for him to take her again, until she shall have married another husband; and if he also divorce her, then shall no blame attach to them if they return to each other, thinking that they can keep within the bounds fixed by God. And these are the bounds of God; He maketh them clear to those who have knowledge.

(So much for romance. Other injunctions have a more legalistic flavour:)

Mothers, when divorced, shall give suck to their children two full years, if the father desire that the suckling be completed; and such maintenance and clothing as is fair for them, shall devolve on the father. No person shall be charged beyond his means. A mother shall not be pressed unfairly for her child, nor a father for his child: And the same with the father's heir. But if they choose to wean the child by consent and by bargain, it shall be no fault in them. And if ye choose to have a nurse for your children, it shall be no fault in you, in case ye pay what ye promised her according to that which is fair. Fear God, and know that God seeth what ye do.

And marry not women whom your fathers have married: for this is a shame, and hateful, and an evil way: though what is past may be allowed ... Forbidden to you are your mothers, and your daughters, and your sisters, and your aunts, both on the father and mother's side, and your nieces on the brother and sister's side, and your foster-mothers, and your foster-sisters, and the mothers of your wives, and your step-daughters who are your wards, born of your wives to whom ye have gone in: (but if ye have not gone in unto them, it shall be no sin in you to marry them;) and the wives of your sons who proceed out of your loins; and ye may not have two sisters; except where it is already done. Verily, God is Indulgent, Merciful!

Forbidden to you also are married women, except those who are in your hands as slaves ... And whoever of you is not rich enough to marry free believing women, then let him marry such of your believing maidens as have fallen into your hands as slaves; God well knoweth your faith. Ye are sprung the one from the other. Marry them, then, with the leave of their masters, and give them a fair dower: but let them be chaste and free from fornication, and not entertainers of lovers.

It is not permitted thee to take other wives hereafter, nor to change thy present wives for other women, though their beauty charm thee, except slaves whom thy right hand shall possess. And God watcheth all things.

No blame shall attach to them (your wives) for speaking to their fathers unveiled, or to their sons, or to their brothers, or to their brothers' sons, or to their sisters' sons, or to their women, or to the slaves whom their right hands hold. And fear ye God: for God witnesseth all things.

And speak to the believing women that they refrain their eyes, and observe continence; and that they display not their ornaments, except those which are external; and that they throw their veils over their bosoms, and display not their ornaments, except to their husbands or their fathers, or their husbands' fathers, or their sons, or their husbands' sons, or their brothers, or their brothers' sons, or their sisters' sons, or their women, or their slaves, or male domestics who have no natural force, or to children who note not women's nakedness. And let them not strike their feet together, so as to discover their hidden ornaments. And be ye all turned to God, O ye Believers! that it may be well with you.

As to women who are past childbearing, and have no hope of marriage, no blame shall attach to them if they lay aside their outer garments, but so as not to shew their ornaments. Yet if they abstain from this, it will be better for them: and God Heareth, Knoweth.

13. Wars

And fight for the cause of God against those who fight against you: but commit not the injustice of attacking them first: God loveth not such injustice:

14. Retaliation

O believers! retaliation for bloodshedding is prescribed to you: the free man for the free, and the slave for the slave, and the woman for the woman: but he to whom his brother shall make any remission, is to be dealt with equitably; and to him should he pay a fine with liberality.

This is a relaxation from your Lord and a mercy. For him who after this shall transgress, a sore punishment! But in this law of retaliation is your security for life, O men of understanding! to the intent that ye may fear God.

15. Moneylending

They who swallow down usury, shall arise in the resurrection only as he ariseth whom Satan hath infected by his touch. This, for that they say, 'Selling is only the like of usury:' and yet God hath allowed selling, and forbidden usury. He then who when this warning shall come to him from his Lord, abstaineth, shall have pardon for the past, and his lot shall be with God. But they who return to usury, shall be given over to the fire; therein shall they abide for ever.

God will bring usury to nought, but will increase alms with usury, and God loveth no infidel, or evil person. ... O believers! fear God and abandon your remaining usury, if ye are indeed believers.

16. Debts

If any one find difficulty in discharging a debt, then let there be a delay until it be easy for him: but if ye remit it as alms it will be better for you, if ye knew it.

And disdain not to put the debt in writing, be it large or small, with its time of payment: this will be more just for you in the sight of God, better suited for witnessing, and the best for avoiding doubt. But if the goods be there present, and ye pass them from hand to hand, then it shall be no fault in you not to write it down. And have witnesses when ye sell, and harm not writer or witness: it will be a crime in you to do this. But fear God and God will give you knowledge, for God hath knowledge of all things.

17. Crimes

If any of your women be guilty of whoredom, then bring four witnesses against them from among yourselves; and if they bear witness to the fact, shut them up within their houses till death release them, or God make some way for them.

And if two men among you commit the same crime, then punish them both; but if they turn and amend, then let them be: for God is He who turneth, Merciful!

The whore and the whoremonger, scourge each of them with an hundred stripes; and let not compassion keep you from carrying out the sentence of God, if ye believe in God and the last day: And let some of the faithful witness their chastisement. The whoremonger shall not marry other than a whore or an idolatress; and the whore shall not marry other than a whoremonger or an idolater. Such alliances are forbidden to the faithful.

As to the thief, whether man or woman, cut ye off their hands in recompense for their doings. This is a penalty by way of warning from God himself. And God is Mighty, Wise.

(Mohammed is said to have punished a woman who had been guilty of theft in this manner while on the route to Mecca previous to its capture.)

And therein have we enacted for them, 'Life for life, and eye for eye, and nose for nose, and ear for ear, and tooth for tooth, and for wounds retaliation:' – Whoso shall compromise it as alms shall have therein the expiation of his sin; and whoso will not judge by what God hath sent down, such are the transgressors.

18. Freedom of Belief

Let there be no compulsion in Religion.

(This rather surprising rule appears just once in isolation and does not seem to fit in to the rest of the Koranic injunctions at all.)

THE SUBTEXT

In his introduction to the Reverend Rodwell's translation, the equally Reverend G. Margoliouth says that the Koran was, at first 'not a book, but a strong living voice, a kind of wild authoritative proclamation, a series of admonitions, promises, threats, and instructions addressed to turbulent and largely hostile assemblies of untutored Arabs'.

Before Mohammed, he reminds us, for these untutored nomads there were only disjointed notes, speeches, and the retentive memories of those who listened to them. The Koran changed all that:

Biblical reminiscences, Rabbinic legends, Christian traditions mostly drawn from distorted apocryphal sources, and native heathen stories, all first pass through the prophet's fervid mind, and thence issue in strange new forms, tinged with poetry and enthusiasm, and well adapted to enforce his own view of life and duty, to serve as an encouragement to his faithful adherents, and to strike terror into the hearts of his opponents.

The Koran's influence went beyond the 'turbulent tribesmen' however. Margoliouth says that what European scholars knew of Greek philosophy, of mathematics, astronomy, and like sciences, for several centuries before the Renaissance, was, roughly speaking, all derived from Latin treatises ultimately based on Arabic originals; and it was the Koran which, though indirectly, gave the first impetus to these studies:

Linguistic investigations, poetry, and other branches of literature, also made their appearance soon after or simultaneously with the publication of the Koran; and the literary movement thus initiated has resulted in some of the finest products of genius and learning.

Margoliouth, like many after him, suggests that even if 'the shortcomings' of the moral teaching contained in the Koran seem appalling to many today, a 'much more favourable' view can be arrived at if comparison is made between the ethics of the Koran and the moral tenets of Arabian life at the time.

This is true, and certainly the Christian church has only comparatively recently reinvented itself as the church of forgiveness and love; but the moral teachings of the Koran must nowadays also be compared with contemporary standards, and not merely the standards of desert tribes 1,500 years ago. In any case, to say that most people at the time thought something does not make it a reasonable judgement. If Hitler advocates hatred of Jews and blacks, it is not compelling to explain that 'most people' thought the same way at the time. Margoliouth also says that 'the Moslems themselves consider the book the finest that ever appeared among men. They find no incongruity in the style. To them the matter is all true and the manner all perfect.' They respond readily to the 'crude, strong, and wild appeal which its cadences make' and the jingling rhythms of the whole. For them, the Koran, is nothing less than a miracle, 'as great a miracle as ever was wrought'.

However, for many others today, accustomed to notions of objectivity, experiment and scientific truth, rational debate and, of course, fundamental rights, the appeal of the Koran as a political text remains impenetrable, and hard to understand. Perhaps it was mere coincidence, perhaps it was drought and famine, rather than any desire of conquest activated by religious convictions, but certainly, by the end of the seventh century, Islam had conquered Persia, and by the end of the ninth it had spread along the northern coast of Africa to a large portion of Spain in the west, and to the Punjab and nearly the whole of India in the East. The simple shepherds and wandering Bedouins of Arabia had been transformed, as Margoliouth puts it, 'as if by a magician's wand, into the founders of empires'.

And it is worth remembering, in assessing the Koran's influence, that Europe, in the Middle Ages, owed much of her knowledge of dialectical philosophy, of medicine and of architecture to Arabian writers and the Koran, even if, today, the Koran seems also to have become an anchor dragging its followers back to a different and harsher era.

KEY IDEAS

- Church authority supercedes that of human judgement in all areas of life.
- Women are inferior to men, and unclean.
- The pursuit of wealth is an ignoble pursuit.

SOURCE

The Koran, translated from the Arabic by the Revd J. M. Rodwell (London, 1861) with an introduction by the Revd G. Margoliouth. I have used the Project Gutenberg e-book for quotations, which is freely available on the World Wide Web.

Timeline:
From Algebra to Political Calculation

751 CE

The first known 'printed book', a copy of the Buddhist *Diamond Sutra*, is produced.

AROUND 850 CE

In Persia, the mathematician Al Khwarizmi develops the first 'algorithms' and early 'algebra' – both named after him. Later, in the Middle East, the physicist Alhazen (965–1039) lays the foundations for the studies of mirrors and lenses.

1042

First known use of movable type recorded in China. It is not until 1454 that Gutenberg uses movable type and an adapted wine press to print religious indulgences for Europeans.

AROUND 1100

The rise of the city in the west, particularly in Italy and northern Europe. Settlements such as Venice, Paris, Bruges and London contain populations over 10,000.

1315–19

Two significant technological breakthroughs in the west. The invention of the verge and pallet escapement enables mechanical clocks to be installed on church towers, dividing up the day for the general public. (The Chinese had been using water clocks since around 1000 CE.) Also at this time, the first guns capable of killing someone (other than their owners) are developed.

1430

Joan of Arc, the simple shepherd girl whose 'vision' inspires the French resistance enough to enable them to defeat the English invaders at Orleans, is captured by her fellow countrymen – the

Burgundians – who sell her to the English. They burn her at the stake a few years later.

1434

Cosimo di Medici becomes de facto ruler of Florence, and founds a dynasty that lasts until 1737, with the exception of a brief period when an 'anti-corruption' Friar, Savonarola, seizes power. This is the period of Italy's great 'Renaissance' of learning and culture.

1502–07

Leonardo da Vinci, as well as making a number of important discoveries and inventions, paints the Mona Lisa.

1508

And Michelangelo paints the Sistine Chapel.

1513

Machiavelli begins *The Prince*, the classic statement of the art of politics, published in 1532.

5
Machiavelli's Psychopathic State

Ironically perhaps, for one writing of 'princes', Machiavelli is the first writer to move away from the paternalism of traditional society towards something closer to our own notions of 'democracy'. In his writings, the masses, ignorant and vulgar though they may be, are better guardians of stability and liberty than individuals can ever become. And despite his reputation for cynicism, Machiavelli reminds us that injustice threatens the foundations of society from within, and urges that it always be combated – wherever it appears and whoever it affects.

THE CONTEXT

Sixteenth-century Italy contained a number of elements that made it, like Greece centuries before, peculiarly fertile ground for the arts, for philosophy and for political thinking.

Out of the whole of Europe, it was the least feudal, the most wealthy and the most politically diverse land. Its culture was sophisticated, urbane and secular, its administrative structure made up of city states or 'communes' presided over by their own 'princes' and governing cliques. As a result, the country was a patchwork quilt of oligarchies, like that in Venice, and tyrannies, like that in Milan. But in some states (although in rather few) a third system had taken root.

One such was Florence, the magnificent Italian city where Dante had written some centuries earlier not only of his vision of hell, the 'inferno', but of the politics of human society. Dante had asked the question: Why should people want to live peacefully and collectively together, when they could often gain more by either striking out alone, or by competing one against the other? And he answered it by supposing that social life was the best, indeed the only way, for them to develop their rational nature. But by the fifteenth century the ruling family in Florence, the Medicis, their name a byword for over-indulgence and corruption, had instead for a century promoted conflict between small traders and large powerful guilds as a means to gain and retain control. The opportunities for the people to develop their rationality had to wait until the Medicis were displaced by a

Dominican friar, Savonarola, who took control of the city in the people's name.

Early auguries for his democratic system were not promising, however. Concerned only with morality and not at all with politics, let alone with consolidating his own position, Savonarola neglected to prepare his defences, and when the poor began to tire of him, as in a democracy they will, the displaced rich were able to make a comeback. In 1498 the moral crusader was executed. His experiment, however, lasted a little longer – until 1512 when the Medici returned to power. And Savonarola left another legacy: Niccolò Machiavelli. Machiavelli was a middle-ranking civil servant who had worked for the new Florentine democracy, gaining there his experience of being involved with the real issues in government.

In fact, during the purge following the Medici's return, Niccolò Machiavelli was arrested, and then tortured, by the triumphant new administration. Only when finally acquitted was he allowed to retire peacefully and concentrate on writing up his political ideas. Two of the most notorious political works ever written, *The Prince* (*Il principo*) and the *Discourses* (*Discorsi sopra la prima deca di Tito Livio – Discourses on the first Ten Books of Titus Livy*) followed in due course.

THE TEXT

The Prince is often said to have been an unsuccessful bid to regain favour, and indeed is dedicated in glowing terms to 'Lorenzo the Magnificent', son of Piero de Medici (presumably a deliberate, punning association with the earlier, more famous, prince of the same name). Machiavelli introduces it with the words:

It is customary for those who wish to gain the favour of a Prince to endeavour to do so by offering him gifts of those things which they hold most precious, or in which they know him to take especial delight. In this way Princes are often presented with horses, arms, cloth of gold, gems, and suchlike ornaments worthy of their grandeur.

What can Machiavelli, a retired (deposed) civil servant, offer? He confides:

I have been unable to find among my possessions anything which I hold so dear or esteem so highly as that knowledge of the deeds of great men which I have acquired through a long experience of modern events and a constant study of the past.

Thus he manages the difficult task of combining obsequiousness with pomposity.

Having in this respectful manner set out his stall, and indeed the style for his investigations, Machiavelli announces his intention to leave discussion of republican government to 'another place'. This is, in fact, the *Discourses*, which, although less celebrated, is his longer and more substantial work. It even contains some additional, liberal, ideas at odds with pleasing the Medici, but there is no essential contradiction between the works: indeed, there is a great deal of duplication.

Machiavelli's most important and original points are usually considered these days to relate to the dry matter of the analysis of the conditions for republican government, but he also allows himself to spend much time and many pages discussing military tactics. 'When an enemy is seen to be making a big mistake it should be assumed that it is but an artifice', he warns, before describing 'the rival merits of fortresses and cavalry', all the while utilising his main literary device of self-serving name-dropping. Despite these other personal aims and interests, his analysis of government is still far more detailed than that of either Plato or Aristotle, and there is, after all, no one (in the European context) to compare with him in the centuries in between.

And indeed his writings have stood the test of time too. If Machiavelli writes of, and for, a pre-industrial society, his notions are still – sometimes strikingly – relevant. In sixteenth-century Italy, society and power were split between three groups: the land and peasantry, industry (such as it was), and the bureaucracy, of which Machiavelli had been a member. All of which is a surprisingly timeless arrangement. Even Machiavelli's discussion of military adventures can be taken as a metaphor for the strategies and effects of economic competition today. Taken literally, Machiavelli may be 'off message', but if we take him more thoughtfully (reading between the lines, as we need to read all medieval texts), his discussions are not so far from today's needs.

Unfortunately, Machiavelli has rarely been read thoughtfully – or even read at all – before being condemned. His reputation is far worse than he merits. Rather than being a 'Doctor of the Damned', recommending immoral behaviour whenever necessary or convenient, his name a synonym for 'cunning, amoral and opportunist' behaviour, there is much in his writings to suggest a fundamentally good man trying to understand human society in its political form. But Machiavelli would probably, in any case, have taken his bad press philosophically. As he sardonically observes at one point: 'genuine virtue counts in difficult times, but when things are going well, it is rather to those whose popularity is due to wealth or parentage that men look'. And he had neither. Elsewhere, Machiavelli dismisses as worthless the apparently successful but unscrupulous activities of Agathocles the Sicilian, who rose by means of wickedness from 'the lowest and most abject position' to become king of Syracuse. Agathocles it was who had the habit of playing tricks, such as calling the people and senate to discuss something, and then giving a signal to his soldiers to have them murdered. The real Machiavelli's conclusion is that the Sicilian may have succeeded in achieving power, but not 'in gaining glory'; the apocryphal Machiavelli is imagined to praise him.

Perhaps Machiavelli's most controversial and unscrupulous claim is that if a prince must choose to be either feared or loved, it is better that he be feared, for 'love is held by a chain of obligation which [for] men, being selfish, is broken whenever it serves their purpose; but fear is maintained by a dread of punishment which never fails'. In this sense, he is Hobbes a century later, or even Mao Zedong in the twentieth century (the Mao equally notorious for his aphorism that power comes out of the barrel of a gun). But, rather unlike Mao, Machiavelli's advice for princes includes the guidance that when

a Prince is obliged to take the life of any one, let him do so when there is a proper justification and manifest reason for it; but above all he must abstain from taking the property of others, for men forget more easily the death of their father than the loss of their patrimony.

Of course, as Machiavelli notes, 'the pretexts for seizing property are never wanting, and one who begins to live by rapine will always find some reason for taking the goods of others, whereas causes for taking life are more fleeting'.

Actually, much of Machiavelli's notoriety probably relates to his attacks on the Roman Church, the body that he blames for the political ruin of Italy, even though, on his deathbed, he asked for – and received – absolution (although this might of course have been just a ploy). At one point (pre-dating Nietzsche, for example, by some 400 years) Machiavelli writes: 'Our religion has glorified humble and contemplative men, rather than men of action. It has assigned as man's highest good humility, abnegation, and contempt for mundane things ...' The advice Machiavelli offers to would-be rulers in Renaissance Europe instead is to transcend conventional values:

it is as well to ... seem merciful, faithful, humane, sincere, religious, and also to be so; but you must have the mind so disposed that when it is needful to be otherwise you may change to the opposite qualities ... [and] do evil if constrained.

Here, Machiavelli heralds the tactics of the emerging secular societies in redefining their relationship with the moral authority of the Church, and is very clear: the prince has a 'higher' morality, rather than no morality at all. This is not just a Machiavellian view – many societies depend on just such a contradiction, resorting to the claim that the end justifies the means, even if the means fall below the publicly held standards of morality. Even Plato allowed it in his 'noble lie', used to explain the different upbringing and roles of the citizens. Machiavelli is simply enunciating plainly what most governments prefer to keep secret and hidden. 'Everybody sees what you appear to be, few feel what you are', Machiavelli says of his prince's duplicity. Some centuries later, in the turmoil of the Second World War, the philosopher Bertrand Russell would comment: 'such intellectual honesty about political dishonesty would hardly have been possible at any other time'.

Yet 'Doctor of the Damned' or not, one of Machiavelli's strongest and most consistent themes is the perils of ignoring injustice. He urges princes to 'consider how important it is for every republic and every prince to take account of such offences, not only when an injury is done to a whole people but also when it affects an individual'. Typical of this concern is his retelling of the story of the Greek noble, Pausanias, who was brutally raped by one of the king's other favourites. His attacker is later promoted. The victim vents his anger against the king by killing him on the way to the Temple, even though this involves 'all manner of dangers' and entails Pausanias' own downfall. The story purports to demonstrate that it is not in the prince's interests to allow the injustice.

'As we have remarked several times,' Machiavelli continues, warming to his theme, 'in every large city there inevitably occur unfortunate incidents which call for the physician, and the more important the incidents the wiser should be the physician one looks for.' He recalls several incidents in Rome, for instance, which were 'both curious and unexpected'. On one occasion all the ladies of the city conspired to kill their husbands, and indeed quite a number of the unpopular husbands were found actually to have been poisoned, with poison ready waiting for many more! Naturally, a prince cannot kill all the ladies of the city. On the other hand, when ancient Rome was threatened by other conspiracies, such as that in the Bacchanals during the Macedonian war, it was only (Machiavelli thinks) the resolution of the city's rulers in pronouncing sentence of death 'on a whole legion at a time' that saved the day. Equally, the practice of decimating an army – selecting by lottery one in ten of a mutinous force and executing them, had been shown to be effective in quelling insurrections, while leaving something intact to lead.

For when a great number of people have done wrong, and it is not clear who is responsible, it is impossible to punish them all, since there are so many of them; and to punish some, and leave others unpunished would be unfair ... the unpunished would take heart and do wrong at some other time – but by killing the tenth part, chosen by lot, when all are guilty, he who is punished bewails his lot, and he who is not punished is afraid to do wrong lest on some other occasion the lot should not spare him.

Advice like this leads even sympathetic commentators like Bernard Crick to say that Machiavelli would not have recognised the merits of the famous words inscribed on the Old Bailey in London: 'Let justice be done though the heavens fall.' But in another sense, Machiavelli is insisting precisely that justice must be done. Machiavelli may be immoral, but surely history is wrong to condemn him as simply amoral.

Machiavelli's writings are primarily a historical and contemporary political analysis of how power is won, maintained and lost. Italy in the fifteenth century had many examples to offer – mainly to do with misrule. Authority, even for the papacy, rested on corruption in elections, and the use of violence and deceit to manipulate opinion. Machiavelli looks through history for examples of certain incidents, and notes the consequences, good or bad, for the ruler. He then forms a hypothesis, which is tested and either confirmed or disproved. It is in this context that Machiavelli sets out the means to achieve certain ends, irrespective of any virtue or merit in those ambitions. His own ends, were, in fact, quite worthy.

Together, these 'historical experiments' make up the testbed for Machiavelli's theory of society. And the first finding is that the origins of societies in general, and cities in particular, are defensive.

In the beginning of the world, when its inhabitants were few, they lived for a time scattered like the beasts. Then, with the multiplication of their offspring, they drew together and, in order the better to be able to defend themselves, began to look about for a man stronger and more courageous than the rest, made him their head and obeyed him.

The Venetians are an example of this – the city resulted from numerous peoples seeking refuge from the daily wars of Italy after the decline of Rome. Eventually, 'without any particular person or prince to give them a constitution, they began to live as a community under laws which seemed appropriate for their maintenance'.

What sort of communities? What kind of laws? Machiavelli, following Aristotle, says that there are six types of government, of which 'three are bad and three are good in themselves but easily become corrupt'. The good forms are *principato, ottimati e popolare* – principality, aristocracy and democracy – and the corresponding bad ones are tyranny, oligarchy and anarchy. States are perpetually degenerating and regenerating through the various forms, although fortunately, Machiavelli thinks, a state in one of the inferior forms will normally fall under the political control of one better organised.

For would-be princes, the rewards for getting the system of government right are considerable: 'in short, the world triumphant, its prince glorious and respected by all, the people fond of him and secure under his rule'. But similarly, under a bad leader, we find 'princes frequently killed by assassins, civil wars and foreign wars constantly occurring, Italy in travail and ever a prey to fresh misfortunes, its cities demolished and pillaged'. Do not forget the sight of 'Rome burnt, its Capitol demolished by its own citizens, ancient temples lying desolate, religious rites grown corrupt, adultery rampant ... the sea covered with exiles and the rocks stained with blood'. Truly, it is out of fear and self-interest that citizens seek the good in government.

Machiavelli, like the ancients, expects the state to follow a cycle of growth, maturity and then decay. This is in contrast to the happy notion, increasingly prevalent today, of some sort of virtuous evolution in human society, seen as working towards a permanent near-perfect system. This doctrine of 'perfectibility' has been endorsed (through the centuries) by thinkers of different political persuasions. Hegel suggested liberal democracy would prove to be the 'end of history', whilst Marx adapted him to try to demonstrate that Utopia could be attained through socialism and communism. (We shall return to this myth.) But for Machiavelli, since all forms of government are unsatisfactory (the good ones because their life is necessarily so short, the bad ones because of their 'inherent malignity'), a mixture is best. In consequence, prudent legislators must choose a form of government that contains all the elements – principality, aristocracy and democracy – so as to minimise the faults and so that each can 'keep watch over the other'. In this, Machiavelli anticipates the doctrine of the division of powers, to be found most explicitly implemented in the American constitution, where prince (president), oligarchy (Senate) and people (Congress) all keep watch over one another.

Machiavelli adds that it is necessary, as those who governed Florence in the fifteenth century were said to have found, to 'reconstitute the government every five years', because by this time

men begin to change their habits and break the laws, and, unless something happens which recalls to their minds the penalty involved and reawakens fear in them, there will soon be so many delinquents that it will be impossible to punish them without danger.

This is an early perspective on the otherwise recent convention for democracies to hold regular elections. But as to the election event itself, Machiavelli has no romantic expectations. He suggests sadly that, asked to choose a candidate, the populace 'relies on common gossip and on their reputation when it has otherwise no knowledge of them based on noteworthy deeds; or else on some preconceived opinion it has formed of them'.

At the same time, he notes that Aristotle, too, recommended that 'principality, aristocracy and democracy' should all coexist in one state. The success of ancient Rome, for Machiavelli, was in harnessing this synergy, achieving the Greek ideal of active, virtuous citizens, in a united state under sound laws. In the *Discourses* he advises that the constitution should share power between the nobles and people as well as with the princes, 'then these three powers will keep each other reciprocally in check'. The Roman constitution is held up as the ideal one, despite the 'squabbles between the populace and the senate', an inconvenience necessary to arrive at its 'greatness'. Praise for the ancients like this underlines Machiavelli's determination to ignore the Christian tradition of St Thomas Aquinas and other medieval thinkers and to draw instead directly upon the works of Aristotle and (indirectly) Plato.

Although there are six types of government, for Machiavelli there are only two types of state: republics and principalities (constitutional monarchies). Republics flourish when they respect customs and traditions; when town dominates country; when a large middle class exists; when popular power is institutionalised; and when there is plenty of civic spirit. On the other hand, adaptability to circumstance is the central virtue of republican government. 'A republic or a Prince should ostensibly do out of generosity what necessity constrains them to do.' Discord in a state (such as the mobs that characterised Rome) can actually strengthen the republic: 'every city should provide ways and means whereby the ambitions of the populace may find outlet, especially a city which proposes to avail itself of the populace in important undertakings'.

It is really only in times of crisis that a prince is needed – such times as when, for example, a ruthless individual cannot be stopped, or when the state lacks virtue and there is civic injustice, or when the republic has been fashioned from 'unsuitable material'. Unfortunately, in general, though, 'where there is a Prince ... what he does in his own interests usually harms the city, and what is done in the interests of the city harms him'.

The masses have trouble following their own interests too. One section in the *Discourses* is headed with the warning: 'How frequently erroneous are the views men adopt in regard to matters of moment'; it explains that 'men are easily corrupted'; they 'pass from one ambition to another, and, having first striven against ill-treatment, inflict it next upon others'. If, he says sadly,

proposals which have been laid before the populace look like sure things, even though concealed within them disaster lies hid, or when it looks like a bold thing, even though concealed within it lies the Republic's ruin, it will always be easy to persuade the masses to adopt such a proposal.

Likewise,

Human appetites are insatiable, for by nature we are so constituted that there is nothing we cannot long for, but by fortune we are such that of these things we can attain but few. The result is that the human mind is perpetually discontented, and of its possessions is apt to grow weary.

Machiavelli goes on:

This bears out what has been said above, namely, that men never do good unless necessity drives them to it; but when they are too free to choose and can do just as they please, confusion and disorder become everywhere rampant. Hence it is said that hunger and poverty make men industrious, and that laws make them good.

Machiavelli adds that he could 'discourse at length on the advantages of poverty over riches, and how poverty brings honour to cities, provinces and religious institutions, whereas the other thing has ruined them; if it had not already been done so often by others'.

Instead, he offers a rarer insight:

in all human affairs one notices, if one examines them closely, that it is impossible to remove one inconvenience without another emerging. If then, you want to have a large population and to provide it with arms so as to establish a great empire, you will have made your population such that you cannot now handle it as you please.

In all discussions one should consider 'which alternative involves fewer inconveniences and should adopt this as the better course; for one never finds any issue that it clear cut and not open to question'.

THE SUBTEXT

A century later, in the chaos of revolutionary England, Thomas Hobbes would consider people's nature to be so bad that the only way anyone could be assured of safety and security would be to create a strong government capable of suppressing individuals. But Machiavelli is following the tradition of Plato and Aristotle, who had believed in the fundamental goodness of the soul (if not of actual people!), and still sees everyone as having the ability to draw upon this source of natural wisdom. So for Machiavelli, despite his reputation, the role of the state is to help people to fulfil this potential. At the same time, he accepts, like his predecessors, that the psychology of the rulers and the ruled varies depending on the prevailing political system and the structure of the state.

Prior to Machiavelli, medieval writers had based legitimacy on God, who expressed His will through the hierarchy of pope, bishops and priests, or alternatively through the emperor and the royal families of Europe. Machiavelli, in contrast, has no doubt that power is available to all those who are skilful enough to seize it. Popular government is better than tyranny, not for any overriding 'moral' reason, but by reason of its success in bringing about certain political goals: national independence, security, and stability. This means sharing power between princes, nobles and people in proportion to their 'real' power. (For maximum stability, Machiavelli thinks, the people's share should be substantial.)

Like Confucius and Plato before him, and Hegel and Mao later, Machiavelli assumes that people are basically the same everywhere, but that their behaviour differs, as states encourage certain traits and not others. His assessment of the basic motivating forces is remarkably close to Thomas Hobbes a century later in England: man is primarily concerned to impose his will on others – or to impress them – and gain recognition. Aristotle, too, had described man as a political animal, but, unlike Machiavelli's version, as one naturally disposed to work within a community for the common weal, as defined by the aristocrats. The nineteenth-century philosopher Nietzsche would take it further by asserting that the only function of most people is to give the 'heroes' or 'supermen' something to use to glorify themselves. Machiavelli is more generous – he values 'the mob', considers it vital for democracy. He says that every city should provide 'ways and means whereby the ambitions of the populace may find an outlet, especially a city which proposes to avail itself of the populace in important undertakings'. However, because the populace, 'misled by the false appearance of advantage, often seeks its own ruin, and is easily moved by splendid hopes and rash promises', we must remember that 'a crowd is useless without a head'. Nor is it enough to 'first use threats and then appeal for the requisite authority'!

Machiavelli explains that, 'contrary to the common opinion', when the populace is in power and the state is well ordered, it will be 'stable, prudent and grateful', even more so than a wise prince. For even if 'Princes are superior to populaces in drawing up laws, codes of civic life, statutes and new institutions, the populace is superior in sustaining what has been instituted'. He concludes:

Government consists in nothing else but so controlling subjects that they shall neither be able to, nor have cause to, do you harm; which may be done either by making quite sure of them by depriving them of all means of doing you harm, or by treating them so well that it would be unreasonable for them to desire a change of fortune.

Even though the masses may be 'more knowing and more constant than is a Prince', Machiavelli's 'democracy' only extends, like that of the Greeks, to a minority of the richest countrymen, whose job it is to stop others seizing power, perhaps by exploiting the power of the mob. But, because the nobility desire to dominate and control, whereas the common people merely wish to avoid being dominated, 'the latter will be more keen on liberty'. And, although the many are incompetent to draw up a constitution, 'since diversity of opinion will prevent them from discovering how best to do it', once they realise it has been done, 'they will not agree to abandon it'.

Machiavelli is the first major European figure to praise freedom as a primary virtue, writing variously that 'those who set up a Tyranny are no less blameworthy than are the founders of a Republic or a Kingdom praiseworthy' and that 'all towns and all countries that are in all respects free, profit by this enormously'. The year of Machiavelli's death, 1527, marks the time that the Emperor Charles V's armies reach and sack Rome, and marks the passing of the Renaissance period itself.

KEY IDEAS

Machiavelli is often narrowly portrayed as simply promoting the use of force and duplicity, even though his intention was highly moral: to protect the state against internal and external threats and ultimately to promote the welfare of the citizens, not simply the interests of the prince.

In the *Discourses*, Machiavelli advocates 'civic virtue', putting the common good ahead of selfish interests, and identifies that curious feature of collective decision making – that the judgement of the masses may be sounder than that of even enlightened individuals.

- People are all a mixture, none much superior to any other, and no system is perfect either. As even a good prince can become corrupt, so it is best to design the state with a series of checks and balances.
- The state is only as good as its citizens – the rulers must be aware of the dangers of allowing civic spirit to wane.
- Although there are many routes to power, only a few of them are worth following.

KEY TEXTS

Machiavelli's *Discourses* (1531) and *The Prince* (1532)

Timeline:
From Dreams of Utopia
to Dreams of Revolution

1516
Thomas More publishes his account of a 'Utopia' in which landlords are prevented from enclosing pastures and poor people are not hanged for stealing bread, but merely made into slaves.

1530
Copernicus circulates copies of his heretical theory that the Earth in fact revolves around the Sun. (He delays publication for another 14 years, leaving just enough time to see the first printed copy on his deathbed.)

1628
In England, Parliament obtains the 'Petition of Right', the agreement of the monarch never to impose taxes without its agreement, nor arrest citizens without cause.

1572
Appearance of a nova in Cassiopeia shows that even the heavenly firmament is not entirely 'fixed'.

1637
In the Netherlands, the price of tulip bulbs shoots up as fantastic prices are offered for rarer varieties, leading to the first known example of a financial collapse. London's infamous financial crash – the South Sea Bubble – is 83 years after this.

1640
King Charles in England is obliged to recall his troublesome parliament to ask for funds after the kingdom is invaded by the Scots. Two years later there is civil war between the Parliamentary forces and the king's, and in 1645 Cromwell's New Model Army crushes the Royalist forces at Naseby. Charles flees to his former enemies, the

Scots, but they sell him back to the Parliamentarians in 1647 for the very princely sum of £400,000. Two years later, Charles is executed. England becomes a 'Commonwealth' instead.

1651
Thomas Hobbes publishes the *Leviathan*.

6
Hobbes' Wicked World

Aristotle thought that people, being rational, would be naturally inclined to organise themselves voluntarily in societies. Thomas Hobbes, writing nearly 2,000 years later, thought that people, being rational, wouldn't.

THE CONTEXT

Hobbes has a more cynical and, he would say, realistic, view of human nature than the Greeks. Whilst he agrees that people have regard for their self-interest, there is little else he will accept from the ancients. Where Aristotle and Plato imagined that (at least some) people were virtuous (and even Machiavelli at least believed it was worth appearing to be so), Hobbes considers that social life is only a mixture of selfishness, violence and fear, topped with a healthy dollop of deceit – the last there to make things work more smoothly. Hobbes even has the temerity to describe this as the 'state of nature', a shocking phrase calculated to arouse the wrath of the Church, directly conflicting with the rosy biblical image of Adam and Eve in the Garden of Eden before the Fall.

How had Hobbes come to such a negative view of society? After all, for most of the Middle Ages in Europe, virtually the only theorising on these matters had been that of the Catholic theologians in their monasteries and convents. In his commentaries on Aristotle, St Thomas Aquinas (1225–74) had built upon Aristotle's notion of rationality the necessity of a virtuous and divinely inspired social order, which none could challenge without challenging God. For doing this (amongst other reasons) Hobbes was considered by many of his contemporaries to be, if not actually an atheist, certainly a heretic. Indeed, after the Great Plague of 1665, in which 60,000 Londoners died, and the Great Fire straight afterwards, a parliamentary committee was set up to investigate whether heresy might have contributed to the two disasters. The list of possible causes included Hobbes' writings.

One factor, doubtless, was that Thomas Hobbes was born in middle England into a Tudor society which was beginning to collapse into the acrimony of the English Civil War. If much has been made of this fact, as explaining Hobbes' desire for one all-powerful authority, perhaps it is too easy to explain away retrospectively Hobbes' unique contribution to the development of the western model of society. After all, the Greeks lived in circumstances in which governments were continually coming and going, and yet they produced theories favouring quite different aims. It might as reasonably be said by the psychological behaviourists that Hobbes' approach stems from emotional distress at being separated from his father, a vicar, who lost his job after quarrelling with another pastor at the church door. (This certainly would explain his own tendency to battle with the church, yet not disown it.) But this would be pointless speculation. All we need know is that, after that event, the young Hobbes had to be brought up by his uncle, eventually becoming an accomplished scholar at Oxford.

Leaving university with a degree in scholastic logic and, it has been said, several more degrees of contempt for Aristotle in particular, and universities in general, Hobbes obtained a post as tutor to the Earl of Devonshire. He travelled widely with 'the Duke', moving in increasingly aristocratic circles and even meeting the celebrated Italian astronomer Galileo in 1636. Four years earlier, Galileo had published his famous *Dialogue*, setting out some of his conclusions from his observation of the heavens through the newly reinvented telescope, notably his discovery that the moons of Jupiter went around their mother planet and the suggestion that the planets too went around the Sun. Even for this carefully worded suggestion, Galileo was summoned to Rome by the Church, required to recant, and forbidden to make any further astronomical observations. The Earth, the Cardinals reminded him, was the centre of the universe, and did not need to go round anything. But Hobbes admired and to some extent modelled his own writings on Galileo's example. His political system is as radical an upturning of social life as anything the astronomers offered of the solar system.

Hobbes' books are a strange mixture of jurisprudence, religious enthusiasm and political iconoclasm. There is an undertone of guilt reminiscent of St Augustine a thousand years before. Augustine, who had, in his own writings, devoted many thousands of pages to alternately apologising and blaming himself for the wickedness of a soul that had led him, amongst other sins, to steal pears – and, as he solemnly recounts, worst of all, to enjoy them. Other aspects, however, particularly Hobbes' legal points, are innovative and frequently perceptive, even if occasionally dubious in the logic of their argument. Of it all, it is the political theory, the first significant one since Machiavelli's, that is most interesting and, historically, the most influential.

THE TEXT

The starting point for Hobbes' theory of society is a mechanistic view of both the universe and of human life within it. 'Nature (the Art whereby God hath made and governs the World)', Hobbes writes, by way of introduction to the *Leviathan*,

is by the *Art* of man, (as in many other things so in this also) imitated, [so] that it can make an Artificial Animal. For seeing life is but a motion of the limbs, the beginning whereof is in some principal part within; why may we not say, that all *Automata* (Engines that move themselves by springs and wheels as doth a watch) have an artificial life? For what is the *Heart*, but a *Spring*; and the *Nerves*, but so many *Strings*; and the *Joints*, but so many *Wheels*, giving motion to the whole Body, such as was intended by the artificer?

His view is that people are just machines, moved by what he terms 'appetites' and 'aversions'.

These small beginnings of Motion within the body of Man, before they appear in walking, speaking, striking, and other visible actions are commonly called ENDEAVOUR. This Endeavour, when it is toward something, is called APPETITE or DESIRE; the later, being the general name, and the other often times restrained to signify the Desire of Food, namely Hunger and Thirst. And when the Endeavour is fromward something, it is generally called AVERSION.

It follows that automata, the clockwork mechanisms that were such a great feature of the period, appearing like outrageous children's toys on the church steeples of the richest towns, didn't actually look alive, they *were* alive – artificially alive. 'Life itself is but Motion, and can never be without Desire, nor without Fear, no more than without Sense.'

The motion of the automata are no more mindless than the motion of the animal or human being, and the human being is no more free to direct its impulses than the machine is. Some, but not many, of these 'motions' are innate, the rest are the result of experience. Everyone seeks to fulfil these appetites, varying only in degree and particular taste. Hobbes says the 'human machine' is programmed to direct its energies selfishly. He doubts if it is ever possible for human beings to act altruistically, and even apparently benevolent action is actually self-serving, perhaps an attempt to make those who act in this way feel good about themselves. Instead, for human beings, 'in the first place, I put for a general inclination of all mankind, a perpetual and restless desire of Power after power, that ceaseth only in Death'.

This view is often associated with the writings of Nietzsche, sometimes with Hegel, but it is Hobbes who puts it so much more convincingly and elegantly 200 years earlier. This desire for power is the cause of human strife and conflict, the origin of the 'War of all upon all', as Hobbes puts it. It is only through an overarching authority that society can overcome this struggle for power over others, and that requires that people abandon their 'natural' rights in return for protection and stability. So Hobbes begins the *Leviathan* thus:

Art goes yet further, imitating that Rational and most excellent work of Nature, Man. For by Art is created that great LEVIATHAN called a COMMON-WEALTH, or STATE, which is but an Artificial Man; though of greater stature and strength than the Natural, for whose protection and defence it was intended ...

The political nature of human society is revealed by an examination of its earliest origins, in particular the 'invention' of speech, when God teaches Adam the names of the creatures. Hobbes sees two purposes for the lesson. The 'general use of discourse' is to turn our 'Train of our Thoughts into a Train of Words', which he thinks makes the thoughts easier to organise, ideas otherwise being 'apt to slip out of our memory, and put us to a new labour'.

The other use is for communication – to teach, to 'make known to others our wills and purposes, that we may have the mutual help of one another'. And immediately, alongside the opportunities for communication, come opportunities for abuse. People can use words to try to deceive others – or themselves.

For the errors of Definitions multiply themselves, according as the reckoning proceeds; and lead men into absurdities which at last they see, cannot avoid, without reckoning anew from the beginning; in which lies the foundation of their errors. From whence it happens, that they which trust to books, do as they that cast up many little sums into a greater, without considering whether those little sums were rightly cast up or not; and at last finding the error visible, and not mistrusting their first grounds, know not which way to clear themselves; but spend time in fluttering over their books; as birds that entering by the chimney, and finding themselves enclosed in a chamber, flutter at the false light of a glass window, for want of wit to consider which way they came in.

Commentators later made much of Hobbes' lack of academic or indeed scientific rigour, perhaps reflecting the prejudices of his contemporaries who despised his lowly origin; yet perhaps the most striking aspect of Hobbes' political philosophy is that, at a time of elaborate respect for the various authorities of God, the pope, the high-born or whoever, it is resolutely rational in its approach. In his science, Hobbes is impressed by Galileo's rediscoveries of the mountains on the Moon (Democritus had written of them too), the phases of Venus and the movements of the planets, as well as by biological discoveries such as that of the circulation of the blood by Harvey, all of which tended to challenge established opinion. He offers arguments which are based on clearly set out grounds, with the reasoning shown in clear step-by-step terms with no waffle or 'fluttering', and no appeal to mystic or traditional authorities. This is a conscious aim, too, for as he writes of the 'abstruse philosophy' of the Schoolmen:

When men write whole volumes of the stuff, are they not Mad, or intend to make others so? ... So that this kind of Absurdity, may rightly be numbered amongst the many sorts of Madness; and all the time that, guided by clear Thoughts of their worldly lust, they forbear disputing, or writing thus, but Lucid intervals. And thus much of the Virtues and Defects Intellectual.

Hobbes' emphasis on clarity and common sense leads him to his low opinion of Aristotle, and much of the work of the ancients. Whereas Aristotle, and indeed Machiavelli, are often to be found extrapolating conclusions from inadequate data whenever and wherever their 'natural light' inspires them to, Hobbes is much more cautious. In another of the many books he produced during his 91 years, Hobbes writes that experience confirms nothing universally, thus anticipating David Hume by a century in his rejection of induction.

Induction is the theory, as Bertrand Russell has put it, that a chicken may have plenty of evidence for believing that the farmer is its friend (handfuls of grain each morning) and still be mistaken when it attempts to generalise the findings. For one morning the unfortunate bird will emerge to find its 'friend' the farmer not scattering the grain, but wringing its neck.

Hobbes is anxious to avoid such an undignified fate for himself. Instead, he carefully breaks down (by analysis) social phenomena into their 'basic constituents' and only then synthesises these to produce a new theory.

It is this technique, as much as his theory of power as the motivating spring of mankind, that makes Hobbes a distinctly modern thinker. This shows itself, for example, in what he then makes of his first and most basic commitment, the idea that people have internal desires or motions, and are 'of necessity' seeking the power to fulfil them.

The Power *of a Man* (to take it Universally,) is his present means, to obtain some future apparent Good. And is either *Original*, or *Instrumental*. *Natural Power* is the eminence of the Faculties of Body, or Mind; as extraordinary Strength, Form, Prudence, Arts, Eloquence, Liberality, Nobility. *Instrumental* are those Powers, which acquired by these, or by fortune, are means and Instruments to acquire more; as Riches, Reputation, Friends, and the secret working of God, which men call Good Luck. For the nature of Power, is in this point, like to Fame, increasing as it proceeds; or like the motion of heavy bodies, which the further they go, make still the more haste.

There are three things that follow directly from this compulsion, three 'principle causes of quarrel' as Hobbes puts it. The first is *competition*, for gain; the second is *diffidence*, and a compulsion for safety; whilst the final one is the compulsion for *glory*, and for reputation. Yet they all precipitate violence.

The first use Violence, to make themselves Masters of other men's persons, wives, children, and cattle; the second, to defend them; the third, for trifles, as a word, a smile, a different opinion, and any other sign of undervalue either direct in their Persons, or by reflection in their Kindred, their Friends, their Nation, their Profession, or their Name.

Of course, people see that they are at risk from their fellow beings, and live perpetually both in danger and in fear.

Hereby it is manifest, that during the time men live without a common power to keep them all in awe, they are in that condition which is called War; and such a War as is of every man, against every man. For WAR, consists not in Battle only, or in the act of fighting; but in ... the disposition.

Every man becomes 'Enemy to every man', living without any security other than 'what their own strength, and their own invention shall furnish them with'. In such conditions, Hobbes observes,

there is no place for Industry; because the fruit thereof is uncertain: and consequently no Culture of the Earth; no Navigation, nor use of the commodities that may be imported by Sea; no commodious Building; no instruments of moving, and removing such things as require much force; no Knowledge of the face of the Earth; no account of Time; no Arts; no Letters; no Society; and which is worst of all, continual fear, and danger of violent death; And the life of man, solitary, poor, nasty, brutish, and short.

To those of his contemporaries who dispute this nature for Man, perhaps asking why God should create such a race, Hobbes challenges them to go to sleep with their doors and money chests unlocked. Anyway, he says, he is not accusing man's nature so much as man's actions. 'The Desires, and other Passions of man, are in themselves no Sin.' Because, in the

war of every man against every other man, this also is consequent; that nothing can be Unjust. The notions of Right and Wrong, Justice and Injustice have there no place. Where there is no common Power, there is no Law: where no Law, no Injustice.

Notions of 'justice' or 'fairness' and 'rights' are 'Qualities that relate to men in Society, not in Solitude'. Morality requires society. The solitary man is not moral. Only through society can 'the solitary man' achieve any relief from fear, any peace and security: 'Fear of oppression, disposes a man to anticipate, or to seek aid by society: for there is no other way by which a man can secure his life and liberty.'

Even exceptionally strong or ruthless leaders needs society, unable to escape from their essential equality with their fellows:

Nature hath made men so equal, in the faculties of the body, and mind; as that though there be found one man sometimes manifestly stronger in body, or quicker in mind than another; yet when all is reckoned together, the difference between man and man is not so considerable.

Although many may believe the differences in intellect to be great, this is but a 'vain conceit'. 'For they see their own wit at hand, and other men's at a distance.'

For individuals are all mortal and all fallible. This fundamental equality makes it impossible for anyone to feel secure from others, except by creating the overriding power of the state. Partly because of this human fallibility, the founders of commonwealths will have to implant in the masses the beliefs that the laws are divine, 'from the dictates of some God, or other spirit', or else that they themselves are 'of a higher nature than mere mortals'. Hobbes' 'covenant' (by which the ruled exchange their freedom for security) is just such a virtuous fiction: he does not suppose it to have any actual historical parallel, merely offers it as a convenient rationalisation. Philosophers sometimes raise the objection that the entire social contract raises the question of how it can ever itself be started or got going, as no one is supposed, in Hobbes' view, to act out of anything but immediate self-interest – a kind of 'bootstrap' problem. But such objections are inappropriate. Hobbes himself is making no historical claims, only offering fictions.

However, the laws of nature are real enough. The most fundamental of these laws is that every living thing struggles to survive. Since the best way of doing this is for there to be peace, and not war, the requirement is to seek peace.

The Passions that incline men to Peace, are Fear of Death; Desire of such things as are necessary to commodious living; and a Hope by their industry to obtain them. And Reason suggests convenient Articles of Peace, upon which men may be drawn to agreement. These Articles, are they, which otherwise are called the Laws of Nature.

The transfer of the right to use force from the people to the sovereign authority, 'the mutual transferring of Right' is 'that which men call CONTRACT'. The general expression of the Laws of Nature is that of the biblical commandment, to do unto others only what you would have done unto yourself. And Hobbes draws another contrast with the views of Aristotle on 'political creatures':

It is true, that certain living creatures, as Bees, and Ants, live sociably one with another ... and yet have no other direction, than their particular judgments and appetites; nor speech, whereby one of them can signify to another, what he thinks expedient for the common benefit; and therefore some man may perhaps desire to know why Mankind cannot do the same.

The reason is that men like to compare themselves with each other – unlike the creatures, whose individual interest is more simply identical with the collective interest. Ants and bees do not differ over methods, merely accepting the system, far less do they try to trick each other. The only way, Hobbes continues, to reproduce such a virtuous system with people, is to

confer all the power and strength upon one Man, or upon one assembly of men, that may reduce all their Wills, by plurality of voices, unto one Will ... This is more than Consent, or Concord; it is a real Unity of them all, in one and the same Person, made by Covenant of every man with every man ...

And this is 'that Great Leviathan', the Commonwealth, and it comes about when either one man 'by War subdueth his enemies to his will', or when 'men agree amongst themselves, to submit to some Man, or Assembly of men, voluntarily, on confidence to be protected by him against all others'.

Hobbes quotes the book of Job on the great power God gives the Leviathan: 'There is nothing on earth to be compared with him. He is made so as not to be afraid. He seeth every thing below him; and is *King of all the children of pride.*'

Much of the *Leviathan* is legalistic in tone, as befits a theory based on constructing order out of anarchy. Crucially, there are even restrictions on the all-powerful sovereign. No man 'can be obliged by Covenant to accuse himself' much less to 'kill, wound, or maim himself'.

On the other hand, covenants entered into out of fear are obligatory, just as, Hobbes says, with Machiavellian pragmatism, if someone has agreed to pay a ransom, then they must pay it. 'For it is a contract wherein one receives the benefit of life; the other is to receive money, or service for it.' If it were not so, then it would invalidate the supposed contract between the individual and the sovereign, for this is precisely that of one motivated by fear. However, there is one exception to this, and that is a covenant not to defend yourself from force. This is always void, for 'no man can transfer, or lay down his Right to save himself from Death, Wounds, and Imprisonment'. Indeed, if a man is in danger of dying, 'Nature compels him' to break the law. For the same reason, most sound systems of law do not compel an accused person to testify against their own interests – the citizen has what today we would value as 'the right to silence'.

Hobbes even defends the man who flees court, a position which seems to be based on a low opinion of judges rather than any philosophical consistency. 'The Lords of England were judges, and most difficult cases have been heard and determined by them; yet few of them were much versed in the study of the Laws ...' Hobbes cautions that judges should have a sense of 'equity', a contempt of riches, and be dispassionate and capable of listening patiently and attentively. It is especially important for judges, of all people, to acknowledge equal rights.

No one is obliged to kill themselves. Nor, more surprisingly, can anyone be bound to kill another. Even a soldier may refuse to fight the enemy 'though his Sovereign have the right to punish his refusal with death'. This may seem to be inconsistent, but there, that's autocracy

for you! At least Hobbes, when he says that 'Allowance may be made
of natural timorousness, not only to women ... but also to men of
feminine courage', is more generous than were the generals of the
First World War to their shell-shocked conscripts.

However, Hobbes has no time for 'the poisonous doctrine' that
'every man is a judge of Good and Evil actions', and that listening
to your conscience takes higher priority than following the law. At
the same time, Hobbes bases his law on what he supposes to be the
reality of human psychology, even rejecting the commandment not
to 'covet', saying that this makes a sin out of human nature.

Certain technical repercussions of a system of laws are considered,
such as what happens when someone does not know of the law.
Ignorance of the 'Law of Nature' is no excuse, for the law of nature
is simply that one should not do to others what one would not like
done to oneself. However, ignorance of a civil matter, perhaps like
that of a traveller in a strange country, is an excuse. Ignorance of the
sovereign is never allowable, for the sovereign is always the citizen's
protection, nor is ignorance of the penalty. Ideally, children should
be brought up to obey the law instinctively. On the other hand, no
law made 'after a Fact done', can make something a crime.

In general, premeditated crime is worse than that arising 'from
a sudden Passion' and crimes undermining the law are worse than
those of no effect. Punishment must be sufficient to deter a rational
criminal, whilst being essentially positive in its aims, a notion which
includes, for example, the deterring of others.

Hobbes recommends a series of limitations on the power of the
law to punish. Punishments should not constitute revenge, but only
restitution, that is, righting wrongs. They should inflict no pain unless
it can be offset against some future good – perhaps persuading others
not to behave similarly. But, the punishment must be greater than
the benefits of the crime, and any ill effects that by chance strike
the wrongdoer are not to be offset against the eventual sentence, for
these are not 'inflicted by the Authority of man'.

The final Cause, End or Design of men, (who naturally love Liberty, and Dominion
over others,) in the introduction of that restraint upon themselves ... is the
foresight of their own preservation and of a more contented life thereby; that
is to say, of getting themselves out from that miserable condition of War,
which is necessarily consequent ... to the natural Passions of men, when there
is no visible Power to keep them in awe, and tie them by fear of punishment

to the performance of their Covenants ... Covenants without the Sword are but Words.

And the sword has great range and freedom in Hobbes' civil society. To begin with, any man who fails to consent to the decrees of the Leviathan may 'without injustice be destroyed by any man whatsoever' (with the exception of 'natural fools, small children and madmen, who do not understand the injunction in the first place'). At the same time, anyone with sovereign power cannot justly be punished, for whatever they do is by definition just. It is not even acceptable to question their actions, for that is to superimpose a new authority over the sovereign. 'It belongeth to him that hath the Sovereign Power, to be Judge.'

There is one exception possible, when the Sovereign 'licenses' another to exercise power 'to certain particular ends, by that Sovereign limited'. (When a colony is founded, the sovereign may need to license them to govern themselves.) Anyway, people are bad judges.

For all men are by nature provided of notable multiplying glasses, (that is their passions and Self-love,) through which, every little payment appeareth a great grievance; but are destitute of those prospective glasses, (namely Moral and Civil Science,) to see afar off the miseries that hang over them, and cannot without such payments be avoided.

Hobbes says there are just three ways to organise society. There is that of just one ruler, which is a monarchy; then there is that of an 'Assembly of All', which is a democracy; and lastly, there is that of an assembly of just part of society, which is an 'Aristocracy'. Any other forms identified by the Greeks (that Aristotle again) are simply the same ones misnamed, because they are 'misliked'. Thus the Greeks dubbed an unpopular monarch a 'tyrant', a disliked aristocracy an 'oligarchy' and a rogue democracy 'anarchy'. Hobbes has no time for such false distinctions. They only encourage 'sedition against the state'.

Of the various forms of government, Hobbes is not in principle opposed to assemblies, but monarchies, he thinks, are less likely to be subject to factionalism than assemblies, although there is one monarchic 'inconvenience' – that the crown may sometimes 'descend upon an infant'. When he writes of parliamentary government, Hobbes seems to have in mind a body made up of unelected individuals serving for life, rather than a body of representatives removable in the event of public dissatisfaction – the House of Lords rather than the House of Commons, in the English context.

What of social policy in the commonwealth? Hobbes thinks that those incapable of work should be helped and looked after, but those unwilling must be compelled. His egalitarianism extends to the distribution of 'Things that cannot be shared out': these must be held in common (or else distributed by lot).

State and church should be united – and then the laws will be unambiguous. It is not possible for the sovereign to be accused of holding a heretical opinion, for the sovereign's opinion will be the highest and holiest. Most of the deliberate heresies are due to the 'vain and erroneous philosophies' of the Greeks, especially Aristotle, whom Hobbes cannot resist having a final go at in the *Leviathan*.

Their Logic which should be their method of reasoning, is nothing else but Captions of Words, and Inventions how to puzzle such as should go about to pose them ... there is nothing so absurd that the old Philosophers ... have not some of them maintained. And I believe that scarce anything can be more absurdly said than that which now is called Aristotle's Metaphysics; nor more repugnant to Government, than much of that he hath said in his Politics; nor more ignorantly, than a great part of his Ethics.

Contempt is due because the 'Heathen Philosophers' define good and evil by reference to the 'appetite of men', by which measure, Hobbes has already said, there is no law, and no distinction between right and wrong. The next mistake is to have not men, but laws, governing. For who thinks that 'words and paper' hurt more than the hands and the swords of men? Finally, by extending the laws to cover thoughts the Greeks allow government to exceed the proper role of the institution.

After this outburst, Hobbes piously hopes that there is nothing too controversial in his views, and brings to an end his 'Discourse of Civil and Ecclesiastical Government, occasioned by the disorders of the present time' with the respectful wish that it might some day in the future be adopted by a sovereign as a partial guide. 'I ground the Civil Right of Sovereigns, and both the Duty and Liberty of Subjects, upon the known natural Inclinations of Mankind, and upon the Article of the Law of Nature; of which no man ... ought to be ignorant.'

However, as John Locke was to write a century later, because of the arbitrary powers it gives to the sovereign, for many people Hobbes' social contract is actually worse than the state of nature it is supposed to help them to rise above. Who, Locke asked, would sign a contract to escape from 'polecats and foxes', if the result was to be put 'at the mercy of lions'?

THE SUBTEXT

Many of the ideas in the *Leviathan* have been fluttered over by philosophers. Nietzsche misappropriated the 'will to power', John Rawls borrowed the idea of a social contract to explain moral decision making, and social determinism in general is today often echoed, for example in talk of 'the selfish gene' that is sometimes claimed to explain human behaviour.

Thomas Hobbes provides an antidote to the high-minded reasoning of the schoolmen and indeed the ancients. Starting from a pragmatic assessment of human nature, he strengthens the case for a powerful political and social apparatus organising our lives. And with his interest in the methods of geometry and the natural sciences, he brings a new style of argument to political theorising that is both more persuasive and more effective. But from Hobbes we also obtain a reminder that social organisation, however committed to fairness and equality it may be intended to be, being motivated by a struggle between its members, is also inevitably both authoritarian and inegalitarian.

Hobbes' influence is profound. For the first time individual rights are deduced and derived from a supposed 'fundamental right' to self-preservation. Together with the works of the Dutch lawyer and politician, Hugo Grotius, he both set the style and laid the foundations for future work in the areas of political theory, social ethics and international law.

KEY IDEAS

- People are motivated by selfishness. Left to their own devices they always come into conflict.
- Self-preservation is the highest law. Not even the state can overstep this mark.

KEY TEXT

Hobbes' *Leviathan* (original text 1651)

Timeline:
From the English Dictatorship
to the First Taxes

1641
Following up its early constitutional foray of *Magna Carta* (1215), the English Parliament pass the Habeas Corpus Act which deprives England's sovereigns of their previously assumed right to arrest and imprison citizens without trial.

1653
The Commonwealth becomes a dictatorship as Cromwell seizes total power and calls himself 'Lord Protector'. When Cromwell dies, England restores the monarchy.

1667
Locke's *Essay Concerning Toleration* is published. The French army develop the use of hand grenades.

Between 1680 and 1690
Locke works on his 'Two Treatises' on Civil Government, and sure enough the first 'civil government' in Britain, a constitutional monarchy, appears in 1689. In this year, Parliament even passes a 'Bill of Rights', which remains, formally, the only one the British have.

1695
The first universal tax is unveiled in France, a tax on windows is developed in England and, in 1698, a tax on beards in Russia. By the 1720s there will be riots in France against the *'cinquantième'* or 2 per cent tax on incomes.

7

Locke's Feudal Freedom

John Locke was born in a quiet Somerset village into a well-off Puritan trading family, and into a rather less quiet period of civil war between Parliament and Royalists. His political theory starts, like Plato's, with a search for moral authority. 'All being equal and independent, no one ought to harm another in his life, health, liberty, or possessions', he proclaims.

THE CONTEXT

Locke is a kind of 'lowest common denominator' of political philosophy, a role that befits a thinker of a naturally orthodox turn of mind. If, as with Hobbes, the upheaval of the English Civil War is the background to his writings, Locke still seems to have enjoyed a placid enough childhood, undisturbed by the activities of the rebellious parliamentarians, who included his father amongst their number. Even the execution of King Charles in 1649, whilst he was a schoolboy, failed to radicalise him. Instead Locke rose steadily up through English society, particularly after rather fortuitously saving the Earl of Shaftesbury's life by performing a hazardous but successful operation on him. (At this time, of course, any successful operation had the nature of something of a miracle, requiring lavish rewards.)

Shaftesbury would go on to have three notable political achievements: he led the opposition to Charles II; he founded the Whig Party, the forerunner of the Liberals; and he pushed Locke into politics. Really rather unexpectedly, Locke eventually became one of the most acclaimed figures of his century, the intellectual forebear of much of today's political orthodoxy, and one of the most influential political philosophers of all time.

Locke's political life begins around the time of the Black Death, when London was burning in the Great Fire, as the son of a Puritan trading family at last abandons the life of polite debate within academia or the Church that had been beckoning. Instead, apparently undergoing something of a 'Damascene' conversion, Locke decided to write what amounted to a work of sedition – which was a very dangerous thing to do in the seventeenth century. Of Locke's immediate circle, Shaftesbury would flee for his life in 1682 to Holland, whilst poor Algernon Sidney, Lord William Russell and the Earl of Essex would all be imprisoned for spreading the wrong sort of (politically controversial) views. Sidney and Russell eventually met their deaths on the scaffold, to the end insisting unheeded on their right to resist tyrants, whilst Essex cheated the hangman – but only by taking his own life whilst languishing in the Tower of London.

But John Locke fitted the times very well (Bertrand Russell even described him as the 'apostle of the Revolution of 1688'). His philosophy was actively adopted by contemporary politicians and thinkers; his influence was transmitted to eighteenth-century France through the medium of Voltaire's writings and inspired the principles of the French revolution. And his views would spread still more widely through the writings of Thomas Paine, eventually shaping the American revolution too.

For Locke, the significance of the Civil War itself was that it represented a flare-up in the perennial battle between the king and the aristocrats and bishops. Through Parliament, both were always seeking a greater role, particularly in the setting of tariffs and the levying of taxes, as well as in the conduct of religious affairs. At this time, matters hinged on the relative influence of two factions in the country: the Independents, who were politically moderate, but who sought a state church and wished to abolish bishops; and the Presbyterians, who insisted, on the contrary, that every congregation should be free to choose its own theology. Eventually the dispute was resolved on the battlefield by Cromwell's New Model Army in favour of the Independents. After this, the hopes of 'moderates' for a compromise with the king were dashed. Cromwell happily assumed the role of Napoleon the pig in *Animal Farm*, Orwell's classic allegorical novel (of a much later, communistic revolution), who, having led the farmyard animals in revolution against their human master, ends up walking on two legs, eating and sleeping in the farmer's old house.

After a period of increasingly less democratic parliaments, the rule of the 'Lord Protector' rapidly descended into a personal dictatorship. As a result, by the time of Cromwell's death, most English were relieved to have Charles' son return as, effectively, their first constitutional monarch, bound to Parliament by the principles of habeas corpus and the need to seek its approval for new taxes. And perhaps there was another, more subtle, legacy of the Civil War – a fear and dislike of over-powerful individuals.

THE TEXT

Fortunately for John Locke, at the time of the revolutionary purges that netted his friends, he himself was of such trifling political importance that he was allowed to slip away abroad (to Amsterdam) largely unnoticed and completely unheeded. Not that his views were particularly radical even when noticed. His political writing is presented in academic style as a response to issues raised by earlier writers such as Hugo Grotius, the Dutch lawyer and statesman with a special interest in ethics and international law, or by the English political theorist (pundit, we might say today), Sir Robert Filmer. Filmer's royalist tract, *Patriacha* (published 1680) earned him a knighthood from Charles I. It also earned him a particular notoriety in the eyes of the parliamentarians, who later, during the war, vented their pent-up frustration by ransacking his house not just once but ten times.

It is with Sir Robert's comfortable, traditionalist thesis in mind, with its philosophy that people are *naturally* born unfree and unequal, and rulers are equally naturally over them (directly descended from the First Man, Adam (who had been given dominion over all creation by God himself), that John Locke begins his political writings. The *Two Treatises (Concerning the True, Original Extent and End of Civil Government)*, written around 1690, start by declaring that 'it is impossible that the rulers now on earth should make any benefit, or derive the least shadow of authority, from that which is held to be the fountain of all power, Adam's private dominion and paternal jurisdiction'.

This, Locke says, is now recognised as a trick played by governments on citizens designed to blind them to the reality

that all government in the world is the product only of force and violence, and that men live together by no other rules but that of the beasts, where the strongest carries it, and so lay a foundation for perpetual disorder and mischief, tumult, sedition and rebellion.

Locke challenges the prevailing view, exemplified by Sir Robert, that the state, through its officers, has the same sort of authority over the citizen as a father (in a patriarchal society) has over his children, or a squire over his servant, or a lord over his slave – or a man over his wife. If elsewhere he writes in favour of such hierarchies, in the *Essay Concerning the True, Original Extent and End of Civil Government*, at least, Locke rejects all these pillars of traditional society. He urges that slavery is 'so vile and miserable an Estate of Man' and 'so directly opposed to the benevolent temper and spirit of the nation' that it was 'hardly to be conceived that any Englishman, much less a Gentleman, should plead for't'. However, this is a departure from Locke's *Second Treatise of Civil Government*, also dated 1690, which contains a special discussion of slavery. Much of this work is given over to an account of the 'state of slavery'; this explanation in turn depends on his account of the 'state of nature' and of the 'state of war', which together take up most of Chapters 2, 3, 4 and 16. In Chapter 3, Locke says that:

there is another sort of servants, which by a peculiar name we call slaves, who being captives taken in a just war, are by the right of nature subjected to the absolute dominion and arbitrary power of their masters. These men having, as I say, forfeited their lives, and with it their liberties, and lost their estates; and being in the state of slavery, not capable of any property, cannot in that state be considered as any part of civil society; the chief end whereof is the preservation of property.

The ambiguity would be essential to Locke's personal morality and investments and to future generations of Americans. But apart from the philosophical interest of the discussion, Locke may have had more specific reasons to include it at length in his political writings. One hypothesis is that Locke thought he needed an account of 'legitimate' slavery to show that the English Royal family were illegitimately attempting to enslave the English people. As one of the aims of his political philosophy is to distinguish between legitimate and illegitimate civil government, the account of slavery may be simply a variation on this theme. A second reason may have been that Locke considered it his patriotic duty to explain and justify an activity so profitable and useful to the national power of England. Or a third reason may simply have been that Locke, like Aristotle and so many others before him, simply considered some people to be naturally greatly inferior and so any theory of natural rights need not apply to them.

Nowadays philosophers don't dwell too much on Locke's view of slaves. But that does not mean the subject was an irrelevance. Because in Locke's philosophy, property is the key to 'civil' society, and the key to property is labour. Indeed, as morality for him starts with the institution of property, slavery is a very peculiar but significant case. Indeed, in the 'original state', Locke writes, it is only this property that gives individuals freedom. In section 63 of the *Second Treatise of Civil Government*, Locke crucially adds a new requirement to being able to be free: 'The freedom then of man, and liberty of acting according to his own will, is grounded on his having reason.' At this time, most authorities, following Aristotle, considered women to lack powers of reason.

At least Locke tries to avoid this interpretation. Quoting in his support the Christian commandments of Exodus to honour both 'thy father and thy mother', Locke suggests that 'it might perhaps have kept men from running into those gross mistakes they have made' if they had remembered that there was another equal authority in the world. Even a monarchy, he goes on, should properly be understood as that of more than one person, for where there is a king, there needs must be a queen. And Locke points out that the hereditary principle itself is dubious and flawed as it would appear to allow only one true heir to Adam, with all the other supposed kings left exposed as frauds. On the other hand, any weakening of the literal hereditary system, say one that simply allows power, like property, to be handed down from father to son, cannot provide the stability that the 'descent from God' principle does. Unlikely though this political debate may seem to modern eyes, the notion of 'direct descent' does hang on even now, for example in the Japanese royal family, in the 'political families' such as the Kennedys and the Bushes in America, and (at least until the end of the last century) in the British House of Lords. In the seventeenth century, the idea that some people are naturally suited to rule over others was widely accepted as the uncontroversial and literal truth.

To justify his radicalism, Locke, like Hobbes (who published the *Leviathan* whilst Locke was preparing to study at Oxford), goes back to consideration of the 'state of nature'. Again like Hobbes, he imagines this as a situation of lawlessness, where all may do as they will, without 'asking leave, or depending on the will of any other man'. It is a state of equality, yet not total anarchy, for there is one rule – the 'sacred and unalterable law of self-preservation'. Thus far, then, thus unremarkable. But now Locke extracts a palatable dish from Hobbes' bitter brew.

The state of nature has a law of nature to govern it, which obliges everyone: and reason, which is that law, teaches all mankind, who will but consult it, that being all equal and independent, no one ought to harm another in his life, health, liberty or possessions.

This is because we are all the work of the 'one omnipotent Maker', all 'furnished with like faculties, sharing all in one community of nature', and so 'any such subordination among us, that may authorise us to destroy one another, as if we were made for one another's uses, as the inferior ranks of creatures are for ours' cannot be justified. It follows that, in the state of nature, no one may interfere with another's liberties – 'we are born free, as we are born rational' – but if once one transgresses another's rights or property, then, be warned, everybody has a right to 'punish the transgressors of that law to such a degree, as may hinder its violation'. But this punishment must still be 'proportionate', and will only be just in as much as this serves to undo the original harm or to prevent future occurrences. For Locke's state of nature has two faces. It is a benign, cooperative existence originally, until an individual or group (like Cromwell and the Independents) seeks power over others. Then it becomes a state of war, with individuals entitled – nay, obliged – to use any means to regain their freedom.

Freedom is the kernel of Locke's philosophy: 'The freedom ... of man and liberty of acting according to his own will, is grounded on his having reason which is able to instruct him in that law he is to govern himself by.'

This is freedom from 'absolute, arbitrary power', not necessarily freedom to do anything. It is the liberty to follow one's own will and volition, except where a rule, 'common to everyone of that society, and made by the legislative power erected in it', prohibits such action. To which extent his doctrine is an early kind of utilitarianism, the engine of a machine with the aim of increasing the sum of human happiness. Locke has in mind only the enlightened self-interest of individuals. But in the priority he gives to individual rights, Locke appeals to a moral conception which is beyond self-interest, and which lies at the heart of political liberalism.

This new morality starts with the institution of property. The earth, and 'all inferior creatures', belong to everyone in common. However, there is one important exception. Each individual does own one thing: they have property in their own person. 'This nobody has any right to but himself', Locke adds, neglecting, it would seem, the contradictions exposed by the issue of slavery and indeed his own investments in the Royal Africa slaving company, doing a profitable trade for him at the time. Consequently, 'the labour of his body, and the work of his hands', are rightly considered to belong to each individual. 'Whatever people produce through their own effort, using the commonly owned raw materials of nature, are also (properly) theirs.' This apparently socialist principle, anticipating Marx's Labour Theory of Value by some centuries, Locke amplifies further:

for 'tis labour indeed that puts the difference of value on everything; and let anyone consider, what the difference is between an acre of land planted with tobacco, or sugar, sown with wheat or barley; and an acre of the same land lying in common, without any husbandry upon it.

But this, Locke appreciates, is jumping ahead in time from the true state of nature to agrarian society. In the beginning there was only hunting and gathering. Yet, even there, labour is the key.

He that is nourished by acorns he picked up under an oak or the apples he gathered from the trees in the wood, has certainly appropriated them to himself. Nobody can deny but the nourishment is his. I ask then, when did they begin to be his? When he eat? Or when he boiled them? Or when he brought them home? Or when he picked them up? And 'tis plain, if the first gathering made them not his, nothing else could.

The labour of picking up the acorns makes them the gatherer's, as 'of private right'. Nor is it necessary to seek the approval of the whole of mankind for it.

Locke sails close to the wind here, as on other occasions, for the rights of 'non-landowners' to 'commons' in seventeenth-century England was a sensitive matter. Common ownership of land had already been taken rather further by the Diggers, active during the first part of Locke's life, with their 'alternative' communities. Commons, perhaps underused but, by definition, unenclosed areas available for grazing or, indeed, collecting acorns, were always being threatened by the aristocracy, who wished to appropriate the common land to themselves. The English commons gave rural labourers the ability to produce food for themselves directly, which they would otherwise have only been able to achieve as payment for their labour on their lord's estates. In the rest of Europe, where there was no equivalent tradition of common land, the suggestion that people had a 'right' to the products of their labour would have been even more scurrilous and revolutionary. Even so, all Locke has in mind is a limit on appropriation. No one should take 'more than they are able to make use of' before it spoils. Whatever is beyond this 'is more than his share, and belongs to others'. Of course, Locke hastens to add, gold and silver do not 'spoil', and therefore there is no harm in *their* accumulation.

Locke also assumes an effectively unlimited supply of property (as with the gold and silver), thereby avoiding the more problematic issues his theory raises.

Nobody could think himself injured by the drinking of another man, though he took a good draught, who had a whole river of the same water left him to quench his thirst. And the case of the land and water, where there is enough of both, is perfectly the same.

Locke likes to advance, as an example of this, the unlimited acres of America, ignorant or uncaring of the effects of European 'property rights' on the native Americans with their long-established communal use and management of the land. Indeed, through most of the medieval period, settlements in the Americas were larger and more sophisticated than the European equivalents. But, most likely, Locke would have followed the prejudices of his time, even if he had considered there to be a conflict in ownership. Locke says that God gave the world to 'the industrious and rational', and the native Americans might well have been found wanting in his eyes – seen as lazy and neglectful of their natural inheritance, and consequently living in poverty.

'In the beginning the whole world was America', explains Locke, meaning that the world was an unexploited wilderness, before, through the efforts of people, there came farms and manufactures and buildings and cities. With these come trade, and money. But although property is the foundation of political society, Locke traces its origin back not to commerce, but to 'the conjugal union'. The first society was between man and wife, and later their children.

Conjugal society is made by a voluntary compact between man and woman: and though it consists of right in one another's bodies, as is necessary to its chief end, procreation; yet it draws with it mutual support, and assistance, and a community of interest too, as necessary not only to unite their care, and affection, but also necessary to their common offspring, who have a right to be nourished and maintained by them, till they are able to ... shift and provide for themselves.

This rule which, Locke notes, the infinitely wise Maker has set, is obeyed by all the 'inferior creatures' too, even though many of their offspring can fend for themselves almost as soon they are born. In the

Two Treatises, Locke argues that where a person is unable to provide the basic means of sustenance for themselves, they have a right to the surplus goods of others, and, indeed, people have an obligation 'by charity' to offer them this. And the handover must be done without exacting an undue toll, for

a man can no more make of another's necessity, to force him to become his vassal, by withholding that relief God requires him to afford to his brother, than he that has more strength can seize upon a weaker, master him to his obedience, and with a dagger at his throat offer him death or slavery.

Like Hobbes, Locke assumes a kind of 'social contract' between ruler and ruled. He imagines that people join voluntarily together as one society, giving up their natural rights in the area of law-making or what he terms the 'executive power of the law of nature'. In the *Two Treatises*, as in other earlier writings, he is content to take these issues as fairly self-evident, and leave the details of 'natural law' unexplored, the better to press on with drawing his conclusions.

Men being, as has been said, by nature, all free and equal and independent, no one can be put out of this estate, and subjected to the political power of another, without his own consent ... when any number of men have, by the consent of every individual, made a community, they have thereby made that community one body, with a power to act as one body, which is only by the will and determination of the majority ... to move ... whither the greater force carries it.

The American constitution is founded on the comforting declaration that certain truths are 'self-evident': it is Locke who provides much of the philosophical impetus for this dubious, if happy, notion.

Society is thus authorised by each individual to 'make laws for him as the public good of the society shall require'. The 'inconveniences' of anarchy ensure that this is a free decision quickly taken. The state of nature now gives way to the laws made for the common weal. This, Locke adds, demonstrates that absolute power, as for instance recommended by Hobbes, and generally present in the principle of monarchical rule, is not actually part of civil society, indeed not part of civil government at all. Where there exists no independent judge to ensure that justice is done, rulers and the ruled remain in a state of nature. Indeed slightly worse. 'For he that thinks absolute power purifies men's blood, and corrects the baseness of human nature, need read but the history of this, or any other age to be assured of the contrary.'

And so,

whoever has the legislative or supreme power of any commonwealth, is bound to govern by established standing laws, promulgated and made known to the people, and not by extemporary decrees; by indifferent and upright judges, who are to decide controversies by these laws; and to employ the force of community at home, only in the execution of such laws, or abroad to prevent or redress foreign injuries, and secure the community from inroads or invasion. And all this to be directed to no other end, but the peace, safety, and public good of the people.

Even then, Locke has no particular view about the form government should take, as long as it is based on popular consent. It might be a republic, but it could also be an oligarchy and there might still be a monarch. But whatever form the government takes, Locke says it does need to include some 'separation of powers', and he sets out fairly precisely the distinction to be made between the law-making part of government – the legislature – and the action-taking part – the executive. The executive must have the power to appoint and dismiss the legislature, but it does not make the one superior to the other, rather there exists a 'fiduciary trust'.

And, despite the fact that 'rigged justice' was very much a central issue of the 'Glorious Revolution', and after all Locke himself lived through the 'Cavalier Parliament' of 1661–79 – which did little other than pass increasingly totalitarian and repressive laws (mainly against religious freedom) – it was left to Montesquieu (in his *Spirit of the Laws* some half a century later, 1748) to argue the need for the additional separation of judicial power characteristic of the American constitution. In England, before the Civil War, judges could be dismissed at will by the king. Afterwards, they were removable only with the consent of both houses of Parliament.

Locke argues too that because self-defence is the foundation of the law of nature, people must always be allowed to protect themselves from an unjust or tyrannical government. (Observers of the changes of 1989 and later in Eastern Europe have claimed that these were 'Lockean' revolutions, in that the people – a political community, not just a class – withdrew their assent from their governments after years of waiting and biding their time.) Locke himself considers various objections to this final and most desperate liberty (the right to resist an unjust government) and finds them unconvincing. He quotes Barclay, 'the great champion of absolute monarchy':

But if anyone should ask, must the people then always lay themselves open to the cruelty and rage of tyranny? Must they see their cities pillaged, and lain in ashes, their wives and children exposed to the tyrant's lust and fury, and themselves and families reduced by their king to ruin and all the miseries of want and oppression, and yet sit still? Must men alone be debarred the common privilege of opposing force with force, which nature allows so freely to all other creatures?

Apparently not. Locke's social contract is different from Hobbes' in being not a once-and-for-all act, but an ongoing bargain between people and sovereign. If a king 'sets himself against the body of the commonwealth, whereof he is head, and shall, with intolerable ill-usage, cruelly tyrannise over the whole, or a considerable part of the people; in this case the people have a right to resist and defend themselves'. But not to go any further. For example, not to revenge themselves, or to lose their sense of respect for the royal authority.

As to the great question of who shall be judge of whether the government or the prince or legislature is acting contrary to the trust bestowed in them by the people, Locke says: 'To this I reply, the people shall be judge.' The only further appeal lies in Heaven.

In Locke's times, taxation had proved just such a cause. ''Tis true,' Locke ruefully acknowledges, 'that governments cannot be supported without great charge', so taxes may be levied, as long as it is with the consent of the people, or their representatives. But Locke sets himself firmly against the practice advanced so catastrophically by Charles I in precipitating the Civil War, and sought still by his son, that the royal prerogative allows the monarch to tax without seeking consent. After all, the 'great and chief end therefore, of men's uniting into commonwealths, and putting themselves under government, is the preservation of their property'.

The relevance and appeal of Locke's philosophy to the revolutions of the seventeenth century was his own achievement. But little more of Locke might have been heard, had it not been for one of his fellow countrymen, Thomas Paine (1737–1809), some years after his death. Through Paine, Locke's liberal individualism became something much more potent, contributing the ideals as well as the language of the two events that heralded the modern world – the French and American Revolutions.

THE RIGHTS OF MAN

Paine himself was from a rather more parochial mould than Locke, primarily concerned with practical matters, such as bridges. Born in

Norfolk, the young Paine worked variously as a 'staymaker', a civil servant, a journalist and a school teacher. It was whilst working for the Excise Board in Lewes in Sussex that he became interested in politics, and started serving on the town council, and holding heated political discussions of Locke's ideas in the White Hart Inn. Actually, Paine once remarked rather dismissively of his debt to his political forbear, that he had 'never read any Locke, nor ever had the work in my hand', but it was certainly Locke's ideas that made the running in those political debates in the White Hart.

Paine soon left quiet, half-timbered Lewes for the New World, on the recommendation of Benjamin Franklin himself, whom he had met in London, and at the same time moved from talk to action. On settling in Philadelphia, he immediately began to set out his ideas on paper: Lockean ideas of equal rights for men and women, for African and European – and (if not full rights) at least fair treatment for animals. Where Locke invested substantially in shares in the slave trade, Paine was one of the first in America to press for the abolition of slavery. His book *The Rights of Man* is rightly considered a political classic, rising above Locke's ponderous prose, whose ideas in it he so largely borrowed.

Paine was also interested in the detail of government. 'In the first place,' he writes, 'three hundred representatives, fairly elected, are sufficient for all the purposes to which legislation can apply, and preferable to a larger number.' They may be divided into a number of houses, or meet in one, as in France, 'or in any manner a constitution shall direct'. He even worked out neatly, in double entry book-keeping form, exactly how much the government would cost, which was not to be very much. In fact, when finances are done his way, there is, happily, enough money to pay something to all the poor people of the country. This money, Paine points out, is no more than remission of their own taxes, from hidden taxation imposed by duties on imports and so on. Furthermore, those who cannot work deserve state support, as the benefits of relieving parents of the twin burdens of paying for the very young and the very old (and the sick – all right, three burdens) enable them to cease being dependent on others, and society is restored to its natural state of being an engine for the production of prosperity.

Paine adds that, as representation is always considered in free countries, 'the most honourable of all stations', the 'allowance made to it' should merely be to 'defray the expense which the representatives incur by that service, and not to it as an office'. This, as with so many other ideals, has been a principle sadly lost somewhere along the line.

But it would be the novel issue of national self-determination that made the name of Thomas Paine historically significant – the issue that John Adams, second president of the United States, once described as a dreadful 'hobgoblin', 'so frightful … that it would throw a delicate person into fits to look it in the face'. Paine's nationalistic pamphlet *Common Sense* acted as a spark in a tinderbox, starting a fire that would eventually destroy far more than the English claim to America.

Locke's influence again is apparent in the writings of one of Paine's contemporaries and one of the first of the feminist philosophers, Mary Wollstonecraft. Writing, as it were, in parallel with Paine, Wollstonecraft produced an anonymous *Vindication of the Rights of Man* days before Paine's work and later, in 1798, even entitled one of her books: *The Wrongs of Women*. Wollstonecraft offered a radical personal narrative, endorsing the aims of the French Revolution even as many of her immediate circle were being led to the scaffold. Another work, *A Vindication of the Rights of Women* (1792), pushed forward Locke's liberal hypothesis on women's political importance, with a wide-ranging denunciation of 'male' rationality and power, criticising Rousseau in particular. For this, Wollstonecraft earned the dislike of many prominent male intellectuals of the time, and the particular soubriquet of 'hyena in petticoats' from Horace Walpole. But it was only a journalist like Paine, not a novelist, even a radical one like Wollstonecraft, far less an academic like Locke, who found the words to trigger change. Paine it was who wrote:

Why is it that scarcely any are executed but the poor? The fact is a proof, amongst other things, of a wretchedness in their condition. Bred without morals, and cast upon the world without a prospect, they are the exposed sacrifice of vice and legal barbarity. The millions that are superfluously wasted by governments, are more than sufficient to reform these evils, and to benefit the condition of every man in a nation … It is time that nations should be rational, and not be governed like animals, for the pleasure of their riders. To read the history of kings, a man would be almost inclined to suppose that government consisted in stag-hunting, and that every nation paid a million a year to a huntsman … It has cost England almost seventy millions sterling, to maintain a family imported from abroad, of very inferior capacity to thousands in the nation. (*The Rights of Man*, 1791)

THE SUBTEXT

Many notable contemporaries thought highly of Locke. The brilliant mathematician and physicist Sir Isaac Newton, who otherwise shunned company, cherished Locke's thoughts. The celebrated English physician Dr Thomas Sydenham worked with him on many medical explorations, declaring that here was 'a man whom, in the acuteness of his intellect, in the steadiness of his judgement ... I confidently declare to have, amongst the men of our time, few equals and no superiors'. The French philosopher Voltaire called Locke a man of the greatest wisdom, adding, 'What he has not seen clearly, I despair of ever seeing.' A generation later, in America, Locke's reputation had risen still higher. Benjamin Franklin thanked him for his 'self-education'; Thomas Paine enthusiastically borrowed and spread his radical ideas about rights; and Thomas Jefferson credited him as one of the 'greatest philosophers of liberty' of all time.

KEY IDEAS

Locke creates a picture of the world in which 'rationality' is the ultimate authority, not God, and certainly not, as Hobbes had insisted, brute force. He insists that people all have certain fundamental 'rights' and also attempts to return the other half of the human race, the female part, to their proper, equal place in history, the family and in government. He places individual judgement firmly above that of both church and state, limiting the latter's role to protecting property. Locke's legacy is the first, essentially practical, even legalistic framework and analysis of the workings of society. That is his own particular contribution to its evolution.

- Property is the key to 'civil' society, and the key to property is labour. The more you work, the more you own.
- The powers of government must be strictly limited, in particular by separating the ability to make laws from the ability to make policy.

KEY TEXT

Locke's *Essay Concerning the True, Original Extent and End of Civil Government* (1690)

 Timeline:
From 'Free Trade' to the Slave Trade

1703

Lahonton's idea of the 'noble savage' is celebrated by many 'Enlightenment' thinkers throughout Europe.

1707

The largest free trade area in Europe, and the most significant one in the world, is created by the Act of Union between England and Wales and Scotland.

1711

The steam engine is invented by Thomas Newcomen.

1719

Daniel Defoe describes the adventures of Robinson Crusoe and two years later Jonathan Swift begins writing *Gulliver's Travels*.

1721

Russian factories buy peasants as slave workers.

1727

The Quakers demand the abolition of slavery, 222 years after the first shiploads of black slaves were unloaded in the newly discovered Americas.

1747

A 'carriage tax' is introduced in England.

1748

Montesquieu's *Spirit of the Law* inspires later revolutionaries.

1765

Publication of the *Discourse on Inequality* sets Rousseau firmly against the optimism of the times.

8
Rousseau's Ode to Liberty

The Discourse on Inequality *is a brilliant work. This despite being wrong on almost every factual point and in many a supposed reference. It is not science – it is art, but then, so is politics. Fortunately, the author himself declares his intentions honestly, beginning his book with magnificent disdain, 'Let us begin by putting aside the facts, as they do not affect the question.'*

Thus far, what has been remarkable is the degree of consensus over the forces that shape history and therefore society. It is there in the comforting notion of 'progress' that all the philosophers seem to share. It is there in the admiration for science, and the respect for the institutions that created social life. But as the eighteenth century drew to an end, many of its values looked increasingly tarnished. The low opinion the rulers had of the ruled, the emphasis on privilege, and the aristocratic assumption that it was better not to work than to do so, along with a new indifference to practical problems such as public health and crime, all became increasingly anomalous and insupportable. New ways of looking at the world were needed, and a young Franco-Swiss philosopher, Jean-Jacques Rousseau, offered a complete reversal of the values of the time.

Rousseau did not think anything of civilisation, nor was he impressed by the achievements of science. He instead thought primitive man had been happier and better off. And he measured people's value not by their possessions, but by the divine spark that he saw in them all, the immortal soul of 'natural man'. His philosophy offers a more spiritual, romantic view of the world.

And it was anathema to many. Voltaire refused to abandon 'civilisation', to accept what he called an invitation to 'go down on all fours' saying that after 60 years or so, he had lost the habit. Dr Johnson said of Rousseau and his supporters, 'Truth is a cow that will yield them no more milk, so they have gone to milk the bull.'

But many others were entranced and inspired.

THE CONTEXT

Rousseau was a thinker who had many hats. He was an expert on music, and on education; one of the key figures in the Romantic movement in the arts, and the standard-bearer of the romantic tradition. But he was also an unscrupulous and selfish man who, despite the fine words of his child-centred educational philosophy, packed his own five illegitimate children off to the harsh world of the local foundling home, and refused even to see them. Rousseau was insecure too, convinced that everyone was out to get him, and often suspected offers of help to be trickery. He constantly complained of being 'misrepresented' and by the end of his life seemed to be suffering from the madness of full-blown paranoia.

At least he was sometimes able to see himself for what he was. Once, having wickedly accused a servant, a maid, of stealing something in fact he himself had taken, he admitted later, in his *Confessions*, that what he had done was actually the cowardly product of his childish resentment at being rebuffed by her.

But these confessions are also a self-indulgent work. His two most influential essays were written for others. The *Discourse on Inequality* and *The Social Contract* are dedicated to his fellow free citizens of Geneva, and to the 'Magnificent and Most Honoured Lords' who governed what was then a tiny, independent state. Not that he lived there for long, or that relations with the unappreciative burghers of Geneva were particularly good. *The Social Contract* was publicly burnt in the City Square of Geneva in 1762, along with Rousseau's idealistic work on education, *Emile*.

But things were rarely entirely straightforward for Rousseau. Born in 1712, in Geneva, his mother died just a week later from illness resulting from complications following the birth. So Rousseau had to be brought up by his father, Isaac, a watchmaker, and his aunt, and instead of going to school was educated at home. Jean-Jacques' older brother, François, did not like this arrangement, and ran away from home at the first opportunity, never to return. The younger Rousseau, however, had nothing but praise for his father, admiring him to a point little short of adoration. Unfortunately, at the age of ten, Jean-Jacques lost his father too, after the patriot unwisely challenged a gentleman to a duel, and was expelled from the city as a result. Jean-Jacques was then sent to the care of his uncle, which meant living just outside the city walls, where it was intended he would continue a rarefied 'Romanesque' education until the time came for him to be an apprentice engraver.

But before this plan could come to fruition, Rousseau rebelled, refusing what he considered to be a demeaning trade, and, using a tactic his city had demonstrated some years before to gain its independence, changed his religion, becoming the ward of the de Warens of Savoy, some benevolent Catholic aristocrats. It was here, in the library of the French family, that Rousseau drank eagerly from a deep well of subversive writing drawn from the works of the great political philosophers, Hobbes, Machiavelli and Locke amongst them.

After reading Locke, as well as after his perusal of Sir Francis Bacon, Rousseau became part of a loose grouping with a peculiar form of political analysis, known as the Encyclopaedists. The group was so called because celebrated members, such as Montesquieu and Voltaire, had contributed articles to the huge *Encyclopédie* of 1751–66. But Rousseau never really agreed with their fundamental position, typical of the Enlightenment, which was that religion and conventional philosophy were 'all empty' and should be swept away to allow for a more logical and rational, scientific calculation of the best way to organise life on earth. In addition, the Encyclopaedists believed, as many have since (completely unlike Rousseau) that new technology would usher in a better age, if given half a chance. Science would be the salvation of all mankind; unlike the religious creeds which only ever promised salvation to a minority.

At the age of 32, Rousseau arrived in Paris where he began to move in the sort of circles he felt he belonged in – being, after all, a citizen of Geneva and, as he never tired of telling people, born free. He became secretary to another aristocratic family, found a mistress, and began to write.

His first major work was, in fact, an attack on the ideas of the Encyclopaedists, and indeed the whole basis of the Enlightenment. In the *Discourse on the Sciences and Arts*, Rousseau takes on the scientists, and says that, far from being our saviours, they are ruining the world, and that any notion of progress is an illusion even as we move further and further away from the healthy, simple and balanced lives of the past. The *Discourse on Sciences* is a conscious salute to the kind of society advocated by Plato, two millennia earlier, and both a contrast with and a challenge to the prevailing orthodoxy of his times. Notwithstanding, or probably (in France) because of that, the essay was considered a great success, and earned Rousseau the Dijon prize.

With this was also bestowed upon him, at last, a certain status as that creature the French, above all, cherish – the *philosophe*.

• THE TEXT

When the Academy of Dijon requested new essays on the theme: 'What is the origin of inequality amongst men, and is it authorised by Natural Law?' Rousseau took up his quill again (attentive readers will have noted the invention of the fountain pen was only in 1782, some years after Rousseau's death), developing the idea he had sketched in the *Discourse on Sciences*, that man in his natural state, far from being greedy, or fearful, as described by Hobbes, is actually living in a peaceful, contented state – truly free. This is a freedom with three elements. The first is free will, the second is freedom from the rule of law (as there are no laws), and the third is personal freedom. It is this last that is the most important.

Rousseau says that the first people lived like animals. He says this not in any derogatory sense, merely in the sense that the original people sought only simple fulfilment of their physical needs. They would have had no need of speech, nor concepts, and certainly not property. Rousseau points out that much of the imagery in both Hobbes and Locke belongs to a property-owning society, not to the supposed 'natural state' prior to the invention of property rights. By realising this, 'we are not obliged to make a man a philosopher before we can make him a man'. The first time people would have had a sense of property (he thinks) is when they settled in one location, when they built huts to live in. Even sexual union, Rousseau notes pragmatically, as well as reflecting on his own experience, is unlikely to have implied any exclusivity, being more likely to have been just a lustful episode no sooner experienced than forgotten, remembered least of all in terms of the children. Neither the father nor the mother is likely to know whose children they beget, he argues, assuming that paternity is the defining characteristic and neglecting the mother's very definite knowledge!

Since this primitive state is actually superior to those which followed it, Rousseau goes on to suggest that the only reason why this early society ever changed must have been as a result of some sort of disaster, perhaps one causing shortages of food or other hardship. This would have forced people to start identifying certain areas as theirs, and maybe to start living in groups. This in turn would imply increased communication, and the development of language. And there is a second dimension to these changes: people began to judge themselves by a new criterion – how others thought of them. To Rousseau, this last is a change of the utmost significance, for it is self-consciousness that was the downfall of Adam and Eve in the Garden of Eden. And it is this self-consciousness that makes humankind permanently unhappy with its lot, and resentful or fearful of others.

After this, most unfortunately, 'the whole progress of the human race removes man constantly further and further from his primitive state'. According to Rousseau, at this point following Hobbes, society necessarily leads people to hate each other, in accordance with their different economic interests. But Hobbes' so-called 'social contract' is, in fact, made by the rich, as a way of doing down the poor. Actually, not even the rich benefit from it, as they warp themselves and become increasingly out of touch with nature's harmony, raised needlessly above their own proper state, just as the poor are pushed below theirs. Justice instead, for Rousseau, is not, to be sure, crude equality, but rather the correct placing of individuals according to their talents and abilities – according to their merit. Unfortunately, society disrupts this balance (which is also the problem discussed by Plato in his *Republic*). And Rousseau considers the very notion of the social contract to be flawed:

Since we have so little knowledge of nature and such imperfect agreement about the meaning of the word 'law', it would be very difficult to concur on a good definition of natural law. All the definitions we find in books have, besides the defects of lacking uniformity, the further defect of being derived from several ideas which men do not have naturally, and the utility of which they cannot conceive until after they have emerged from the state of nature.

Rousseau suggests instead just two laws, or principles, that could be said to be 'antecedent to reason'. The first (as with Hobbes) is a powerful interest in self-preservation and our own well-being; the second, however, is 'a natural aversion to seeing any other sentient being perish or suffer, especially if it is one of our own kind'.

The only time 'natural man' would hurt another is when his own well-being requires it. In saying this, Rousseau is drawing a parallel for humankind with the animals who – unlike their masters – never harm each other out of malice alone. If, in fact,

I am obliged to refrain from doing any harm to my neighbour, it is less because he is a reasonable being [i.e. one capable of reasoning] than because he is a sentient one; and a quality which is common to beast and man ought to give the former the right not to be uselessly ill-treated by the latter.

Significantly, *On Inequality* is introduced by Rousseau with the observation that the most important challenge in philosophy is the injunction posed by the Oracle at Delphi: 'Know thyself.' 'The most useful and least developed of all sciences seems to be that of Man', he writes. 'It is this ignorance of man's nature which creates such uncertainty and obscurity as to the correct definition of natural right.' So long as we have no knowledge of natural man, 'we shall wish in vain to ascertain the law which he has received from nature or that which best suits his constitution'.

And the preamble continues by promising to 'defend the cause of humanity' from what at that point is only a shadowy and undefined enemy. The crime is never made entirely clear either, but by the end of the essay, 'the rich', the 'law makers' and various fellow travellers appear to have been accused, found guilty and indicted, even if not actually guillotined.

Rousseau begins his task by distinguishing 'two kinds of inequality'. The first is 'natural or physical inequality', consisting in differences of age, health, strength and intelligence; the second is 'moral or political' and consists of 'the different privileges that some enjoy to the prejudice of others' – things such as wealth, honour and power.

The philosophers who have examined the foundations of society have all felt it necessary to go back to the state of nature, but none of them has succeeded in getting there. Some have not hesitated to attribute to men in that state of nature the concept of just and unjust, without bothering to consider whether they must have had such a concept, or even that it would be useful to them. Others have spoken of the natural right each has to keep and defend what he owns without saying what they mean by the word 'own'. Others again, starting out by giving the stronger authority over the weaker, promptly introduce government, without thinking of the time that must have elapsed before the words 'authority' and 'government' could have had any meaning.

Those who talked ceaselessly of 'greed, oppression, desire and pride' failed to realise that they were introducing into nature ideas that only originated in society. Rousseau, having up to this point veiled his references in suitably opaque language, suddenly becomes more specific: it is Hobbes that is the intellectual enemy, along with all those who imagine man to be a timid creature, 'always trembling and ready to run away at the least noise he hears or the smallest movement'. Although Hobbes also said that man is naturally intrepid and seeks 'only to attack and fight', only Rousseau reveals man as he truly is: the *Noble Savage*.

Let the civilised man gather all his machines around him, and no doubt he will easily beat the savage; but if you would like to see an even more unequal match, pit the two together naked and unarmed, and you will soon see the advantages of having all ones forces constantly at one's command, of being always prepared for any eventuality, and of always being, so to speak, altogether complete in oneself.

This is the favoured notion at the heart of Rousseau's alternative philosophy. To back it up, he tells the story of the Dutch sailor and the African. The sailor, disembarking at the Cape, gives the African a sack of tobacco weighing about the same as a bucket of coal to carry. When they have walked some distance and are alone, the African asks the sailor if he knows how to run. 'Run?' answers the Dutchman, 'Of course, I can run, and very well!' 'We shall see', says the African, and making away with the tobacco disappears over the horizon almost at once. The sailor, Rousseau finishes, 'bewildered by such marvellous speed', does not think of chasing him, and never sees again either his porter or his tobacco.

This imaginary story is offered to demonstrate the superiority of the natural man over the civilised man. But what of all the other supposed advantages of civilisation? Rousseau deals unceremoniously with them. They are but:

the extreme inequality of our ways of life, the excess of idleness among some and the excess of toil among others, the ease of stimulating and gratifying our appetites and our senses, the over-elaborate foods of the rich, which inflame and overwhelm them with indigestion, the bad food of the poor, which they often go without altogether, so that they over-eat greedily when they have the opportunity; those late nights, excesses of all kinds, immoderate transports of every passion, fatigue, exhaustion of mind, the innumerable sorrows and anxieties that people in all classes suffer, and by which the human soul is constantly tormented.

Rousseau says that another of Hobbes' great mistakes is to have imagined that the savage shared civilised man's greeds and passions. Instead, Hobbes should have realised that the state of nature was a happy one. It requires a sophisticated, rational knowledge of good and evil to make civilised man so wicked:

let us not agree with Hobbes that man is naturally evil just because he has no idea of goodness, that he is vicious for want of any knowledge of virtue, that he always refuses to do his fellow men services which he does not believe he owes them, or that on the strength of the right he reasonably claims to things he needs, he foolishly imagines himself to be the sole proprietor of the whole universe.

For, even in the dark heart of the savage, there is already (what others, such as Adam Smith, also considered to be) the central humanising characteristic: pity, and concern for others. It is there in the savage, because it is there in the animal too. Rousseau says that horses avoid trampling living creatures, that no animal ever passes 'the corpse of a creature of its own species without distress', and that there are even animals which give their dead a sort of burial. The 'mournful lowing of cattle entering a slaughterhouse reveals their feelings in witnessing the horrible spectacle that confronts them'. What, Rousseau asks, are generosity, mercy and humanity but compassion applied to the weak, or to the guilty – or to the human race in general? Even if it were true, he adds, that 'pity is no more than a feeling that puts us in the place of the sufferer', it is still the natural sentiment that ultimately allows the preservation of the species. It is only the philosopher who 'puts his hands over his ears and argues a little with himself' whilst another is murdered outside his window.

Rousseau's point is both original and subversive. Unfortunately, it has not been politically very influential. During the twentieth century, it was a sophisticated and highly rational system that devised and implemented the extermination camps, and even at the end of the century, in a series of 'hands over ears' incidents, it was the intellectuals at the top of the United Nations who approved the abandonment both of ill-omened 'safe havens' in the Balkans, as well as of almost a million Rwandans to their deaths at the hands of carefully planned and centrally coordinated mobs and militias. Either there are more philosophers around than Rousseau realised, or his 'natural sentiment' to prevent suffering is a very weak one.

But back to a more simple kind of savage man. He, Rousseau writes, would wander in the forests without work, speech, home, or war, without relationships, without either need nor fear of his fellows, concerned only for a few simple physical needs. 'A savage may well seize the fruits which another has gathered', Rousseau imagines, or he may even try to enslave another he comes upon, but he cannot stop the other slipping away into the forest to gather some more for himself once his vigilance slackens. The tragedy of human existence is that someone eventually came upon a more permanent way of exploiting their neighbour. Someone invented private property.

'The first man who, having enclosed a piece of land, thought of saying "This is mine" and found people simple enough to believe him, was the true founder of civil society', says Rousseau. Before there was property, he adds, perhaps misquoting Locke (who speaks of injustice), there could be no injury.

So, men 'ceased to doze under the first tree', and instead developed tools from stones and branches, and used these to till the land and create huts, in the process developing their notions of property, from which inevitably 'quarrels and fights were born'. And so, soon, society required 'a language more complex than that of crows or monkeys'. And then there were other consequences. The conventional, 'nuclear' family was created, producing not only (what he at least professed to consider) the desirable by-product of men and women living together in conjugal and paternal love, but also some less desirable gender differences. Notably, women becoming 'more sedentary' as they become accustomed 'to looking after the hut and children whilst men go out to seek the common sustenance'. But the men too, become rather sedentary:

This new condition, with its solitary life ... left men to enjoy a great deal of leisure, which they used to procure many sorts of commodities unknown to their fathers; and this was the yoke they imposed upon themselves, without thinking about it, and the first source of the evils they prepared for their descendants.

Not only did such commodities 'continue to soften both body and mind', but they themselves 'almost lost through habitual use their power to please', and as they had at the same time degenerated into actual needs, 'being deprived of them became much more cruel than the possession of them was sweet; and people were unhappy in losing them without being happy in possessing them'.

Thus it was that Man, who was formerly free, was diminished into subjection, slave to a multitude of 'new wants' and ambitions. Above all, the 'burning desire to enlarge his own fortune, not so much from real need as [from the desire] to put himself above others', as Rousseau puts it, in words with echoes today for consumer societies. In due course, this urge to dominate becomes like blood lust. The consumers are like 'ravenous wolves which, having tasted human flesh, refuse all other nourishment'. The rich use their old slaves to subdue new ones, and dream only of ever greater subjugation and exploitation of their fellows.

Rousseau paints a mocking portrait of the rich man, seeking to protect his gains by pretending concern for his victims. 'Let us unite,' says his rich man, 'to protect the weak from oppression, to ensure for each that which he owns, and create a system of justice and peace that all shall be bound to, without exception.' Rousseau thinks his explanation of civil law is more convincing than those based on some imaginary universal social contract for, as he puts it, the poor have only one good – their freedom – and voluntarily to strip themselves of that without gaining anything in exchange would appear to be absolute folly. The rich, on the other hand, have much to gain. For that reason, it seems reasonable to suppose the thing to have been invented by them, 'by those to whom it was useful rather than by those to whom it was injurious'.

Rousseau's version of the origins of the division of labour is similarly perverse and even bizarre. Instead of the use of iron improving agriculture, he sees it as a burden on the producers of food. 'The more the number of industrial workers multiplied, the fewer hands were engaged in providing the common subsistence, without there being any fewer mouths to feed.' Then we must consider all the unhealthy trades of modern society – labouring in mines, preparation of certain metals (such as lead) – and the general migration to the cities, before we can claim society has improved people's lives. Not that Rousseau is saying we should return to 'living with the bears', a conclusion he hastens, as he says, to forestall.

However, natural man, outside society, will not tolerate subjugation, 'as an unbroken horse paws the ground with its hooves' and rears at the approach of the bit, or animals break their heads against the 'bars of their prisons' – yet civil society reduces all to slaves. And the explanation offered by such as 'Mr Locke' that the government is but like a father to us, Rousseau dismisses too, for, 'by the law of nature, the father is master of the child only for such time as his help is necessary and that beyond this stage, the two are equals, the son becoming perfectly independent of the father'. In fact, by giving up liberty, a man degrades his being.

Moving from the small picture to the larger one, Rousseau offers a 'hands-off' state. The only way that the sovereign and the people can have a single and identical interest, so that all the movements of the civil machine tend to promote the common happiness, is for them to be one and the same. (Actually, in later writings, notably *The Social*

Contract, Rousseau suggests that a way around the selfishness could be through a system of majority voting in which each individual's wishes become instead part of a 'general will', rather than reflecting directly anyone's particular desires.) No one can be outside the law, for once they are, all the others are 'at their discretion'. Furthermore, there should be few laws, and new ones introduced only with the greatest circumspection, so that 'before the constitution could be disturbed, there would be time enough for everyone to reflect that it is above all the great antiquity of the laws that makes them sacred and inviolable'.

And what of Rousseau's political philosophy 'in practice'? The *Discourse*, as we have just seen, is dedicated to Geneva, a city that retained its independence in the face of a Europe of much larger nation states, not by any pretensions of military power, but by playing the religious card at the appropriate and opportune time, and defecting from the other Catholic areas of Switzerland towards Protestant worship, under the protection of Lutheran Berne. This protection allowed Jean Calvin, the French theologian, time to reorganise the city state of Geneva along democratic lines, with a general assembly of all citizens (but not all adults), a Council of Two Hundred, and an executive council. Rather than change the system, the self-styled radical continues to stress instead the respect due to the governing magistrates:

The people must have respect for their leaders, for the magistrates of Geneva afford an example of moderation, of simplicity in morals, of respect for the laws, and the most sincere spirit of reconciliation. There is not in the universe a body of men more upright, more enlightened, more worthy of respect.

He finishes, sanctimoniously:

Magnificent and Most Honoured lords, the worthy and revered magistrates of a free people, allow me to offer you in particular my homage and my respect. If there is in the world a rank capable of conferring glory on those who occupy it, it is undoubtedly one acquired by your talent and virtue, the rank of which you have proved yourselves worthy and to which your fellow citizens have raised you.

Rousseau adds mysteriously to his readers: 'Beware, above all, of ever listening to sinister interpretations and malicious rumours, the secret motives of which are often more dangerous than the actions they report.' In fact, more generally, Rousseau is troubled by the fact that the views of a majority of a people does not necessarily represent the views of its most intelligent citizens. Indeed, he agrees with Plato that most people are stupid. Thus the general will, while always morally sound, is sometimes mistaken. Hence Rousseau suggests the people need a lawgiver – a great mind like Solon or Lycurgus or Calvin – to draw up a constitution and system of laws. He even suggests that such lawgivers need to claim divine inspiration in order to persuade the dimwitted multitude to accept and endorse the laws it is offered. Conventionally, it is claimed amongst political philosophers that where Plato asked, 'Who should rule?', up to Rousseau the answer was, 'The prince should rule', but that after Rousseau the answer becomes, 'The people (the general will) should rule.' But that is not Rousseau's view here.

As for Geneva, Rousseau considered Calvin to be a great lawgiver in the mould of the Romans. But Calvin's state was in fact not so progressive, and it quickly degenerated into the rule of the executive council – an oligarchy. Calvin himself persecuted religious dissenters, expulsion from Geneva became the norm, and executions were not out of place in the free city. Calvin never considered women to be citizens, and as time went by the majority of men were not counted as such either.

Rousseau's view of women is no more egalitarian than Calvin's – at best it is romantic in an unenlightened sort of way. In *Emile*, he confines the education of the fair sex to domestic science and recommends training from an early age in habits of docility and subservience. He writes:

Could I forget that precious half of the commonwealth which assures the happiness of the other, and whose sweetness and prudence maintain its peace and good morals? Lovable and virtuous women of Geneva, your destiny will always be to govern ours. Happy are we so long as your chaste power, exerted solely within the marriage bond, makes itself felt only for the glory of the state and well-being of the public!

But despite the unsavoury undercurrents, and irrespective of the truth or otherwise of the sinister rumours, the Geneva that Rousseau had reluctantly left in his youth and which remained the backdrop to his philosophising, was a successful and contented one: business was good and taxes were moderate. There was even a social security system, and corruption was almost unknown.

However, the details of institutions of government are not of much interest to Rousseau once their essentially malign character has been identified. He merely adds that if law and property are the first stage in human society, and the institutions of government are the second, then the third and last stage is the transformation of legitimate into arbitrary power. Human society leads people to hate each other in proportion 'to the extent that their interests conflict'. People pretend to do each other services whilst actually trying to exploit them and do them down. 'We must attribute to the institution of property, and hence to society, murders, poisonings, highway robbery and indeed, the punishments of those crimes.' That is at the individual level. On the national scale, 'Inequality, being almost non-existent in the state of nature ... becomes fixed and legitimate through the institution of property and laws.' When society has, as it inevitably will, degenerated into tyranny and all are slaves again, the circle is complete, for 'all individuals become equal again when they are nothing'. And at the same time 'civil man' torments himself constantly in search of ever more laborious occupations, working himself to death, 'renouncing life in order to achieve immortality'.

Civil society is, in fact, a society of people 'who nearly all complain and several of whom indeed deprive themselves of their existence'. This is the logic of property ownership and capitalism.

THE SUBTEXT

What, then, is the legacy of Jean-Jacques Rousseau? His influence is greater than is perhaps often realised. Philosophically, he crystallises that particularly French concern with *la conditione humaine* and, in particular, with individuals' attempts at finding their true selves. Freedom, the French challenge us, is actually within, obtained from finding our true identity, not from having satisfied social conventions and stereotypes. It requires having the opportunity to live the kind of life we want to live.

Rousseau offers a view of social evolution in which the human animal is being moulded by its environment, deriving its attitudes and values from its surroundings. With regard to human nature, Rousseau is the optimist to Hobbes' pessimist. All people are born with the qualities that will lead them to success and happiness – given the right conditions. In *Emile*, as part of his account of bringing up a child, he makes this even more explicit, describing how the child acquires needs and feelings different from those it is born with, as an effect and result of its environment. If the child is unhappy, it is because of a fault with its surroundings, and the same is true, he thinks, for adults.

The *Discourse* itself is an essay that somehow manages to be already at least 1,000 years out of date even when it is written, in the early years of the Industrial Revolution – and yet also surprisingly contemporary. Rousseau not only, as he promises to, 'put aside' the facts but also seems to have 'put aside' such niceties as an overall theory and logical structure. Yet *On Inequality* is still, for all that, undoubtedly magnificent; and more than that, it contains truths about human nature which other philosophers somehow failed to see. The common people to whom it is addressed did, however, recognise them, and it is for that reason that Rousseau's tract became one of the most influential works not only of its time, but of all time. That, surely, is the true measure of a political work.

Rousseau died in 1778, the same year as his critic Voltaire, possibly by his own hand, and certainly in sad and lonely circumstances. But as Goethe commented: 'with Voltaire an age ended; with Rousseau, a new one began'.

KEY IDEAS

Rousseau's recipe for human society can be expressed in just one word: 'Freedom'. Rousseau offers us a fairly implausible idea of what this might be, and supposes it to be in conflict and opposition to the structures of modern societies. But Rousseau's legacy is still important as a reminder of non-material values, and an optimistic if somewhat romanticised notion of humanity. What he offers us may be largely false and is often hopelessly impractical, but it is also always an important, alternative understanding of ourselves.

- People were more happy and satisfied in the 'state of nature', before the invention of property brought about competition, inequality and conflict.
- Most of the desires and wants of modern society are artificial, pointless and ultimately self-destructive.

KEY TEXT

Rousseau's *Discourse on Inequality* (1753)

Timeline:
From the (Re)discovery of America,
to the Boston Tea Party

AROUND 1000 CE
In North America, early cities like Cahokia exceed medieval London
and Paris in size and sophistication.

1492
Columbus sets off in search of China and discovers the West Indies.
Ten years later he explores the central American coastline between
Honduras and Panama. In fact, despite poetical imaginings of the
'discovery of America', he never visits the North American continent.
After all, his mission for the Queen of Spain was to find a way *through*
the Americas to the rich markets of Asia.

1505
The first black slaves are brought to the 'New World', at
Hispaniola.

1520
Meanwhile, back in the 'Old World', Martin Luther denounces the
pope, and two years later produces an alternative version of the
Bible. The Christian Church splits into two, the 'Protestants' and the
'Catholics'. Many of the former group will eventually leave Europe
and settle in North America instead.

1540
An expedition led by Coronado explores much of the south-west of
the future United States and discovers the Grand Canyon.

1561
Start of the 'Slave Trade'. John Hawkins establishes the principle of
exporting European manufactures to Africa, slaves to the Caribbean
and American raw materials back to Europe.

1585–87
First attempts to found colonies on the eastern seaboard of the future United States by Sir Walter Raleigh fail. A second more serious effort at Jamestown based on the cultivation of tobacco and supported by regular exchanges of replacement settlers slowly establishes itself more solidly. A carefully planned attack by the indigenous North American Indians is repulsed with heavy losses on both sides. But from then on, the Europeans have the Indians on the retreat.

1620
The Pilgrim Fathers, having set sail from Plymouth in England, land on the East coast of the future United States at what is also called 'Plymouth' in 'Massachusetts'. Over the next century there is a rapid acceleration of European settlement of North America coupled with the comprehensive and systematic destruction of the indigenous communities. In 1734, for example, 8,000 Protestants expelled from Salzburg in Germany arrive in Georgia as settlers. In two centuries some 10 million North American Indians are reduced to a few hundred thousand living in 'reserves'.

1664
The English grab 'New Amsterdam' from the Dutch and rename it 'New York'.

1673
England passes the last of its 'Navigation Laws', placing restrictions on the goods the colonies can export. Trade, however, blossoms and by 1763 Philadelphia becomes the first settlement in the New World to exceed 20,000 people.

1752
Benjamin Franklin demonstrates that lightning is, in fact, electricity.

1765
The 'Stamp Act' taxing legal documents infuriates the colonies, being the first 'direct' tax they had ever had imposed on them. The Virginia Assembly and delegates from the nine colonies draw up a declaration of rights and liberties. The British government yields and adopts custom duties instead.

1770

Five 'patriots' threatening to loot the Boston Customs House are killed by British troops attempting to enforce the new duties on tea. This becomes known somewhat fancifully as the 'Boston massacre'. An organised response known as the 'Boston Tea Party' comes five years late when 150 patriots, dressed up as Indians, tip the imported tea into the river.

1775

The War of American Independence begins; it will end a few years later in total success for the colonists after heavy defeats of the English. The distinctive federal constitution of the United States is signed into existence at Philadelphia in 1787.

9
The Founding Fathers' Constitutional Recipe

While Adam Smith was working on a theory of society that revolved around money, on the other side of the Atlantic, Britain's rebel colonies were drawing up a formal political blueprint, legalistic in style and intention, to do just that. The US constitution is a remarkable document, but it is philosophically neither innovative nor original. Rather, its success is in its simplicity and efficiency. All the more surprising as it was the product not of a single individual but of a committee.

THE CONTEXT

So who were the authors anyway? If George Washington is the most famous of the 'Founding Fathers' who made up the committee that drafted the American constitution, he himself was by no means the most important influence on the document. Indeed, it is James Madison, whom Washington dubbed 'a withered little Applejohn', who has been elevated by history to become 'the Father of the Constitution', which must make him the 'Founding Grandfather'. Madison, despite having no legal training and still in his mid twenties, had helped write the constitution of Virginia. This was the document that would become the basis for the US constitution. Madison had been too short to be allowed to enroll in the Revolutionary Army and had had to fight the British with paper instead. But thus he was behind the important series of amendments to the constitution that became the Bill of Rights, and was one of the four Founding Fathers to become president (1809–17). Perhaps to make up for his inability to serve in the army, his term involved a disastrous attempt to annex Canada.

Another influential figure was Benjamin Franklin, who, having been born in 1706, was the oldest delegate at the Constitutional Convention. He was also one of the three chosen to sign the treaty that ended the original revolutionary war against England. Franklin was suspicious of centralised governments, be they run by kings or by presidents, and advocated instead a three-person presidential committee rather than a single figure. Having a sole leader, he warned, would risk a government that would be 'well-administered for a number of years, [but] can only end in despotism'. At the end of the Convention he cautioned: 'Our Constitution is in actual operation. Everything appears to promise that it will last. But in this world nothing is certain but death and taxes.'

It is Roger Sherman who is credited with introducing the 'great compromise' of representation between the larger states and the pint-sized ones, as befits a consummate negotiator who once counselled: 'When you are in a minority, talk; when you are in a majority, vote.' After all, the Founding Fathers did not agree on many fundamentals. On the contentious issue of the rights of individuals, Sherman suggested that the question was, 'not what rights naturally belong to man, but how they may be most equally and effectually guarded in society'. The sole Founding Father to refuse to sign the eventual document, George Mason, did so saying that it failed to protect individual rights.

George Morris, who is said to have been primarily responsible for the wording of the constitution, was a writer and diplomat. As befits a man with a wooden leg, he spoke more often at the Convention than anyone else, mainly warning against the sharing of too much power with 'the mob'. 'The mob begin to think and reason – Poor reptiles! They bask in the sun, and ere noon they will bite, depend on it!' He favoured significant property qualifications for political influence. He was supported by others amongst the Founding Fathers, such as Alexander Hamilton, who agreed with Morris that an aristocracy should rule the masses. Another delegate, James Wilson, a lawyer and also a democrat, thought on the contrary that the 'government ought to possess not only first the force but secondly the mind or sense of the people at large'. Wilson favoured individual rights over 'property rights' and opposed slavery.

In the event, the constitution that emerged envisaged a powerful Senate of prominent – indeed aristocratic – individuals kept in line by a more humble House of Representatives. In this design, the Founding Fathers consciously followed the division of the British parliament into a house of 'Lords' and a house of 'Commoners'. The arrangement left open the question of the powers of the president, which the committee wished to keep strictly limited. Several of them, particularly Edmund Randolph, credited with influencing the design of the bicameral (two chambers) structure of the legislative body, favoured a three-person presidency. Yet the role of the president is barely discussed in the eventual document, and it failed to anticipate the changes that would rapidly reduce both the House of Representatives and the Senate to the status of followers to presidential prerogatives.

So why did the Constitutional Convention eventually replace the British monarch with a sole president? And more dangerously still, one unambiguously in sole control of the armed forces? Although the constitution stipulated that Congress alone would have the power to declare war, this has proved a nominal authority – both the Korean and Vietnam wars were conducted for years before the formality of a 'declaration'. (Since the War Powers Act of 1974, the president has been obliged to seek Congressional approval after 60 days.) Yet the one thing all the delegates shared was a concern to protect their respective colonies from the great European powers. And even as they planned the early days of the new republic, George Washington, victorious general of the Revolutionary Army and the first president, spent most of his time during the Constitutional Convention in splendid isolation at the luxurious mansion of Robert Morris. Morris was at the time the richest man in America, and Washington was establishing the link between personal wealth and political power that defines the United States as much as any more theoretical values.

On becoming the first president, Washington delivered an inaugural speech of just 143 words – slightly shorter even than the preceding paragraph! – and refused to shake hands with anyone else, preferring to bow graciously instead. This tradition was continued by his successor as president, John Adams (1797–1801), until the more liberal-minded Thomas Jefferson reinstated the handshake.

On the divisive issue of slaves, Washington is credited with a suitably ambiguous policy of having profited from them during his lifetime, but of anticipating his reception in heaven by planning for them to be set free after his death. This was not a particularly generous gesture in any case, but in fact his will delayed the slaves' emancipation until after his wife too decided that she had no need for them, and she not only kept them while alive, but chose in her will not to free them. Black America has long been asked to accept this sort of compromise!

If this seems hypocritical, John Adams, a lawyer and the second president, is remembered for saying, 'Let the human mind loose. It must be loosed. It will be loose. Superstition and despotism cannot confine it', as well as for signing the 'Aliens and Sedition Acts' which made it an imprisonable offence to criticise the government. Adams was also the first president to live in a new, rather grandiose and neo-classical 'White House', despite having become a grammar school teacher after graduating from Harvard, and writing:

My little school, like the great world, is made up of Kings, politicians, divines, fops, buffoons, fiddlers, fools, coxcombs, sycophants, chimney sweeps, and every other character I see in the world. I would rather sit in school and consider which of my pupils will turn out be a hero, and which a rake, which a philosopher and which a parasite, than to have an income of a thousand pounds a year.

The third president would be Thomas Jefferson. It was Jefferson who had drafted the ringing Declaration of Independence, although he was serving as ambassador to France as the constitution itself was drafted. Washington and Adams were unattractive, but Jefferson was tall, slim, 'carrot-topped' (red-haired) and something of a 'Renaissance man' who spoke seven languages fluently, didn't believe in God, and (like Bill Clinton's flourishes with the sax centuries later) was celebrated for having wooed his wife with a violin serenade. He lived flamboyantly – the wine bill for his eight years as president (1801–09) came to $11,000, an incredible figure for those times. But politically, he was a progressive who advocated equal rights for women and free education for all. Despite being a poor speaker, he was an effective negotiator who managed to persuade France to sell Louisiana, thereby doubling the size of the fledgling United States. It is Jefferson's skills that gave the unanimous Declaration of the 13 United States of America, on 4 July 1776, something of the myth-making capability that the constitution lacks.

THE TEXTS

The *Declaration of Independence* starts with the famous preamble:

We hold these truths to be self-evident, that all men are created equal, that they are endowed by their Creator with certain unalienable Rights, that among these are Life, Liberty and the pursuit of Happiness. That to secure these rights, Governments are instituted among Men, deriving their just Powers from the consent of the governed, – That whenever any Form of Government becomes destructive of these ends, it is the Right of the People to alter or to abolish it, and to institute new Government, laying its foundation on such principles and organising its powers in such form, as to them shall seem most likely to effect their Safety and Happiness.

There is then offered a justification for being disloyal, which is summarised finally as the 'history of the present King of Great Britain is a history of repeated injuries and usurpations, all having in direct object the establishment of an absolute Tyranny over these States'. To prove this, it continues, 'let facts be submitted to a candid world'. These facts are a series of gripes (which the US constitution reflects), accusing the British monarch of

- cutting off our Trade with all parts of the world;
- imposing Taxes on us without our Consent;
- depriving us, in many cases, of the benefits of Trial by Jury;
- and transporting us beyond seas to be tried for pretended offences.

In fact, 'He has plundered our seas, ravaged our Coasts, burnt our towns, and destroyed the lives of our people.' Thus, as the British 'have been deaf to the voice of justice and of consanguinity', America must, 'therefore, acquiesce in the necessity, which denounces our Separation, and hold them, as we hold the rest of mankind, Enemies in War, in Peace Friends'.

We, therefore, the Representatives of the united States of America, in General Congress, Assembled, appealing to the Supreme Judge of the world for the rectitude of our intentions, do, in the Name, and by Authority of the good People of these Colonies, solemnly publish and declare, That these United Colonies are, and of Right ought to be Free and Independent States; that they are absolved from all Allegiance to the British Crown, and that all political connection between them and the State of Great Britain, is and ought to be totally dissolved; and that as Free and Independent States, they have full Power to levy War, conclude Peace, contract Alliances, establish Commerce, and to do all other Acts and Things which Independent States may of right do.

It is then signed, with 'firm reliance on the protection of Divine Providence' by various worthy American figures, central amongst whom of course is Jefferson himself. In later years, when Jefferson devised his own epitaph he wanted it to read: 'Here was buried Thomas Jefferson, author of the Declaration of Independence, of the statute of Virginia for Religious Freedom, and the father of the University of Virginia.' His role as president he did not consider worth mentioning.

The *Constitution of the United States* starts loftily enough by promising the people of the United State that it will, 'in order to form a more perfect Union, establish Justice, insure domestic Tranquility, provide for the common defence, promote the general Welfare, and secure the Blessings of Liberty to ourselves and our Posterity'. Then it gets straight down to business.

The document is structured in legal style as a series of seven sections or 'articles'. Article 1 describes the structure of the new government. 'All legislative Powers herein granted shall be vested in a Congress of the United States, which shall consist of a Senate and House of Representatives'. The House of Representatives shall be composed of 'Members chosen every second Year by the People'. There will be one representative for every 30,000 citizens, and each state 'shall have at least one Representative'. The Senate of the United States will be made up of two senators from each state, 'chosen by the Legislature thereof', for six years, and each of whom shall have just one vote. 'The Congress shall assemble at least once in every Year, and such Meeting shall be on the first Monday in December, unless they shall by Law appoint a different Day.'

Thus the stage is set. But what shall the new leaders do exactly? The document continues:

Each House shall be the judge of the elections, returns and qualifications of its own members. Each House may determine the rules of its proceedings, punish its Members for disorderly behaviour, and, with the concurrence of two-thirds, expel a Member, and each House shall keep a Journal of its proceedings.

Procedural rules and a Journal! Not to forget, of course, that 'The Senators and Representatives shall receive a Compensation for their Services', to be paid out of the Treasury of the United States. They are also given certain limited legal privileges to guard against harassment and arbitrary arrest.

Some minor restrictions are imposed on membership, notably that

No Person shall be a Representative who shall not have attained to the age of twenty five years, and been seven years a Citizen of the United States, and no person shall be a Senator who shall not have attained to the age of thirty years, and been nine years a Citizen.

As for presidents, they, like Plato's Guardians, will have to be at least 35 years old (and, additionally, to have lived in the United States for at least 14 years).

The activities of the House of Representatives are not described, other than that they shall 'choose their Speaker and other Officers;

and shall have the sole power of Impeachment'. This, evidently, was a matter of considerable import to the Founding Fathers, doubtless a reflection of the recent turmoil in Britain and France regarding their respective heads of state, resolved in the cases of both countries only by cutting off the heads of their kings.

The Senate is given

the sole power to try all Impeachments. When sitting for that purpose, they shall be on Oath or Affirmation. When the President of the United States is tried, the Chief Justice shall preside: And no person shall be convicted without the concurrence of two-thirds of the Members present.

Reasonably enough,

Judgement in cases of Impeachment shall not extend further than to removal from Office, and disqualification to hold and enjoy any Office of honor, trust or profit under the United States: but the Party convicted shall nevertheless be liable and subject to indictment, trial, judgement and punishment, according to Law.

Article 1 then continues to the next most contentious issue: how to raise taxes. It states that 'All bills for raising revenue shall originate in the House of Representatives; but the Senate may propose or concur with Amendments as on other Bills.' The Founding Fathers seem not to have envisaged how an all-powerful president, controlling both Senators and Representatives through the alternative political structures of 'parties', would seize control of the nation's finances. Indeed, it continues naively to outline the likely sequence of events as follows:

Every Bill which shall have passed the House of Representatives and the Senate, shall, before it become a Law, be presented to the President of the United States; If he approve he shall sign it, but if not he shall return it, with his Objections to that House in which it shall have originated, who shall enter the Objections at large on their Journal, and proceed to reconsider it. If after such Reconsideration two-thirds of that House shall agree to pass the Bill, it shall be sent, together with the Objections, to the other House, by which it shall likewise be reconsidered, and if approved by two-thirds of that House, it shall become a Law. But in all such Cases the Votes of both Houses shall be determined by Yeas and Nays, and the Names of the Persons voting for and against the Bill shall be entered on the Journal of each House respectively.

The Congress takes decision, and the president advises. A final provision clearly indicates that the Constitutional Convention intended the president's role to be inferior to that of Congress:

If any Bill shall not be returned by the President within ten Days (Sundays excepted) after it shall have been presented to him, the Same shall be a Law, in like Manner as if he had signed it, unless the Congress by their Adjournment prevent its Return, in which Case it shall not be a Law.

In fact, though, the very first president, George Washington, decided he would take decisions and that Congress would follow. Washington asserted 'executive privilege' by issuing Presidential Proclamations – policies which are not formally laws, but still have the effect of statutes. Congress did a little better in attempting to guard for itself the practical jobs of government. Section 8 of Article 1 explains that: 'The Congress shall have Power To lay and collect Taxes, Duties, Imposts and Excises, to pay the Debts and provide for the common Defence and general Welfare of the United States', as well as the following:

- To borrow Money on the Credit of the United States;
- To regulate Commerce with foreign Nations, and among the several States, and with the Indian Tribes;
- To establish an uniform Rule of Naturalization, and uniform Laws on the subject of Bankruptcies throughout the United States;
- To coin Money, regulate the Value thereof, and of foreign Coin, and fix the Standard of Weights and Measures;
- To establish Post Offices and post Roads;
- To promote the Progress of Science and useful Arts, by securing for limited Times to Authors and Inventors the exclusive Right to their respective Writings and Discoveries;
- To declare War, grant Letters of Marque and Reprisal, and make Rules concerning Captures on Land and Water;
- To raise and support Armies, but no Appropriation of Money to that Use shall be for a longer Term than two Years;
- To provide and maintain a Navy; and
- To provide for calling forth the Militia to execute the Laws of the Union, suppress Insurrections and repel Invasions.

That is, amongst other things. There is only one small effort at protection to individual rights noted, namely that the 'privilege of the

Writ of Habeas Corpus shall not be suspended', but this is immediately qualified: the provision is voided in 'Cases of Rebellion or Invasion' or when 'the public Safety may require it'. But then the constitution is concerned with institutions. It is only the amendments that are concerned with rights. Although not entirely: with regard to the technicalities of taxation the constitution does protect certain 'rights', saying that no 'Bill of Attainder or *ex post facto* Law' can be passed; no 'capitation, or other direct tax' can be laid, 'unless in proportion to the Census or Enumeration herein before directed to be taken'; and no tax or duty can be imposed on articles exported from any state, nor other trading preferences given to one state over another. It also states firmly that: 'No Title of Nobility shall be granted by the United States.'

All of this is in Article 1 and is concerned with Congress. It is Article 2 that first introduces the president: 'The executive power shall be vested in a President of the United States of America.' Along with his vice-president, he is to be elected for four years by a complicated mechanism which is stipulated:

Each State shall appoint, in such manner as the legislature thereof may direct, a number of Electors, equal to the whole number of Senators and Representatives to which the State may be entitled in the Congress.

The Electors shall meet in their respective States, and vote by ballot for two persons, of whom one at least shall not lie an inhabitant of the same State with themselves. And they shall make a List of all the persons voted for, and of the number of votes for each; which List they shall sign and certify, and transmit sealed to the Seat of the Government of the United States, directed to the President of the Senate. The President of the Senate shall, in the presence of the Senate and House of Representatives, open all the certificates, and the votes shall then be counted. The person having the greatest number of votes shall be the President.

Before he starts, the president has to take the special 'Oath' or 'Affirmation':

I do solemnly swear (or affirm) that I will faithfully execute the Office of President of the United States, and will to the best of my Ability, preserve, protect and defend the Constitution of the United States.

Section 2 bestows the title, so beloved of recent presidents, of 'Commander in Chief' of the Army and Navy of the United States (and of the Militias of the several states). It also gives him certain specific powers, notably:

- the 'Power to grant Reprieves and Pardons for offenses' against the United States, except in Cases of Impeachment;
- to make Treaties, provided two-thirds of the Senators present concur;
- and to appoint Ambassadors and other public officials.

The most important of these appointing powers turns out in many ways to be that of appointing the Judges of the Supreme Court. After all, President George W. Bush obtained his position over candidate Al Gore in 2000 not by the number of votes cast in his favour in the country, or even according to the supposed procedures of Congress, but by the number of votes cast in his favour in this court, which was made up with judges who were not only politically partisan but had been appointed by ... his father, George Bush Senior. So much for judges avoiding conflicts of interest!

Another appointing power that the president is allowed by the constitution is the authority to fill up 'all Vacancies that may happen during the Recess of the Senate, by granting Commissions which shall expire at the End of their next Session', a power which has been increasingly used (particularly by George W. Bush) to circumvent the Constitutional role of Congress.

This is all very far from the vision of the Founding Fathers of a president merely there 'from time to time' to 'give to the Congress Information on the State of the Union, and to recommend to their Consideration such Measures as he shall judge necessary and expedient'. Except in times of war, of course. It is perhaps no coincidence that the United States is the world's most belligerent nation, involved in a constant series of wars. As one US academic has noted, since the Second World War alone it has fought China twice (1945–46, 1950–53), Korea (1950–53), Guatemala twice (1954, 1967–69), Indonesia (1958), Cuba (1959–60), the Belgian Congo (1964), Peru (1965), Laos (1964–73), Vietnam (1961–73), Cambodia (1969–70), Grenada (1983), Libya (1986), El Salvador (1980s), Nicaragua (1980s), Panama (1989), Iraq (1991–99), Bosnia (1995), Sudan (1998), Yugoslavia (1999). At the time of writing the United States is conducting two wars, in Afghanistan and Iraq, along with about half a dozen minor conflicts elsewhere.

But back to peacetime matters. Article 2, Section 1 is concerned to regulate relations between the government and the governed, and describes the administration of justice. It states that 'the judicial Power of the United States, shall be vested in one supreme Court, and in such inferior Courts as the Congress may from time to time ordain and establish'. It continues:

The Trial of all Crimes, except in Cases of Impeachment, shall be by Jury; and such Trial shall be held in the State where the said Crimes shall have been committed; but when not committed within any State, the Trial shall be at such Place or Places as the Congress may by Law have directed.

Article 4, on the other hand, is concerned with regulating relations between the national authority and the constituent states and it starts by promising that 'the United States shall guarantee to every State in this Union a Republican form of Government, and shall protect each of them against invasion'. Next, Article 5 creates the potential for change and adaptation in the political future of the United States, as opposed to say the religious statutes of the Koran (which are concerned to prevent and pre-empt future changes), by allowing that 'The Congress, whenever two-thirds of both Houses shall deem it necessary, shall propose amendments to this Constitution.' The Koran is of course concerned with religious truth, which is by definition eternal and unchanging, so fittingly enough, when Article 6 makes one important exception to this future flexibility, it is that 'no religious test shall ever be required as a qualification to any Office or public trust under the United States'.

The final article, Article 7, is the 'Ratification'. The list of delegates starts with George Washington, deputy from Virginia, the revolutionary general who, as in most Republics born in war, now becomes the first president, reigning, as it were, from 1789–97.

So what happened to the individual citizen's rights that sparked the war of independence and that the US constitution is so celebrated for protecting? These, and all the other contentious issues, had to be left to be incorporated later as amendments. Because the Founding Fathers were initially concerned to balance the powers of the states, the protection of individual rights had to be left on one side. Secondly, as almost all of the state constitutions contained bills of rights, the federal constitution was seen as potentially undermining or opposing those rights.

It is only the First Amendment that offers individuals freedom of religious choice and freedom of speech. It states that

Congress shall make no law respecting an establishment of religion, or prohibiting the free exercise thereof; or abridging the freedom of speech, or of the press; or the right of the people peaceably to assemble, and to petition the Government for a redress of grievances.

Thomas Jefferson later wrote (in an 1802 letter to a Baptist association) that the First Amendment erected a 'wall of separation' between the church and the state, and the term stuck. Jefferson did not have a hand in the authoring of the constitution, nor of the First Amendment, but he was an outspoken proponent of the separation of church and state, going back to his time as a legislator in Virginia. In 1785, he drafted a bill that was designed to squash an attempt by some to provide taxes for the purpose of furthering religious education. He wrote that such support for religion ran counter to a natural right of man:

no man shall be compelled to frequent or support any religious worship, place, or ministry whatsoever, nor shall be enforced, restrained, molested, or burthened in his body or goods, nor shall otherwise suffer, on account of his religious opinions or belief; but that all men shall be free to profess, and by argument to maintain, their opinions in matters of religion, and that the same shall in no wise diminish, enlarge, or affect their civil capacities.

However, religion in America, as elsewhere, continues to be a divisive issue. Over the years the pendulum has swung from the religious conservatives to the secular reformers, often meeting in battle on the terrain of otherwise obscure legal points in the Supreme Court. The culmination of all such battles is said to be a 1971 case, *Lemon v. Kurtzman*, that established criteria for testing whether laws have the 'effect of establishing a religion'. These are known as 'The Lemon Test'. The Supreme Court wrote:

In the absence of precisely stated constitutional prohibitions, we must draw lines with reference to the three main evils against which the Establishment Clause was intended to afford protection: 'sponsorship, financial support, and active involvement of the sovereign in religious activity.' Every analysis in this area must begin with consideration of the cumulative criteria developed by the Court over many years. Three such tests may be gleaned from our cases. First, the statute must have a secular legislative purpose; second, its principal or primary effect must be one that neither advances nor inhibits religion; finally, the statute must not foster 'an excessive government entanglement with religion'.

For example, in 2001, a case known as *Good News Club* v. *Milford Central School* led the Supreme Court to decide that a school should not exclude a religious club from using facilities in the school, after school hours, just because the club was religious. If the Chess Club could use the school library, they mused, the 'Good News Club' should be able to do so too. Otherwise it would be the application of a religious test in reverse. A year later, a more central part of American school life, the 'Pledge of Allegiance', was brought to its attention. Since 1954, all American schoolchildren have been obliged to recite this at the start of classes, including the words 'under God'. When it went to the District Court it seemed obvious that 'the Pledge' did not pass the test. The lower Court noted that:

In the context of the Pledge, the statement that the United States is a nation 'under God' is an endorsement of religion. It is a profession of a religious belief, namely, a belief in monotheism ... The text of the official Pledge, codified in federal law, impermissibly takes a position with respect to the purely religious question of the existence and identity of God.

Then, on 14 June 2004, the Supreme Court overturned its ruling on a technicality, leaving the 'Pledge' obligatory on all American school children. In this way, another of the key planks of the US constitution is daily disregarded even as it is saluted.

Many of the other amendments are controversial too. Amendment 2, which says that 'A well regulated Militia, being necessary to the security of a free State, the right of the people to keep and bear Arms, shall not be infringed', is accused of being responsible not so much for the security of the people as for their continued insecurity. Certainly, since the Second World War, a staggering 1 million Americans have been shot dead by their fellow countrymen. And like many of the ideas of the constitution's authors, it matters not a whit that the amendment clearly protects the right to have guns for one purpose only – in order to allow individual states their militias.

The key protections of the constitution in Amendments 4, 5 and 6 have likewise always been bitterly contested. Amendment 4, which protects the 'right of the people to be secure in their persons, houses, papers, and effects, against unreasonable searches and seizures', has regularly been violated, starting with the unfortunate Cherokee Indians, and continuing most recently as part of the emergency provisions of the so-called 'War on Terror'.

As for Amendments 5 and 6, which offer various legal rights, notably a right to trial by jury (and what is more, by an ' impartial' one), black Americans have often found themselves being tried by prejudiced white jurors. But then, the historical origin of this provision was that juries should be composed of 'one's peers' – a protection intended more for the aristocracy than for the commoner. A similarly well-intentioned but ineffectual protection is offered in Amendment 8, which seeks to outlaw 'cruel and unusual punishments', but nonetheless has never been able to prevent the routine application of various cruel and unusual punishments, including forms of execution.

Yet if the amendments have not been as effective as those who proposed them might have hoped, who is to blame for that? Today, as part of the doctrine of the division of powers, the Supreme Court is seen as overseeing and guarding the constitution. But none of this is written there. Article 3, Section 1 specifies that there will be a Supreme Court, Article 1, Section 3 mentions the Chief Justice, and Article 2, Section 2 mentions the 'Judges of the Supreme Court', but nowhere is it said what the Court should or can do, let alone how it can enforce its rulings. When the Cherokee Indians (at the time a constitutional entity within America, recognised in treaties) successfully convinced the Supreme Court that the 'Indian Removal Act', which confiscated their lands and obliged them to relocate to the west, was unconstitutional, the then president contemptuously ignored it, saying 'Let the Court enforce its rulings' and ordering the army to move against the Indians. Nor is the Court impartial. Although judges are appointed for life, nowhere is it stated how many judges are to be appointed at any one time, and so the political make-up of the Court has been regularly influenced by expanding the total number of justices. In fact, now that a series of administrations have ensured a conservative bias in the Court, it would equally be possible for a liberal or radical administration to appoint several extra judges to the Court in order to escape the influence of past presidents.

Nor does the constitution have anything to say about 'politics'. At the time of the Articles of Confederation, there weren't any political parties. There were regional blocs and temporary affiliations, but nothing like political groupings around shared manifestos. For this reason, details of how to vote, how parties choose their candidates, and even how to arrange things like Congressional Districts are not part of the constitution.

And what about the slaves? At the time of the Constitutional Convention in 1787, as the census of 1790 records, there were slaves in nearly every state. Of a total national population of 3.8 million people, 700,000 of them, or 18 per cent, were slaves. Only Massachusetts and the 'districts' of Vermont and Maine had none. In the southern states, with economies based on cultivating cotton, rice and tobacco, the proportion was far higher. Their representatives considered slavery to be not only sanctioned by the Bible, but what was more, an economic necessity.

Oliver Ellsworth, one of the signers of the constitution, wrote of the matter at the time: 'All good men wish the entire abolition of slavery, as soon as it can take place with safety to the public, and for the lasting good of the present wretched race of slaves'; and Thomas Jefferson, who had written the opening words of the *Declaration of Independence*, added that

There must doubtless be an unhappy influence on the manners of our people produced by the existence of slavery among us. The whole commerce between master and slave is a perpetual exercise of the most boisterous passions, the most unremitting despotism on the one part, and degrading submissions on the other.

Nonetheless, Jefferson, being a southerner, owned slaves, over 200 of them. If Jefferson, like Washington (who, as mentioned already, held over 300 slaves), was uncomfortable with the practice, he was not uncomfortable enough to do anything about it. Least of all, in the constitution.

Even Benjamin Franklin, a scientist and writer, not a farmer, held several slaves during his lifetime. In 1789, he said, 'Slavery is such an atrocious debasement of human nature, that its very extirpation, if not performed with solicitous care, may sometimes open a source of serious evils.' His compromise was to set one of his slaves free after his death. But even this slave was never freed, as he died before his master – lazy fellow! The practical result was that despite the freedoms claimed in the declaration, the constitution and the Bill of Rights, slavery was not only tolerated in the constitution, but was incorporated into it.

The real negotiation was over the number of representatives to be given to each of the 13 original states. The calculation was based on population – and in calculating that population, slaves, called 'other persons', were only counted as three-fifths of a person. The northern states wanted the slaves to be treated as property, like mules and horses, and left uncounted. Southerners, however, wanted to have them included in their state populations to avoid losing influence. Counting each slave as three-fifths of a person was thus the great compromise of the US constitution, agreed with little debate.

There are other small compromises on the issue too. Article 1, in Section 9, expressly prohibits the 'importation' of slaves, that is the slave trade – but delays implementation until after 1808. At the same time, the Fugitive Slave Clause obliged any state in which an escapee was found to deliver the slave back to the state he or she had escaped from. It is only Amendment 13 in 1865 that finally gets around to outlawing slavery. 'Neither slavery nor involuntary servitude, except as a punishment for crime whereof the party shall have been duly convicted, shall exist within the United States, or any place subject to their jurisdiction.'

Amendment 15 further attempts to protect the right of former slaves to vote, saying: 'The right of citizens of the United States to vote shall not be denied or abridged by the United States or by any State on account of race, colour, or previous condition of servitude.' However, many states have been creative in circumventing this. The shorter restatement of Amendment 19 has not helped much either: 'The right of citizens of the United States to vote shall not be denied or abridged by the United States or by any State.'

The Fourteenth and Fifteenth Amendments were actually national reactions to 'Black Codes' enacted in the south just after the Civil War. Legally, constitutionally, blacks were equal. But to counter this a series of so-called 'Jim Crow' laws were enacted, most of which aimed to deny blacks the vote by means that did not explicitly use race, but which would be racist in effect. Poll taxes, historical criteria, requirements for 'good character', literacy tests and other tactics were developed to remove blacks from the voting registers.

By 1910, the southern state that had been part of the Confederacy had a complex and complete system of Jim Crow laws in place. In addition, widespread lynchings and other acts of violence were tolerated by the authorities. Apartheid-style laws were passed, such as the 1958 Alabama law which stated, 'It shall be unlawful for white and coloured persons to play together ... in any game of cards, dice, dominoes, checkers, pool, billiards, softball, basketball, football, golf, track, and at swimming pools or in any athletic conference.' In Alabama too, by 1965, Jim Crow laws had reduced black participation in elections to just 19.6 per cent of the total potential black population, as compared with the near 70 per cent rate for whites. Many appeals and many acts have attempted to 'enforce' the Fourteenth and Fifteenth Amendments, most importantly the Civil Rights Act and Voting Rights Act of 1964 and 1965 respectively, but segregation and disenfranchisement continue to be the daily reality for many in the United States.

Take the already mentioned election in 2000 of George W. Bush, a conservative southerner. The low voting rates of blacks in the southern states again seemed to tip several states in favour of political conservatives. But then, in one state, Florida, a state governed by his brother, 'felons' were barred from voting unless they petitioned successfully to get their rights back. Seven other states did this – of which all but two were southern. Preventing felons from voting means preventing proportionately far more blacks than whites. Curiously, in the case of Florida, out of a list of 48,000 felons banned from voting, only 61 Hispanics were included. Curious because Hispanics made up about 11 per cent of the prison population, yet only 0.2 per cent of the list. But then as a rule Hispanics are strongly conservative. George Bush eventually won Florida by just a few hundred votes, and as appeals against the manipulation of voting rolls were dismissed (by a divided Supreme Court voting along party lines) the issue behind the Fifteenth Amendment was clearly still a live one.

The idealism of the constitution is kept tightly under control – except in one place. Amendment 18 is an unsuccessful foray into the universe of Plato's *Republic* which states optimistically:

After one year from the ratification of this article the manufacture, sale, or transportation of intoxicating liquors within, the importation thereof into, or the exportation thereof from the United States and all territory subject to the jurisdiction thereof for beverage purposes is hereby prohibited.

The failure of the 'Prohibition Amendment' is often taken as an example of why social issues should stay out of the constitution. Amendment 21 followed inevitably, saying only: 'The eighteenth article of amendment to the Constitution of the United States is hereby repealed.' Pragmatism clearly dictates Amendment 22 too. This usefully imposes one restriction on individual power, saying that 'No person shall be elected to the office of the President more than twice.'

THE SUBTEXT

Simon Jenkins, writing in the *Guardian* newspaper (London) in 2007, surely reflected a commonly held view when he declared, 'the noblest testament to freedom is the American Constitution'. In fact the constitution is quite the opposite. It is a remarkable document, indubitably both far-sighted and successful – yet its aims were not at all to protect individual liberties, let alone 'freedom'. It left black Americans as slaves, and indigenous Americans on reserves. It left women without civil rights. Instead, it reflects its origins, in reconciling various points of views in constructive compromises. Its central aim seems to have been to create 'checks and balances' against the dominance of one point of view.

The US constitution created both the world's richest and most innovative nation – and its most powerful. But if power is always the politician's goal, policy is often their later downfall. The authors of the documents of the American revolution were more concerned with power than with its application. As a result, the United States is a country where morality is the province of the elite, and where 'the pursuit of happiness' has led to extremes of wealth and power, where 'might is right'. But then the roots of the United States are firmly and indisputably in the cruelty and excesses of the ethnic cleansing of America zealously undertaken by the European Protestant settlers, followed up by the importation of millions of Africans to work as slaves on the plantations. The violence of its origins continues to influence society today, amplified by the baleful influence on government of what a conservative – not a radical – president dubbed, the 'military–industrial complex'. Military adventurism coupled with economic expansion is also the legacy of the US constitution.

KEY IDEAS

Two phrases have made their indelible mark on political philosophy. The first, from the *Declaration of Independence*, is that all 'men' (but alas, not all people)

- are created equal, that they are endowed by their Creator with certain unalienable Rights, that among these are Life, Liberty and the pursuit of Happiness.

The second is the pledge in the constitution itself that

- Congress shall make no law respecting an establishment of religion, or prohibiting the free exercise thereof; or abridging the freedom of speech, or of the press; or the right of the people peaceably to assemble, and to petition the Government for a redress of grievances.

KEY TEXTS

The Constitution of the United States (Philadelphia, 1787) and *The Declaration of Independence* (1776)

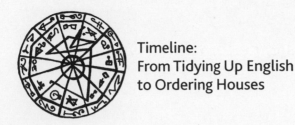

Timeline:
From Tidying Up English
to Ordering Houses

1755

Samuel Johnson's book of words, the 'dictionary', standardises English.

1759

Voltaire publishes *Candide*, a cynical portrait of a Dr Pangloss, who believes that everything is always for the best in the 'best of all possible worlds'.

1760

The face of rural Britain changes for ever after the Enclosure Acts take away the traditional rights of commoners. This is the year conventionally taken as the beginning of the Industrial Revolution.

1764

Houses in London are numbered.

1776

Wealth of Nations published.

10
Mr Smith's Excellent Inquiry into Money

From Smith, we gain a new perspective on human society. Where others saw society as determined by human decisions and choices, whether altruistic, as in Plato and Locke, or selfish, as in Machiavelli and Hobbes, Smith argues that economic forces have a power all of their own, and that our political arrangements, indeed our values, are only a consequence of these subtle forces.

THE CONTEXT

The English, American and French revolutions, momentous though they seemed, were only so many puffs of smoke, the superficial, political aspects of a far greater, but hidden, subterranean economic volcano that had been slowly building up pressure in the preceding centuries.

The first person to examine the significance and impersonal power of these economic forces was not, as is sometimes said, the iconoclastic revolutionary, Marx, in the nineteenth century, but the highly conventional son of a civil servant lawyer a century earlier. It is Smith who first writes of the Industrial Revolution and predicts that, like the most fearsome lava flow, it will sweep over the industrial landscape, incinerating all the old political certainties as so much dead wood, destroying all that it touches.

As with so many political activists, Smith's childhood was uneventful enough. He was brought up alone in Kirkcaldy, on the eastern coast of Scotland, by his mother, Margaret. His father had died before he was born, although it is only for psychologists to discern any effects here. But, certainly, the maternal bond was a particularly strong and lifelong one, and the father of laissez-faire economics also has a caring side.

Smith proceeded smoothly from Kirkcaldy school to Glasgow and then Oxford universities, although he had a low opinion of the English institution. He describes it, disgustedly, as a place where 'the greater part of the public professors have, for these many years, given up altogether even the pretence of teaching'. When, years later, he himself became professor of moral philosophy at Glasgow, he was a most scrupulous lecturer, not above putting on extra sessions of related topics that students might find interesting or useful. His 'public' lecture was given first thing each weekday, followed by seminar discussions the rest of the morning, with additional lectures in the afternoon, finally finishing off with extra tutorials for selected students. (As a perk, not a punishment, of course.) Not to mention the time taken up with the considerable amounts of extra administrative work that he found for himself. At this time, students paid the bulk of a professor's salary directly to the lecturer in the form of fees, and the story goes that when Professor Smith had to leave the university just half way through the session of 1764, the students refused to accept reimbursement of their monies, saying that 'the instruction and pleasure received' was already more than they could ever repay.

Had they known that Smith merely planned a 'grand tour' of Europe in charge of two young dandies, a privilege offered in return for acting as their chaperone, they might have changed their minds. But in any case, for Smith, the leisured life deprived of his teaching and administrative duties was so dull that, early on in the tour, at Toulouse, he wrote home that he had decided to write a book 'to pass away the time'. So it was that the bestselling work of its time, and one of the most important economic analyses of all time, *An Inquiry into the Nature and Causes of the Wealth of Nations*, came to be written.

Smith is a philosopher in the mould of Plato and Aristotle. He is prepared to deal with all types of question, all types of evidence, untrammelled by notions of sticking to a narrow discipline. He is a philosopher, but he is also a social scientist, a historian and a natural scientist too. (His *History of Astronomy* is counted very highly by historians of science.) Smith's method is to examine the research and findings of others and to make new connections, new discoveries from them. He is aware that any theory he puts forward, just as with any straightforwardly 'physical' theory, such as Newton's, remains just theory, always capable of refutation. His writing is philosophy as a way of thinking, applied to real issues and questions – not philosophy as an esoteric body of obscure knowledge, as it so often is for lesser academicians.

The *Inquiry* is also the result of another grand journey, one that had started for Smith with the question of 'justice', tackled in the process of cataloguing the history of law. On this journey, he had explored the nature of ethics in *The Moral Sentiments*, before arriving in due course at economics, which is, for Smith, the hidden set of rules that govern society. Additionally (again anticipating Marxism), he believed economic realities could be observed in the changing nature of the overt laws of the judicial system.

The geographical tour itself hinged on Paris, which Smith and his two companions found much the most agreeable part. And here Smith discovered a group of French intellectuals to discuss economics with. The French held that agriculture and mining were fundamentally the source of national wealth because they alone permitted a genuine conversion of labour into production: other processes, such as manufacturing, merely turned one sort of product into another. Smith was highly impressed by this, later describing it as 'perhaps the nearest approximation to the truth that has yet been discovered on the subject of political economy'.

When the tour eventually finished, Smith returned to the British Isles and completed his book, aided by discussions with other intellectuals, such as Benjamin Franklin, who was then visiting London and, amongst other things, dispatching Thomas Paine to the New World to start a revolution. Indeed the *Wealth of Nations* itself was published in 1776, the year of American independence. At the time, Smith was concerned that his work might be felt to be controversial – after all, he described it ironically in a letter as a 'very violent attack ... upon the whole commercial system of Great Britain' – but his worries proved to be unnecessary. The book simply became a bestseller, highly sought after and popular, with its author a correspondingly popular and increasingly wealthy man. Yet, in line with his dry reputation, Smith continued to live quietly and gave away most of his new-found riches to charity – anonymously.

THE TEXT

So what did this bestseller reveal? In the *Inquiry*, Adam Smith writes of four stages in society: an age of hunters, one of shepherds, an agrarian age, and finally an age of commerce. Society, he says, only begins to need laws and government in the second stage. The 'Age of Shepherds' is where government commences. 'Property makes it absolutely necessary', as he puts it in one of his 'Lectures on Jurisprudence':

The wood of the forest, the grass of the field, and all the natural fruits of the earth, which, when land was in common, cost the labourer only the trouble of gathering them, come ... to have an additional price fixed upon them.

Animals begin to belong to people, and shepherds, unlike hunters, are concerned with future planning as well as with the present. In seeing the need to protect property as the origin of government, and hence of society, Smith is following Locke. However, unlike Locke, he also sees the process as bearing rather unequally on the citizens: 'Civil government, so far as it is instituted for the security of property, is in reality instituted for the defence of the rich against the poor, or of those who have some property against those who have none at all.' This is a radical insight.

This is also a little like Rousseau, who had spoken of the rich man's advantage over the poor. But Smith's perspective on 'savage man' is very different. He writes, in what could be an impassioned plea for the welfare state:

Among the savage nations of hunters and fishers, every individual who is able to work, is more or less employed in useful labour, and endeavours to provide, as well as he can, the necessaries and conveniences of life, for himself, or such of his family or tribe as are either too old, or too young, or too infirm to go a hunting and fishing. Such nations are, however, so miserably poor that, from mere want, they are frequently reduced, or at least, think themselves reduced, to the necessity sometimes of directly destroying, and sometimes of abandoning their infants, their old people, and those afflicted with lingering diseases to perish with hunger, or to be devoured by wild beasts.

Smith's starting point is that the central motivation of mankind is a desire for approval by others. 'Sympathy' creates a social bond. Here, it should be explained that the ordering of the chapters in his books reflects Smith's view of the importance and explanatory role of the concepts. So, the first chapter of the *Wealth of Nations* is entitled: 'Of the Division of Labour'; the first chapter of *The Theory of Moral Sentiments*, his other major work, if rather less influential, is entitled 'Of Sympathy'. Human beings, Smith explains there, have a spontaneous tendency to observe others. From this, we turn to judging ourselves, and the moral identity of the individual develops, in this way emerging from social interaction. 'Sympathy', or 'awareness of other's feelings' (we might say 'empathy'), explains morality; the division of labour explains economics. A human being growing up

in isolation, Smith thinks, will have no sense of right and wrong
– nor any need for the concept:

without any communication with his own species, he could no more think of his
own character, of the propriety or demerit of his own sentiments and conduct,
of the beauty or deformity of his own mind, than of the beauty or deformity
of his own face.

In his ethics, as in his economics, Smith is scientific in intention.
He is aware of the possibility of self-deception, in both studies, and
curses it as the source of 'half of the disorders of human life'. If only,
he wrote in the *Moral Sentiments*, we could see ourselves as others see
us, 'a reformation would be unavoidable. We could not otherwise
endure the sight.'

However, it is self-interest that underpins the economic system. In
his most famous epigram, he says: 'it is not from the *benevolence* of
the butcher, the brewer, or the baker, that we expect dinner, but from
their regard to their own interest'. The individual does not intend to
promote the public interest, but 'intends only his own gain, and he is
in this, as in many other cases, led by an invisible hand to promote
an end which was no part of his intention'.

Smith illustrates the role in economics of the division of labour
by considering the increase in productivity possible by changing
the process of manufacture of a pin in a pin factory. Acting alone,
one man could 'scarce, with his utmost industry, make one pin a
day, and certainly could not make twenty'. But if the work can be
divided up –

one man draws out the wire, another straights it, a third cuts it, a fourth points
it, a fifth grinds it at the top for receiving the head; to make the head requires
three distinct operations; to put on is a peculiar business, to whiten the pins is
another; it is even a trade in itself to put them into the paper

– ten people, he suggests, could produce

about twelve pounds of pins a day. There are in a pound upwards of four thousand
pins of middling size. Those ten persons, therefore, could make upwards of forty-
eight thousand pins a day. But if they had all wrought them separately ... they
could certainly not each of them make twenty, perhaps not one pin a day.

Smith then goes on to relate this to the accumulation of capital, the
increase of employment and finally the emergence of mechanisms
to control the resulting tendency for wages to increase. So great are
the advantages of this industrial approach that even the humblest

member of 'a civilised country' is part of a complex system providing sophisticated goods and services.

Compared indeed, with the more extravagant luxury of the great, his accommodation must no doubt appear extremely simple and easy; and yet it may be true, perhaps, that the accommodation of a European Prince does not always so much exceed that of an industrious and frugal peasant as the accommodation of the latter exceeds that of many an African king, the absolute master of the lives, and liberties of ten thousand naked savages.

Another of the advantages of dividing up labour – specialising – is that people then think of ways of improving that specific task, improvements otherwise obscured by the complexities of the whole process. And the first chapter ends with the observation:

if we examine, I say, all these things, and consider what a variety of labour is employed about each of them, we shall be sensible that without the assistance and co-operation of many thousands, the very meanest person in a civilised country could not be provided, even according to, what we falsely imagine, the easy and simple manner in which he is commonly accommodated.

Lurking behind Smith's view of capitalism is the Panglossian belief that everything is for the best in all possible worlds, mocked acerbically by Voltaire in his novel *Candide* (where no matter what disaster befalls the main character, he insists all is serendipity): 'All is for the best in the best of all possible worlds' ('Tout est pour le mieux dans le meilleur des mondes possibles').

If this is a controversial element of Smith's analysis, he is only following a long tradition that can be traced back to the Stoics of ancient Greece and Mesopotamia – indeed, before them, to Eastern notions of harmony. The tendency of supply and demand to reach an equilibrium and of the market price to reflect the underlying 'natural price' are part of this philosophy.

Smith is sometimes vilified by those who (at least) aspire to be 'do-gooders', for advocating laissez-faire economics – leaving things to sort themselves out without government interference. It is not so often recognised that this was because he himself certainly believed that if this were done the outcome would be not just acceptable, but (*vide* Dr Pangloss) the best possible for everyone. Free trade encourages countries to specialise in what they are good at, and forces them to give up doing what they are not. This results in more goods being produced in total (because they are produced more efficiently). The same applies on a regional level too. For example, within a state, improving road links may remove physical obstacles to trade, with the effect of making a region's special wine or woolly jumpers worth transporting to the rest of the country. (However, as poorer regions know, the reverse is also true: large efficient companies outside the region can move in and displace even the last few small cottage industries of the local communities. The overall gains may still be at the clear expense of the small region.)

There are practical restraints on this policy, but it provides a set of clear economic targets to aim at. As the market is so good a master, in domestic affairs, the state is left with only a minimal role, although for Smith this is not just in defence and law and order, but also in providing many of those services that commerce will not bother with – such as building sewers or bridges and providing elementary schools. And not all enterprises are even best in private hands – Smith offers transport as an example. A privately owned road can be profitable even when poorly looked after by the unscrupulous, so it is better for the state to provide them and maintain higher standards. Conversely, canals *must* be maintained, otherwise the private owner can make no money out of them, so they can be left in private hands. As far as education goes, Smith recommends the practice current then in Scotland (which he himself had experienced) of making teachers and professors depend upon the satisfaction of their classes for their wages. Where this link is broken, Smith warns, slackness obtains (as at the rich colleges of Oxford).

With taxation, Smith lays down four principles. (Smith generally has something of a quaternate turn of mind.) First, taxes should be based on 'ability to pay'. Second, tax policy should be made publicly known and therefore predictable. Third, taxes should be collected with the convenience of the taxpayer in mind. Finally, this should all be done with a minimum of administration or other expense. Today we might add fifth and sixth principles of proportionality and choice: taxes should not be levied on essentials, such as food or water, nor should they be so great as to be effectively punishments for an activity, for example, smoking or drinking alcohol. Environmentalists might amend this with a seventh principle of 'encouraging sustainability' and avoiding damage to the ecology of the country. (In passing, we might note that 'free market' economies today, despite in other things following Smith, invariably design tax policy to press heavily upon the majority of citizens, while leaving a small minority at the top largely untouched.)

Smith notes that the division of labour is limited by the size of the available market. In a village, the specialisation is less, in a town it is more. In the town, carpentry, joinery, cabinet-making, wood-carving are separate occupations of differently skilled people; in the village, one person will do all of them. Smith is not wholly enamoured with the division process however, noting that a worker reduced to performing one task can become 'as stupid and ignorant as it is possible for a human creature to become'; indeed the process even threatens to reduce people to 'riot and debauchery'.

To combat this unfortunate tendency (amongst other reasons), Smith says that the state should provide basic education for all the citizens. 'For a very small expense the public can facilitate, can encourage, and can even impose upon almost the whole body of the people, the necessity of acquiring those most essential parts of education.'

The size of the market does not depend simply on the number of people who live in a particular area. It depends also on the roads or other transport links in the area and on the ability of producers to get their produce to the people. Smith notes the effect that cheaper transport by water was having on trade at the time, recalling that ancient civilisations developed along sea coasts and river banks, and in particular around the Mediterranean Sea. (This, Smith observes irrelevantly, being enclosed and calm, was 'extremely favourable to the infant navigation of the world ... To pass beyond the pillars of Hercules, that is, to sail out of the Straits of Gibraltar, was, in the ancient world, considered a most wonderful and dangerous exploit of navigation.') Smith deduces that if economic growth is to be sustained, the market has to widen continually. This is one of the main reasons, he believes, to support free trade.

What are the mechanisms by which this trade can be carried out? Smith has an indefatigable interest in the detail of the beginnings of money. The exchange of goods can be carried out by barter – the butcher stockpiles some beef, the baker some loaves, and so on – but as there may be a baker who does not eat beef, or other practical shortcomings of the system, this soon gives way to exchange of goods by reference to one particular commodity, such as gold or silver (or salt, which gives us the word 'salary'), and hence to money itself. He describes at some length (one of the most popular parts of the book) the transition to coinage, a process driven by the two related problems of how to stop people from adulterating the metals, or from filing small bits off to make a little extra margin for themselves.

Kings and Royal Mints themselves were past masters at this, of course, with Roman silver coins, in the dying days of the Republic, worth just one twenty-fourth of what they had started out as. Smith, ever frugal himself, indignantly condemns 'the avarice and injustice of princes and sovereign states', who, 'by abusing the confidence of their subjects, have by degrees reduced the quantity of metal which had been originally contained in their coins'.

But if the value of the coin used to depend on the amount of silver in it, what gave the silver its value anyway? Smith says, 'The real price of every thing, what every thing really costs ... is the toil and trouble of acquiring it.' Prices are essentially measures of the amount of labour needed to make the commodity. 'Labour, therefore, is the real measure of the exchangeable value of commodities.' Rents paid in corn, he notes, have held their value far better than rents paid in anything else. 'From century to century, corn is the better measure because, from century to century, equal quantities of corn will command the same quantity of labour more nearly than equal quantities of silver.'

Now, on one level, this is obviously not true. (Ask an artist – or even an author!) But let Smith have his say. He admits it is more complicated than that. It is the 'nominal value' of goods that determines whether trade is profitable – so for example, tea in China is cheap, and worth the while of the European importer to purchase it. It is therefore nominal values that regulate 'almost the whole business of common life in which price is concerned – we cannot wonder that it should have been so much more attended to than the real price'.

But Smith considers there to be a 'real' value for everything, apart from the 'nominal' value, which is something's market valuation, its price. However,

Labour alone, never varying in its own value, is alone the ultimate and real standard by which the value of all commodities can at all times and places be estimated and compared. It is their real price; money is their nominal price only.

He puts it like this:

The labour of the manufacturer fixes and realises itself in some particular subject or vendible [sellable] commodity, which lasts for some time at least after that labour is past. It is, as it were, a certain quantity of labour stocked and sorted up to be employed, if necessary, upon some other occasion.

Various examples are offered. There is the simple case of fish. Those caught from the sea involve only the labour and capital costs, those caught from rivers will also include a 'rent' charge, to the owner of the fishing rights. There is the more sophisticated case of the factory. The owner of the factory requires a return on the investment, which varies with the amount of capital invested. This is because this capital could have been simply put in a bank (where the manager could then lend it to others for a small fee) and left to grow by compound interest. Profit and interest are basically the same sort of thing – return on capital. Rent, Smith sees as different, because rent may simply be a charge imposed without any original investment; although any asset that can be rented can probably be sold too – in which case we might say to Smith that the distinction disappears. But Smith describes the landlord as one who 'loves to reap where others have sowed'. 'They are the only one of the three orders whose revenue costs them neither labour nor care, but comes to them, as it were, of its own accord, and independent of any plan or project of their own.'

It is the nominal value that drives the marketplace. The price someone is prepared to pay is determined by several factors. There is the 'psychological' factor of how much they want it. There is the practical consideration of the manufacturer of how much they have had to spend already to produce the goods. This will include the wages of the workers, the share due to the people who have provided the investment in the machinery and premises for the manufacture, the rent of any equipment or land, and the cost of the raw materials. Smith distinguishes the types of cost because they have different effects. The workers require recompense simply for their time and effort. This aspect he considers to be fairly straightforward.

The difference of natural talents in different men is, in reality, much less than we are aware of ... [that] between a philosopher and a common street porter, for example, seems to arise not so much from nature as from habit, custom, and education. When they came into the world, and for the first six or eight years of their existence they were perhaps very much alike, and neither their parents nor play-fellows could perceive any remarkable differences.

If everyone had to do everything for themselves, as would be the case without the division of labour and the mechanisms for the trading or bartering of goods, people would all appear much the same too. Yet people do in fact get paid very different amounts for jobs; and this is certainly not due to the different amounts of time and effort invested – although largely spurious claims may be made to this effect – nor is it about the rarity of the skills involved in certain kinds of work. (Media stars, university professors, managers and chief executives are amongst today's examples of this self-serving delusion. We might add to Smith's system the general rule that the more people are paid, the more important and unique they believe themselves to be!) Smith himself acknowledges that each factor, such as wages or rent, of the 'natural price' is in itself subject to the influence of demand in relation to supply.

So Smith's economic analysis depends on various kinds of prices that appear to overlap – even to be capable of changing their category. It is a threefold division, which seems to collapse into a twofold one. But there is another more serious problem, too. The price of, say, nails, will depend on their 'usual price', the demand for things made with nails, the demand for other things made with iron suitable for making nails, the demand for things whose manufacture indirectly involves nails or iron ... all of which are competing for the supply, the availability of iron to make nails and blacksmiths to smelt them (or however they are made!) – and indeed all of these things may in turn be affected by the price of nails. When the price of a 'variable' depends on itself, we have what physicists term 'feedback'. (The amount of feedback with the nails may not be very noticeable or significant, but consider the price of houses or postage stamps or shares!) Feedback makes these phenomena behave strangely. In fact, this phenomenon of 'non-linearity' is what makes the stock markets so attractive to investors. Because no one can predict anything reliably, it is always possible for someone to make a large profit by, say, speculating on the price of nails.

Smith accepts that supply and demand are 'complex' and cannot be represented by any simple (linear) relationship. Take wages, for example. The only *real* component of wages, he says, is the amount necessary to keep the worker alive, although Smith does insist that the subsistence wage is actually a bit more – that which is 'consistent with common humanity'. But in any case, in a growing economy, there may be a shortage of workers, obliging the employers to compete for them amongst each other, particularly by raising wages. He compares the experience of the then 'tiger' economies of Britain and America with the static economy of China, and the shrinking one of Bengal, concluding that it 'is not the actual greatness of national wealth, but its continual increase, which occasions a rise in the wages of labour'. This improvement of the 'lower ranks' is not an 'inconveniency' but a moral necessity, for no society can surely be flourishing and happy, when the greater part of the members are poor and miserable. 'It is but equity, besides, that they who feed, cloath and lodge the whole body of the people, should have such a share of the produce of their own labour as to be themselves tolerably well fed, cloathed and lodged.' But in the *absence* of economic growth, Smith predicts that wages will be forced down to the subsistence level.

Smith details the all-important subject of wage levels a bit more precisely too. There are several components. There is the 'unpleasantness' factor. Unpleasant work will be avoided if the worker can subsist without doing it, and therefore the employer must raise the wage to compensate. Smith assumes all work to be basically worse than not working – 'toil and trouble', an assertion which may not be universally true (unemployment itself can be a heavy burden), but surely is a reasonable approximation. Secondly, work which requires skill or training is like work which requires an expensive machine – the cost of hiring a professional must reflect this. Smith thinks work which is irregular may attract an extra premium (although we might argue that this is clearly not the case with 'casual work' such as that epitome of low-paid work, picking harvests for farmers). Jobs requiring people to step back slightly from their own selfish interests, such as being a doctor, also need to be given additional rewards.

Smith observes that people tend to be optimistic about their chances of success in life. In a lottery, for instance, even if the chances of winning may be slightly less than the chance of being run over getting the lottery ticket (to embellish his example), people will remain optimistic and sure that this sort of statistical reality does not apply to them. Indeed, they may behave irrationally by buying several tickets – irrationally, since even if they bought *all* the tickets in the lottery, they would still end up with less money than they had put in. Similarly, Smith notes, people will not pay a small premium for insurance against fire, because they believe that this misfortune will not befall them anyway. For this reason, jobs involving a calculation of risk, such as being a soldier, or even taking on difficult legal cases which require winning, may not obtain the extra premium that the market should determine, if everything was worked out logically.

Locke, too, explained economics in terms of the circulation of goods and materials acted upon by labour. But Smith distinguishes the different characteristics of capital and income, and explains the significance of savings. He begins by observing that capital is of two types, fixed and circulating. Fixed capital is like the lathes in a factory, or the skills of their operators. Circulating capital is the profit from the selling of the products, as this profit can then be used to buy a new carriage for the factory's owner, which involves more profits for the carriage maker, and all their suppliers too. Because of this, it is circulating capital that keeps the economy going, and only certain parts of the economy produce it. Civil servants, teachers and soldiers, for example, do not produce any circulating capital, although they may be useful for other reasons. (It could be said, indeed, that they may facilitate others in the making of circulating capital, thereby increasing the amount of circulating capital.)

On the other hand, the labour of the 'menial servant', such as that of a footman who puts his master's coat on him each morning, Smith says, 'does not fix or realise itself in any particular or vendible commodity. His services generally perish in the very instant of their performance, and seldom leave any trace or value behind them.'

The same goes, Smith adds dismally, for some of the

gravest and most important, and some of the most frivolous professions ... Like the declamation of the actor, the harangue of the orator, or the tune of the musician, the work of all of them perishes in the very instant of its production.

As their activities leave no tangible residue, they are worthless. We must leave aside speculation as to whether Smith would have considered the advent of sound and video recording technology as making these professions any the less transitory and frivolous, but indubitably the entertainments industry today is now a major source of 'circulating capital'. Smith's analysis looks dated and simplistic, but his overall theory is still indispensable.

Smith is actually rather against spending in general (let alone on frivolities): he sees it as usually unnecessary and inferior to saving. Money saved is available for business to borrow, creating new jobs which in turn create new goods and new profits. These new profits more than cover the initial borrowings, creating 'a perpetual fund for the maintenance of an equal number in times to come'. The urge to save, Smith thinks, is 'the desire of bettering our condition, a desire which, though generally calm and dispassionate, comes with us from the womb, and never leaves us till we go into the grave'. Yet what is saved? Just intrinsically worthless lumps of metal or promises to pay.

The *Wealth of Nations* is not just a discourse on the dismal science. It contains many profound insights into sociology, psychology and ethical behaviour. The historian H. T. Buckle said of the work: 'looking at its ultimate results, [it] is probably the most important book that has ever been written, and is certainly the most valuable contribution ever made by a single man towards establishing the principles on which government should be based'.

The book is a great work. But its greatness lies not in its originality, for little in it had not been suggested elsewhere before, and Smith, as a scrupulous scholar, would have been aware of the discussions. It is rather in the clarity and comprehensiveness of his vision.

THE SUBTEXT

In the intervening centuries, following Plato and Aristotle, economics appeared in philosophical and political debate only as a side issue with moral or immediately practical implications. So the scholastic philosophers commented on the ethics of charging interest, and in the seventeenth century there was a vigorous debate about the merits of foreign trade. Smith effectively carved out the whole subject as a new and separate discipline with its own questions, debates and occasionally solutions.

Marx and Engels adopted Smith's problematic theory that the value of something depended on the amount of labour put into it – and then drew revolutionary conclusions about 'surplus value' and 'exploitation'. Marx also follows Smith in distinguishing 'productive' labour from 'unproductive', before going on to derive a parasitical middle class.

Smith's political influence is huge. But it might have been even greater. A major part of *The Theory of Moral Sentiments* concerning lawmaking and government, although laboured over for many years, was never completed to the scrupulous Scot's satisfaction and, just before he died, perhaps thinking of his friend David Hume's famous epigram about works of sophistry and illusion, he stuffed it into the fireplace and 'consigned it to the flames'.

KEY IDEAS

Smith describes the 'hidden hand' of economics that guides all our actions and decisions. In fact, he makes a powerful case for leaving government, especially trading policy, to the hidden hand of market forces. Yet there is also a desire for approval by others – which can lead to conflict and upset the natural order.

- People come together naturally, because of the practical advantages: notably the efficiencies of specialisation and the division of labour as well as out of an awareness of the needs and feelings of others.
- Because civil society is concerned with property rights, it inevitably discriminates against the poor in favour of the rich. The state has a duty to offset this effect.

KEY TEXT

Adam Smith's *An Inquiry into the Nature and Causes of the Wealth of Nations* (1776)

Timeline:
From Air Travel to the First Railways

1780
This year marks the start of a period of great technological advances. But the technological changes also result in great political stresses. In this year, the mundane but important invention of the fountain pen.

1785
The first air crossing of the English Channel – by Blanchard and Jefferies in a hot air balloon. The first successful balloon flight at all had only been two years earlier, by the Montgolfier brothers.

1786
The first interior (gas powered) lights for houses used – in German homes. Meanwhile, in Japan, a famine claims over a million lives.

1788
The first convicts are transported to Australia, where the native peoples are being brutally displaced.

1791
Thomas Paine writes the *Rights of Man* against a background in Europe of the Fall of the Bastille (1789) as part of the French revolution and a clampdown generally on the freedom of its citizens. However, this is also the year a bill is introduced by William Wilberforce in the English Houses of Parliament to abolish slavery.

1793
Meanwhile, in the newly 'United States', a law is passed requiring escaped slaves to return to their owners. In revolutionary France, the Reign of Terror rages – one arguably less terrible effect of which is that compulsory education from the age of six is introduced.

1795
William Pitt introduces income tax in England as an emergency wartime measure (supposedly temporary). In France, Camacérès begins to develop the Napoleonic legal code, and, a year later, the country goes metric.

1800
Britain, now at the height of its Industrial Revolution, produces over a quarter of a million tonnes of iron a year and dubs itself the 'Workshop of the World'. For the first half of the nineteenth century, Britain alone accounts for a quarter of the world's trade. Alessandro Volta invents a portable means of storing electricity – the battery.

1801
The first 'railway' begins to operate – but not for passengers. Horses haul wagons of fruit, vegetables and coal along the rails.

1804
Robert Trevithick builds the first locomotive, although the first commercially useful one has to wait until ten years later and George Stephenson.

1805
The first factory lights enable owners to increase working hours. A year later, the half a million cotton workers of Great Britain are working under the ghostly and inadequate illumination of gas lights.

11
Marx's Messianic Materialism

For all Adam Smith's economic logic, the tidy march of society towards industrial nirvana was to be upset by a scandalous pamphlet produced by two Germans, Karl Marx and Friedrich Engels, whose names would become infamous. For the next 150 years, from the 1840s to the 1990s, the world appeared to split into 'two great warring camps' – a capitalist west, and a communist vanguard, centred on the Soviet Union and China.

THE CONTEXT

The *Communist Manifesto* opens with the famous promise: 'Let the ruling classes tremble at a communistic revolution. The proletarians have nothing to lose but their chains. They have a world to win!'

Alas, of course, reality was never so simple, as many failed communist societies could testify, not to mention failed 'anticommunist' dictatorships. But for a century at least, it seemed as though Marx was right and it would be a straight fight between the workers' forces calling for common ownership of 'the means of production', and an increasingly beleaguered and unpopular elite clinging to private ownership. It also seemed it must be true that certain macro-economic factors were all that created and defined societies and the lives of their citizens.

Karl Marx and Friedrich Engels wrote a great deal, of a largely rather turgid quasi-economic variety. There are not just the three voluminous parts of *Das Kapital*, but also the *Critique of Hegel's Philosophy of Right*, in which Marx and Engels declared that religion was 'the opium of the people', and the *Theses on Feuerbach*, in which it is observed that 'philosophers have only interpreted the world in various ways – the point is to change it'. Not to forget the numerous essays, *On Religion*, *On Literature and Art*, *On Ireland* and so on, nor other documents such as letters and correspondence. From these last, differences of approach between the two men can be seen. Much of historical communism, in fact, followed Lenin's interpretation of Engels, rather than Marx himself. And some scholars now attribute the first draft of the *Manifesto* to Engels, and later versions to Jenny Marx. Perhaps that is why Marx is said to have declared sadly in a letter to a friend towards the end of his life, 'All I know is that I am not a Marxist.' But in this chapter, at least, 'Marx' may be taken as a shorthand for any work that included his name. Anyway, for the workers of the world, 'his views' are essentially encapsulated in just one document – the relatively short and colourful 'manifesto' for the embryonic Communist Party, written in German, printed in London and speedily translated into French in time for the insurrection in Paris of June 1848.

In Europe, 1848 was the 'Year of Revolutions'. Protests rocked not only Paris, but Rome, Berlin, Vienna, Prague and Budapest. The 'Paris Insurrection' in particular started as street protests against royal interference in civil government, fuelled by resentment at the perceived betrayal of the principles of the 1789 revolution, which had promised not only 'liberty' but, more problematically, 'equality' as well. After troops fired on crowds the insurrection did indeed escalate into the provisional government of the Second Republic, which promptly cracked down on the protesters even more harshly than the first one had done.

The other revolutions of that year also fizzled out in failure for the working class, beaten back by the bourgeoisie, as was to happen time after time, to Marx and Engels' frustration. Nevertheless, this was the backdrop to the *Manifesto* – a chaotic period in which there seemed to be a new class of worker, facing a new type of exploitation – a situation which had, to be sure, already engendered the new political movement of 'socialism'. But neither Marx nor Engels ever had much time for socialism, which they considered a middle-class concern, respectable to the bourgeoisie, whereas any decent doctrine should have been subversive. Communism, by comparison, was much better: the unacceptable face of working-class power, presenting a totally alien face to the capitalist class.

Marx and Engels' strategy is summarised in the *Manifesto* for the benefit of the new movement. The 'fundamental proposition' is that 'in every historical epoch' the prevailing 'mode of economic production and exchange' and 'the social organisation necessarily following from it' determine the political structures of society, along with the intellectual beliefs and ideas. That is, economics determines social life, and that decides political positions. In one of the *Manifesto*'s more memorable phrases (and one that has become part of the shared consciousness (true or false) of the modern world), Marx and Engels argue that it therefore follows that 'the whole history of mankind has been a history of class struggles, contests between exploited and exploiting, ruling and oppressed'.

This idea, as Engels ambitiously puts it in the preface to the English version of the *Manifesto*, is comparable to Darwin's theory of evolution. Marxism is the theory of the evolution of societies. It is as impersonal and its conclusions as inevitable as Darwin's biological model of the development of species.

But the *Communist Manifesto* is much more than an interpretation of history as a preparation for the coming of true socialism. As it says, the point is not to understand the world, but to change it. So the *Manifesto*'s emphasis is on the class struggle, and its consequent call for revolutionary action indeed led to Marx being arrested in Cologne in 1849, after the crushing of the 1848 revolutions, and tried for sedition. Although acquitted, Marx spent the rest of his life as an exile in London, supported financially by Engels' Manchester textile business. There he pored over books in the reading room of the British Museum, leaving the frontline action to others. Indeed, Marxism began to stress the inexorable changes in economic production over the role of the proletarians.

Marx, the individual, lived a rather sad and lonely life of straitened circumstances, if not true poverty, apparently deeply affected by the early deaths of four of his seven children, from malnutrition and poor living conditions. The son of a wealthy German lawyer, who had renounced his Jewish faith in order to progress in his career, he married the 'most beautiful girl in Trier', the daughter of the Baron of Westphalen, Jenny, to whom in due course it fell to pawn the family silver (marked with the crest of the Dukes of Argyll) and cope with Marx's unfaithfulness, which had produced an illegitimate child by one of their servants. In between, she had to edit and write out many of the revolutionary scripts. (How great an input Jenny Marx may have had into the *Manifesto* is unknown, but it may well have been more than is conventionally acknowledged.) All the while, Marx vowed never to allow 'bourgeois society' to make him into a 'money-making machine', and money that was given to him or otherwise came to the family was frequently expended rather ineffectually on either revolutionary projects, school fees, or just parties. In many ways, Marx's writings are a substitute for physical activity – revolutionary or otherwise. And in a way, he was a great snob, embittered by personal experience. Just before his death he observed that he was 'the best hated and most calumniated man of his time'. But the *Manifesto* dates from a more optimistic time in his life. It opens with a piece of literary braggadocio: 'A spectre is haunting Europe – the spectre of communism.' It was time, Marx and Engels contended, to 'meet this nursery tale of the spectre' with the publication of the founding principles of the Communist Party.

THE TEXT

Marx and Engels' lifelong collaboration had begun in the early 1840s after a crackdown by the repressive Prussian government began to make life impossible for Marx, then attempting to make a career as a journalist on the *Rheinische Zeitung*. Abandoning Germany for Paris, he had met Engels in 1842 and the two formed the partnership which would prove so productive, at least in literary terms. Marx, who had studied law in Bonn and philosophy and history in Berlin (receiving a doctorate in due course from the University of Jena, for his thesis on the ancient Greek philosophers, Epicurus and Democritus), is generally credited with providing the scholarship, imagination and passion; Engels, with the philosophical rigour and practicality (as well as being the better writer) – not to mention the money. It is Engels who attempted to make Marxism into 'scientific socialism', using the 'best of' philosophy, political science and traditional socialism.

The key elements of this are the division of society into two groups: the bourgeoisie, who are essentially those rich people who either hire others to work for them, or simply own the factories the work goes on in; and the proletariat, those who, 'having no means of production of their own', are forced to sell their labour in order to live.

This division is traced back through time in an effort to show that it is a 'universal truth'. 'Freeman and slave, patrician and plebeian, lord and serf, guild master and journeyman, in a word, oppressor and oppressed', stand in constant opposition to one another, always carrying out a battle, sometimes overt, sometimes covert, 'a fight that each time ended either in a revolutionary reconstitution of society at large or in the common ruin of the contending classes'.

The perennial claim of the liberals that class conflict is always only in the past, and that the world is now all 'middle class', is a sham. 'The modern bourgeois society that has sprouted from the ruins of feudal society,' Marx writes, 'has not done away with class antagonism. It has but established new classes, new conditions of oppression, new forms of struggle in place of the old ones.'

In the 1850s, the *Manifesto* describes society as a whole already increasingly 'splitting up into two great hostile camps, into two great classes directly facing each other: bourgeoisie and proletariat'. Today, 150 years on, this distinction has lost its force. Indeed, the proletariat, or full-time workers, often are the bourgeoisie too. But the words still strike a chord, for even as the workers are 'embourgoisified', there develops what contemporary Marxists have described as the new 'unworking class', of casual labourers, the unemployed, the disabled, the old, the mad and the sick – together making up a new underclass. Even at the time Marx was writing, Bakunin in Russia was predicting that if there was to be an uprising it would be amongst the 'uncivilised' – driven by their instinctive desire for equality. Bakunin, however, also predicted correctly that the revolutionary instinct would be enfeebled by 'civilisation'.

One thing is still the same though, as Marx goes on to say: when we examine the characteristics of the new industrial society, we see that the bourgeoisie has established itself as the supreme power in the modern state, running the government, turning it into 'but a committee for managing the affairs of the whole bourgeoisie'.

The bourgeoisie, wherever it has got the upper hand, has put an end to all feudal, patriarchal, idyllic relations. It has pitilessly torn asunder the motley feudal ties that bound man to his 'natural superiors', and has left remaining no other nexus between man and man than naked self-interest, than callous 'cash-payment'. It has drowned the most heavenly ecstasies of religious fervour, of chivalrous enthusiasm, of Philistine sentimentalism in the icy water of egotistical calculation. It has resolved personal worth into exchange value and, in place of the numberless indefeasible chartered freedoms, has set up that single, unconscionable freedom – free trade.

'In one word,' adds Marx ungrammatically, 'for exploitation, veiled by religious and political illusions, it has substituted naked, shameless, direct, brutal exploitation.' Developing the idea, he says that the bourgeoisie has also stripped occupations such as medicine and the law, the church and teaching, of their 'halos', reducing everyone to paid wage labourers (a transformation which at other points he might have been expected to encourage). Even the family has been reduced by the bourgeoisie to a mere money relation, Marx adds disgustedly. But then the *Manifesto* is sprinkled with barbed and sarcastic asides which are not intended to be wholly consistent with its central arguments. (It is almost as if a doctoral student's philosophical essay had fallen into the hands of an overzealous newspaper sub-editor – a perspective which may, in fact, not be so far from the mark.)

In industrial society, the workers themselves become mere appendages of machines, of whom only the most simple and monotonous activity is required. The 'lower strata' of the middle class, the shopkeepers and tradespeople, sink gradually into the proletariat, as the capitalists render their skills irrelevant by the might of the new methods of production.

The *Manifesto* says that industrial society requires constant change, as opposed to the tranquillity of the feudal and other epochs. 'Constant revolutionising of production, uninterrupted disturbance of social conditions, everlasting uncertainty and agitation distinguish the bourgeois epoch', it warns, in one of its prolonged if rather tiring bouts of ironic, oxymoronic language.

Similarly, bourgeois society relies on a constantly expanding market, a claim we have already seen with Adam Smith's analysis of the creation of wealth. The industries demand raw materials from ever more obscure and remote sources, and must persuade consumers about new and exotic needs, thus creating a world market. The same applies in the intellectual sphere, with the rise of a 'world literature'. Legal systems, governments and methods of taxation must transcend any frontier. The 'most barbarian' nations are dragged into the impossible equation, with the cheap prices of commodities the 'heavy artillery' with which the bourgeoisie forces the barbarians to capitulate. All nations, on pain of extinction, are compelled to adopt the capitalist mode of production.

Modern bourgeois society with its relations of production, of exchange, and of property, a society that has conjured up such gigantic means of production and of exchange, is like the sorcerer who is no longer able to control the powers of the nether world whom he has called up by his spells.

The insatiable forces of production even begin to threaten their 'bourgeois midwives', and, through continual crises, the whole of bourgeois society. But it is not only these forces that undermine the system. By creating the proletariat, the bourgeoisie has already 'forged the weapons that bring death to itself'.

Hitherto, every form of society has been based, as we have already seen, on the antagonism of oppressing and oppressed classes. But in order to oppress a class certain conditions must be assured to it under which it can, at least, continue its slavish existence. The serf, in the period of serfdom, raised himself to membership in the commune, just as the petty bourgeois, under the yoke of feudal absolutism, managed to develop into a bourgeois. The modern labourer, on the contrary, instead of rising with the progress of industry, sinks deeper and deeper below the conditions of existence of his own class. He becomes a pauper, and pauperism develops more rapidly than population and wealth.

At first the counter-struggle is carried out by a few individuals (polite coughs from Marx and Engels), with the labourers still 'an incoherent mass'. But with the growth of industry, the strength of the workers increases, and they become more conscious of this strength and their power. At the same time capitalism is forced to worsen both wages and conditions for its workers, thereby inadvertently causing the growth of workers' clubs to protect their wages. Thus are unions born. And now the tone of the pamphlet changes, as Marx and Engels shift from analysis to activism, seeing in the unions the bourgeoisie's eventual 'grave-diggers'.

It is because the bourgeoisie is incompetent that it is unfit to govern (the *Manifesto* adds, with unusual reasonableness). Unfit, because it cannot stop its slaves sinking into poverty to such a point that it ends up feeding them. 'What the bourgeoisie therefore produces, above all, is its own grave-diggers. Its fall and the victory of the proletariat are equally inevitable.'

Communists are the 'most advanced and resolute' part of the working class and they are just the workers who understand better than the rest that the abolition of the institution of private property is essential, for property represents (as Smith puts it) stored up, or (as the *Manifesto* puts it) expropriated, labour. However, with Marx's definition, since the wage labourer only receives the bare subsistence necessary to continue working, private property necessarily represents exploitation. In the famous phrase of Pierre Joseph Proudhon, Marx's contemporary and the first anarchist, 'property is theft'.

But the *Manifesto* does not believe that revolutionaries need to be prepared to enter into long arguments on economics, advising them to say instead:

don't wrangle with us so long as you apply, to our intended abolition of bourgeois property, the standard of your bourgeois notions of freedom, culture, law, etc. Your very ideas are but the outgrowth of the conditions of your bourgeois production and bourgeois property, just as your jurisprudence is but the will of your class made into a law for all.

Far better simply to enumerate the 'generally applicable' requirements of communist revolution, as Marx and Engels go on to do. These are offered in summary form as a series of short points, simple to remember:

- Abolition of land ownership and rents
- A heavy progressive income tax
- Abolition of all inheritance rights
- Confiscation of the property of all those who no longer live in the state, or who rebel against the new government
- Centralisation of all capital and credit in a state bank
- Central state control and ownership of the means of communication and transportation
- Increased state production through factories and farming; development of underused land
- 'Equal liability of all to labour'; new armies of workers, especially to work the land
- Disappearance of the distinction between town and country: population distributed evenly over the country

And, lastly:

- Free education for all in state-run schools, preparing the children for work in the new industries

In the meantime, the *Manifesto* concludes, communists should support every 'revolutionary movement against the existing social and political order, bringing to the fore, as the main issue, the property question'. This should be done 'no matter what its degree of development at the time': by which Marx and Engels mean the political aspects rather than the economic stage prevailing. Central to their point of view was the naive belief that these impersonal forces had brought the industrial societies to the brink of collapse. (It was left to Mao Zedong in China to make the important doctrinal changes necessary to allow communist theory to apply to pre-industrial peasant societies – the kind of societies in which it actually took root to some extent, as it had done earlier in Russia.) Thus, the *Manifesto* presses for unionisation and makes it clear that for communists the only way forward is the 'forcible overthrow' of existing social structures. ('Let the ruling classes tremble at a communistic revolution. The proletarians have nothing to lose but their chains. They have a world to win!')

According to Marx and Engels, the communists are assured of eventual victory thanks to two things. The capitalist mode of production necessarily results in recurrent economic crises, perhaps creating wealth for a few, but also inevitably increasing poverty for an ever growing working majority. At the same time, Marxism predicts, optimistically, that there will be 'ever growing' realisation amongst the proletarians of their exploitation – that 'law, morality and religion are ... just so many bourgeois prejudices'.

Certainly, even bourgeois economists accept that capitalism has its 'cycles', with recurrent troughs and adjustments – in bad cases, economic depressions. But, as is discussed later, on this crucial, factual claim of increasing absolute poverty, Marxism has simply been wrong. Marx and Engels did not perceive the almost inexhaustible ingenuity of the capitalist system in increasing production through technical progress, and generating within itself apparently unlimited financial resources, making possible high standards of living not only for the tiny minority of mill owners, and the ever expanding ranks of the petty bourgeois, but for the workers too.

Then again, there are those, such as the French former Marxist, André Gorz, who have suggested in recent years that the truly oppressed class of modern capitalism is not that of the workers any more, but of the 'unworkers' – the old, the unemployed and the very young (such as the 'street children' of South America), who cannot work and must rely on state handouts or charity (or crime) for their sustenance. Even at the time that Marx and Engels were writing, this view was being expressed in Russia by Bakunin, who foresaw an uprising of the 'uncivilised', driven by their instinctive desire for equality. Bakunin predicted, in contrast to Marx, that the revolutionary instinct would be enfeebled by 'civilisation', and that violence was part of a primitive urge.

The other important claim of the pocket analysis offered by the *Manifesto* is the so-called 'materialist conception of history', the idea that, in Engels' words, 'men must first of all eat, drink, have shelter and clothing, therefore must work, before they can fight for domination, pursue politics, religion, philosophy [!], etc'. Because of this realisation, attention shifts from the activities of the leaders to the experiences of the led, from the kingly individuals of conventional history towards the social trends of economic science. By deciding that the battles of conventional political history are of little importance, Marxism instead raises to prominence another ongoing struggle, one that changes from epoch to epoch but remains essentially the same – the struggle of the exploited against their oppressors. These are always essentially two classes, defined by the knowledge – consciousness – of the exploited that they *are* oppressed. (Although Marx recognises the gradations of social class, he rejected them as unimportant, as he did also the nationalistic impulse – and the motivation of racism which had produced the slavery of the nineteenth century.)

THE SUBTEXT

In the *Communist Manifesto*, Marx and Engels were confident that each stage of society – Asiatic, ancient, feudal and bourgeois – was both necessary and invariable. Other, earlier, practical social experiments, such as the Diggers of sixteenth-century England, were therefore not of much interest to them. Later, this was a view which they needed to amend, to explain the possibility of revolution in peasant societies – such as Russia.

But what of the other radical, but pre-industrial, social experiments? Revolutionary politics did not start with Marx. In nineteenth-century England alone, there were many currents of radicalism swirling amongst the masses: Jacobinism from the French revolution; Luddism from the battle of factory workers against increasing mechanisation and the unemployment associated with it; legislative battles for trade union rights and the freedom of the press; and popular campaigns for welfare and working-hours protection. But for Marx and Engels, these were all so many false starts, deviant forms of socialism, and for that reason the *Manifesto* takes time to explain exactly what is wrong with each, in sequence:

- *feudal* socialism: merely aristocrats using sympathy for the workers to denounce the bourgeoisie
- *clerical* socialism: mere 'conscience-salving'
- *petty-bourgeois* socialism: nostalgic, unrealistic and ultimately reactionary
- *humanist* socialism: erroneously puts 'humanity' above class struggle
- *bourgeois* socialism: reform by do-gooders

- *utopian* socialism: consists only of fantastical visions of the future, such as those advanced by Robert Owen and Henri Comte de Saint Simon.

What is offered by the *Communist Manifesto* is also a theory of psychological and social relationships. It invokes a kind of *'anomie'* or 'alienation' as a central feature of life in industrial society (to use the terms coined by the nineteenth century's new breed of 'social scientists'). The key to reforming social life, whether its problems are material or spiritual, is therefore, as Marx and Engels see it (and as Rousseau also concluded), to abolish property. With no property, there can no longer be two classes. No bourgeoisie, as they can no longer exist once they no longer have control of the 'means of production'. No proletariat, as they instead become effectively part owners with their former adversaries. With no classes, there is no longer any conflict, and so there is no need either for laws or for the repressive role of the state. Instead of calculations of profit, production can simply be organised for need. Marx and Engels imagine this as being not only more efficient than under capitalism, but also more rewarding for the workers involved. In place of alienation comes involvement and satisfaction.

Actually, as history has shown, these calculations of need are anything but simple. Not only are they are extremely complex and difficult to make, but as the command economies of the former Soviet Union demonstrated, the end result is anything but efficient. It is *possible* to set up a bureaucracy to calculate how many two inch nails to make, and then to provide them at a set price, but there is no guarantee that the calculation will be right.

Marxist freedom is freedom from blind economic forces, replaced by the shared plans and controls of the collectively planned economy. But the shackles of the market are not so easily broken, and Marxism in practice is control by not one but two masters – the detached and unaccountable control of the bureaucracy, and still the irrepressible effects of countless individual market decisions.

But the *Manifesto* is based on several tenets, each of which is independent of the others. So, unlike religious creeds, such as Catholicism or Islam, or indeed western science, it is possible to believe parts of the *Manifesto* to be true, whilst having doubts about other elements. The first of these tenets is that all history is the history of class struggle, in a society shaped by the prevailing mode of production. The second is that these struggles inevitably result in social disorder, and that, in a capitalist society, this disorder leads to the workers seizing power. The third credo is that the final stage will represent the ultimate goal of the human spirit, and further developments will be neither necessary nor possible. Accordingly, communism is the 'end of history'.

The first and second tenets look historically verifiable, but in fact aren't really, as the ambiguity of human events requires interpretation as well as investigation. (And crucially, for the second, there is no fixed 'timescale'.) The third is clearly unverifiable.

So the *Communist Manifesto* (like anarchism, the rival ideology of the times) requires of its adherents a great deal of blind faith. In this, it is more of a religious doctrine than a scientific theory. For this reason, it is not surprising that it was amongst the pre-industrial societies of Africa, China and South America, and in Russia itself, that the words of the *Manifesto* actually took root – amongst the 'rural idiots', as Marx and Engels used to refer to people who worked on the land. Indeed, as the last years of the twentieth century showed, the industrialisation of Russia and China that proceeded under communism actually brought about the collapse of the command economy and the return of capitalism.

Of course, Marxism also took hold amongst that most bourgeois of all bourgeois groups, the university intellectuals, albeit often in a selective form; perhaps adopting the language and images of Marxist 'alienation' or 'false consciousness' to make broadly humanist points. Although Marx and Engels were passionate (at least on paper) about the conditions of the workers, they did not make any appeal in their theory to 'human rights'. They merely maintained that by the laws of economics, capitalism would collapse, producing the workers' state. But then Marx and Engels were not humanists themselves: they genuinely lacked feeling for their fellow human beings, not just wishing to dispense with it in their philosophical system building. Marx even insisted on changing the motto of the Communist League when he joined it in 1847 from 'All Men are Brothers' to 'Proletarians of the World Unite!', not out of creditable egalitarianism to sisters, but because he objected to the implication in the notion of universal brotherhood that it included the enemy. In the years before the tragedy of the First World War, the two revolutionaries looked forward to the last 'great war dance' of the capitalists, expecting, and hoping, that this would usher in revolution.

KEY IDEAS

The *Communist Manifesto* outlines Marx and Engels' theory of society. It is an important document, a rich smorgasbord of social science, philosophy and history. Many of its asides – about globalisation, deskilling, even 'embourgoisification' – seem prescient and far-sighted in the light of subsequent developments, and still speak across the centuries. But it contains far less that is new, far less that is original, than it promises.

The materialist conception of history is, as we have seen, very old, and much of Marx and Engels' writing on this and other matters is merely a reworking of other people's theories. The 'dialectic' itself, with its notion of two classes fighting each other, before destroying themselves to produce a new class, can be seen in non-materialist form in the philosophy of Hegel, along with a version of the evolution of history, and much of that is borrowed from Plato. Many of the *Manifesto*'s economic 'insights' are conventional in both scope and nature. Nonetheless, Marxism has been a powerful force in shaping society, whatever the flaws and inconsistencies in its theoretical base.

- The modern state is controlled by one class – the bourgoisie – acting for its own benefit and advantage.
- The rapacious demands of the market tear down geographical and cultural distinctions and barriers without distinction between the important and useful and the unimportant and outmoded.

Since the 1980s, with the implosion of the Soviet Union, and the conversion of even old communist societies, such as China and Cuba, into proto-capitalist economies, the legacy of the *Manifesto* is today an almost mundane one. The future may reveal Marxism as no more than a historical cul-de-sac. But, if it is, then it is at least one which shifted attention away from the 'bourgeois' agenda of nineteenth-century politics, mitigated by the charitable intentions of paternalists and liberals, towards a more holistic calculation of the respective rights and duties of rich and poor within capitalist society.

KEY TEXT

Karl Marx and Friedrich Engels' *Communist Manifesto* (1848)

Timeline:
From Roads Paved with Tarmac
to Roads Paved with Gold

1806
The US Federal Government bans importation of slaves – but the law is not enforced.

1810
John McAdam begins a road programme in England, giving his name to the new technique of surfacing roads. The first canned food is made – but the process is very risky and prone to poisoning purchasers.

1811
Jane Austen writes *Sense and Sensibility*, published in a year of protests against the gradual mechanisation of factories – known as the Luddite riots after their leader.

1819
The Factory Acts in Britain forbid the employment of children under nine in cotton factories. Even with its limited scope, the law is largely ineffective, and it is not until 1838 that a general restriction on workers under nine years of age comes into force.

1821
James Mill publishes his 'Essay on Government', and James Faraday discovers the principles of the electric motor. Ten years later, Faraday develops the electric dynamo, which enables electricity to be produced more easily.

1825
The first passenger railway – the 43 kilometres of the Stockton to Darlington line – is opened in the north of England. In 1830, the first person will be killed by a train.

1828

Increasingly frequent peasant revolts in Russia, reacting against harsh feudal conditions, herald a generation of uprisings in the rest of Europe which will peak 20 years later.

1829

Niépce and Daguerre's photographic process results in the first true photographs. The daguerreotype, which uses silver salts, follows nine years later.

1831

Charles Darwin travels on *HMS Beagle* as naturalist for a survey of coral formations. Working out the implications will take him another 20 years.

1834

Six Dorset labourers – the Tolpuddle Martyrs – are transported to Australia for their part in an attempt to set up a trade union. Instead, the British devise the workhouse system to deal with the problem of unemployment.

1836

And it is in Britain that the government starts to record the births, marriages and deaths of its citizens centrally by law, the first time this is believed to have been attempted.

1840

The Penny Post is introduced in London. Envelopes are invented shortly afterwards, too. But the 1840s are a period of corn and potato famines in Ireland and throughout Europe, and the railway-led boom collapses.

1841

At this time, the US imports 135,000 slaves a year to toil for its 17 million population (which is now only slightly less than that of Britain).

1842

The Chinese are forced to sign the hated 'Unequal' Treaty of Nanjing, giving the European imperialist powers extensive rights in the East.

1848

Beginning of the Californian gold rush and the start of a massive increase in emigration from Europe to the New World. This is also the year that John Stuart Mill's *The Principles of Political Economy* is published.

12
Mill's Optimistic Liberalism

At the time John Stewart Mill was writing, the new science of economics, inaugurated, at least as a popular subject, largely by Smith, was vexed by problems resulting from the country's involvement in wars against Napoleon. The recently founded Bank of England had defaulted on repayments of the National Debt, new taxes were causing hardship, and inflation was upsetting economic relationships as workers found their wages buying less and less food. It was a situation that required a systematic approach: so step forward the utilitarians.

THE CONTEXT

It was while leafing through a copy of Joseph Priestley's pamphlet, an *Essay on Government*, that Jeremy Bentham had found proposed a system for grounding the authority of the law on the principle of maximising the happiness of the greatest number. This became the guiding light of a new philosophy called 'utilitarianism', and Bentham wrote enthusiastically in favour of it (notably in the *Introduction to the Principles of Morals and Legislation* of 1789), that is, when not working on his attempts to design a large circular prison, the 'Panopticon', in which everything the prisoners did could be watched (amongst other eminently 'useful' projects).

Utilitarianism has become, as much as anything, the founding principle of western liberal democracy. After all, if everyone is equal, and they all have a vote, then the politically shrewd, if not the right, policy will be something pretty close to calculating a method for pleasing the maximum number of people. Bentham, however, the son of a lawyer, had aims that were slightly different. He wanted to 'systemise' the study of society, and only found in the process of this that he had produced a system for evaluating both social and individual action. It fell to John Stuart Mill, whose education was under Bentham's watchful gaze, to adapt and adopt Bentham's 'felicific calculus' in the service of a progressive, egalitarian vision of liberalism. Whilst Bentham became a 'political theorist' only after his attempts to construct the Panopticon were thwarted, Mill's political interests were much deeper.

Mill spent most of his life as a clerk in India House, London, with a brief spell as a member of Parliament, particularly interested in women's rights, constitutional reform and economics. He also believed, unlike Bentham, that some forms of happiness were better than others. Which, essentially, relegated the pleasure principle to second place, behind some sort of notion of values. Mill's version of utilitarianism holds that allowing people to decide for themselves as much as possible increases the general happiness, thereby arriving at a philosophy arguing in favour of liberty of thought, speech and association.

Mill reflects his upbringing by his immersion in utilitarian theory and accepts that the greatest happiness of the greatest number is the goal of sound social policy. However, in his twenties, the effects began to wear off as Mill discovered, like Smith, the importance of the moral sentiment. And for Mill there came a new perspective, due to the influence of his lifelong collaborator on his great political works, Harriet Taylor.

THE TEXT

The *Principles of Political Economy* (*with Some of the Applications to Social Philosophy*) was written in 1848, around the same time as Marx and Engels were fomenting (or attempting to foment) proletarian revolution. It is essentially an attempt to emulate Mill's illustrious Scottish predecessor, Adam Smith, in setting out the workings of the modern state. Unlike Smith, however, Mill is a poor writer and lacks both the insight and the subtlety of the Scot. Despite, or perhaps because of, his famous education at the hands of James Mill (Greek at age three, Latin at eight and Logic at thirteen), Mill has leaden prose (*vide* Book 5, chapter 9, section 8: 'I proceed to the subject of Insolvency Laws ...') and plodding mathematics. Take, for example, his discussion, in Book 4, of the relationship of supply and demand. Mill complains that Smith

overlooked the circumstance that the fall of price, which if confined to one commodity really does lower the profits of the producer, ceases to have that effect as soon as it extends to all commodities; because, when all things have fallen, nothing has really fallen, except nominally; and even compared in money, the expenses of every producer have diminished as much as his returns. Unless indeed labour be the one commodity which has not fallen in money price, when all other things have; if so, what has really taken place is a rise of wages; and it is that, and not the fall of prices, which has lowered the profits of capital.

This is the point about 'feedback' in the economic system that we saw earlier. It is an important criticism, but not well made. Perhaps this is because the whole book took Mill just 18 months to scratch out in manuscript form, a rate of 1,000 words a day, including a six-month break to campaign for peasant rights in Ireland, prompted by awareness of the desperate plight of the Irish peasants during the potato famine of the late 1840s. Since, to all intents and purposes, 'political economy' is inseparably intertwined with many other branches of social philosophy, Mill goes on to suggest a radical political and social agenda from what would otherwise be fairly uninspiring economic theorising.

For example, in this rather dreary way, Mill proceeds to discuss the workings of the quintessential corn market, where he finds that the 'interest of the landlord is decidedly hostile to the introduction of agricultural improvements' and that the 'doctrine that competition of capital lowers profits by lowering prices, is incorrect in fact, as well as unsound in principle'. Yet the deficiency is not merely one of style: Mill himself (a bit later in the work) notes that there actually is a 'tendency for profits to fall' which can only be offset by improvements in production.

Mill's strength is less in the analysis, particularly not the economic one, than in his system building, particularly the ethical one, and his idealism, where he places economic and social claims in a new framework of political rights. For example, he writes, following Smith, that only labour creates wealth, but that capital is stored-up labour, and may be accumulated – or even inherited – quite legitimately. Inheritance is acceptable, even when initially based on an injustice, once a few human generations have passed, as to remedy the injustice would create worse problems than leaving the situation alone. Even so, he says, the inheritance of wealth, beyond the point of achieving 'comfortable independence', should be prevented by the state's intervention and confiscation of assets. People who want to live more than 'comfortably' should work for it.

Mill thought that this 'Benthamite' part of his book would cause more than a little stir, and indeed hoped to become notorious for it. However, tucked away in nearly half a million other words, it attracted little interest. He wrote in a letter to a friend, 'I regard the purely abstract investigations of political economy as of very minor importance compared with the great practical tensions that the progress of democracy and the spread of socialist opinions are pressing on.' It is these elements, largely confined to the end portion of Book 5, which make for the most original parts of the whole work.

Mill is one of the first writers to consider themselves 'social scientists', and was firm in his conviction that these studies were justly related to the natural sciences, and could be pursued using similar methods. Mill, like Plato, distinguished between the study of individuals, which would be largely psychology, and the study of collective behaviour, which would be largely economics and politics. He tried out various terms for summing up his approach, such as 'social economy' and even 'speculative politics' but eventually returned to what he called Comte's 'convenient barbarism' – sociology. This study was to be pursued using deduction from observations and analysis of historical trends.

Like the Enlightenment Encylopaedists and many since, Mill considered himself to be living in an unprecedented age of invention and discovery, but perhaps unlike us he was sure that the discoveries were yet in their infancy, and that 'production is the perpetual, and so far as human foresight can extend, the unlimited growth of man's power over nature'. Of the marvel of telegraphic communication, for example, he writes:

The most marvellous of modern inventions, one which realises the imaginary feats of the magician, not metaphorically but literally – the electromagnetic telegraph – sprang into existence but a few years after the establishment of the scientific theory which it realises and exemplifies.

Mill goes on to say that it is impossible not to look forward to 'a succession of contrivances for economising labour and increasing its produce', as well as, in Bentham-like terms,

a continual increase of the security of person and property. The people of every country in Europe, the most backward as well as the most advanced, are in each generation, better protected against the violence and rapacity of one another, both by a more efficient judicature and police for the suppression of private crime, and by the decay and destruction of those mischievous privileges which enabled certain classes of the community to prey with impunity upon the rest.

As if this wasn't already optimism enough, Mill predicts that generation after generation the people will also become better protected against the 'arbitrary exercise of the power of government'. Taxation would grow 'less arbitrary and oppressive' (although a little taxation is still a good thing) and wars 'and the destruction they cause' will be confined to those 'distant and outlying possessions' in which Europeans come 'into contact with savages'.

As to these latter, Mill is clearly a long way from Rousseau's vision of the 'noble' savage. Although, he concedes, they may individually have superior general abilities to soft, pampered, civilised man, the savage cannot match the 'greater capacity' of 'civilised human beings collectively considered'. What Rousseau saw as a disastrous loss of autonomy for man in the 'state of nature', Mill welcomes.

In proportion as they put off the qualities of the savage, they become amenable to discipline; capable of adhering to plans concerted beforehand, and about which they may not have been consulted; of subordinating their individual caprice to a preconceived determination, and performing severally the parts allotted to them in a combined undertaking.

It is this element of 'cooperation' that is the key to modern societies. From it characteristically follows a great 'flowering of co-operatives' and joint-stock companies.

Towards the end of the *Principles*, in a section headed 'the limits of the *Laissez-faire* or Non-interference Principle', Mill makes his most distinctive contribution to political philosophy, as he turns his mind to the setting out of the limits of government. 'Whatever theory we may adopt,' he writes,

respecting the foundation of the social union, and under whatever political institutions we live, there is a circle around every individual human being which no government, be it that of one, of a few, or of the many, ought to be permitted to overstep ... That there is, or ought to be, some space in human existence thus entrenched around, and sacred from authoritative intrusion, no one who professes the smallest regard to human freedom or dignity will call into question: the point to be determined is, where the limit should be placed; how large a province of human life this reserved territory should include.

Mill himself marks the boundaries very clearly: 'I apprehend that this ought to include all that part which concerns only the life, whether inward or outward, of the individual, and does not affect the interests of others, or affects them only though the moral influence of example.'

Even when the activity appears to affect others, the onus of proof must lie on the defenders of legal prohibitions. For to be prevented from doing what one is inclined to, from acting according to one's own judgment of what is desirable, 'is not only always irksome, but also always tends, *pro tanto*, to starve the development of some portion of the bodily or mental faculties'.

In essence, such prohibitions partake 'in a great or small degree, of the degradation of slavery'. So, although reared as a utilitarian by men who believed in the dispassionate calculation of wants and needs, Mill ends up stating explicitly:

Scarcely any degree of utility, short of absolute necessity, will justify a prohibitory regulation, unless it can also be made to recommend itself to the general conscience; unless persons of ordinary good intentions either believe already, or can be induced to believe, that the thing prohibited is a thing which they ought not to wish to do.

This principle is crucial, for as self-styled democrats tend to forget, experience proves that

the depositaries of power who are mere delegates of the people, that is of a majority, are quite as ready (when they think they can count on popular support) as any organs of oligarchy to assume arbitrary power, and encroach unduly on the liberty of private life.

The public taken collectively, Mill adds, is 'abundantly ready' to impose, not only its generally rather narrow views of its own interests, but even its abstract opinions and aesthetic tastes, as laws binding on individuals.

But there is another, pragmatic, reason to resist the attempts of the state to increase its role and power, a reason that is a consequence of the principle of the division of labour. This is that 'every additional function undertaken by the government, is a fresh occupation imposed upon a body already overcharged with duties'. As a natural consequence,

most things are ill done; much not done at all, because the government is not able to do it without delays which are fatal to its purpose; that the more troublesome and less showy of the functions undertaken are postponed or neglected, and an excuse is always ready for the neglect while the heads of the administration have their minds so fully taken up with official details, in however perfunctory a matter superintended.

The solution to this problem is quite simple – the devolution of power. Small is beautiful:

the inconvenience would be rescued to a very manageable compass, in a country in which there was a proper distribution of functions between the central and local officers of government, and in which the central body was divided into a sufficient number of departments.

So, by way of an example, Mill praises the creation of a British Railways Board, or at least as he imagines it – a separate and independently functioning body carrying out a clearly delineated task for the public. If, in retrospect, such state bodies are today seen to be as effectively unresponsive and uninterested as any central government one, that is not necessarily a criticism of the underlying principle. And the approach appears to be experiencing something of a resurgence with the recent fashion for 'downsizing' and 'privatising' aspects and functions of not only central but local government. Mill's straightforward claim is that 'the great majority of things are worse done by the intervention of government, than the individuals most interested in the matter would do them, or cause them to be done, if left to themselves'.

After all, he argues, even if the government were to be superior in intelligence and knowledge to the most intelligent and knowledgeable individual or group in society, it would still be inferior to all the individuals of the nation taken together. '*Laissez-faire* should, in short, be the general practice; every departure from it, unless required by some great good, is a certain evil.' Mill warms to his theme, observing (what many of us will recognise) 'that, as a general rule, the business of life is better performed when those who have an immediate interest in it are left to take their own course', uncontrolled and unhindered by either the law or 'the meddling of any public functionary'.

But there are exceptions. Mill thinks the most important is in the ability of the 'uncultivated' to judge matters of cultivation, that is to say, 'things which are chiefly useful as tending to raise the character of human beings'. Those individuals, Mill sadly notes, who 'most need to be made wiser and better, usually desire it least'. Even if they could be brought to desire it, they would be 'incapable of finding the way to it by their own light ... Education, therefore, is one of those things which it is admissible in principle that a government should provide for the people.'

However, 'it is not endurable that a government should, either *de jure* or *de facto*, have complete control over the education of the people. To possess such a control, and actually exert it is to be despotic.' And he continues, without apparent irony, as noted above, but certainly with some piquancy: 'A government which can mould the opinions and sentiments of the people from their youth upwards, can do with them whatever it pleases.'

The safety valve is to allow free choice from rival educational institutions, and the right of parents to educate their own children, subject to some unspecified state supervision. Mill then considers the case of those who may suffer when a *'laissez-faire* attitude' is followed. He identifies four particular groups for concern: children, very poor people, such as those incapable of any work, women – and animals. Children, like animals, require special protection from 'the most brutal part of mankind'.

It is by the grossest misunderstanding of the principles of liberty, that the infliction of exemplary punishments on ruffianism practised towards these defenceless creatures, has been treated as a meddling by government with things beyond its province; an interference in domestic life. The domestic life of domestic tyrants is one of the things which it is the most imperative on the law to interfere with.

Even so, Mill sees through the linking of women and children's protection in the Factory Acts as mere mischief. Whilst children are not sound judges of their own interests, 'women are as capable as men of appreciating and managing their own concerns, and the only hindrance to their doing so arises from the injustice of their present social position' – specifically, that the law makes 'everything which the wife acquires the property of her husband, while by compelling her to live with him it forces her to submit to almost any amount of moral and even physical tyranny'.

The women in the factories, Mill argues, are the only women who are not slaves or drudges. Women's rights can only be advanced by opening access to jobs, not by adding limitations. If, for the poor and destitute, he sees a compelling prima facie case for helping, yet the fact remains that

in all cases of helping, there are two sets of consequences to be considered; the consequences of the assistance, and the consequences of relying on the assistance. The former are generally beneficial, but the latter, for the most part, injurious, so much so, in many cases, as greatly to outweigh the value of the benefits.

Worse still, this is most likely to be the case when the need is most extreme. 'There are few things for which it is more mischievous that people should rely on the habitual aid of others, than for the means of subsistence, and unhappily there is no lesson which they more easily learn.'

This is the 'problem' that modern capitalism wrestles with most doggedly. In the liberal democracies, welfare is suspected of creating will-sapping habits of dependence, and instead of charity, either private or state, 'workfare' is increasingly provided.

But there is another way around the problem, one which governments have been less eager to try. Mill puts it this way:

In so far as the subject admits of any general doctrine or maxim, it would appear to be this – that if assistance is given in such a manner that the condition of the person helped is as desirable as that of the person who succeeds in doing the same thing without help, the assistance, if capable of being previously calculated on, is mischievous: but if, while available to everybody, it leaves to every one a strong motive to do without it if he can, it is then, for the most part, beneficial.

Subject to certain conditions, Mill holds it 'highly desirable that the certainty of subsistence should be held out by law to the destitute able-bodied, rather than that they should depend on voluntary charity'. Although Mill is not putting it quite in this form, what he is saying corresponds to the idea of the 'citizen's wage', that is to say, a minimal amount necessary to ensure subsistence, paid as of right to each citizen, leaving each with not only the duty but the practical necessity to find ways to improve their lot further through their own efforts. After all, Mill says:

In the first place, charity almost always does too much or too little; it lavishes its bounty in one place, and leaves people to starve in another. Secondly, since the state must necessarily provide subsistence for the criminal poor while undergoing punishment, not to do the same for the poor who have not offended is to give a premium on crime.

The problem is that the state must act by general rules: it cannot discriminate 'between the deserving and the undeserving indigent'. It owes 'no more than subsistence to the first, and can give no less to the last'. In words which have been well and truly forgotten, Mill warns: 'The dispensers of public relief have no business to be inquisitors.' So Mill concludes Book 5 of the *Principles of Political Economy*:

I have not thought it necessary here to insist on that part of the functions of government which all admit to be indispensable, the function of prohibiting and punishing such conduct on the part of individuals in the exercise of their freedom, as is clearly injurious to other persons, whether the case be one of force, fraud, or negligence. Even in the best state which society has yet reached, it is lamentable to think how great a proportion of all the efforts and talents in the world are employed in merely neutralising one another. It is the proper end of government to reduce this wretched waste to the smallest possible amount, by taking such measures as shall cause the energies now spent by mankind in injuring one another, or in protecting themselves against injury, to be turned to the legitimate employment of the human faculties, that of compelling the powers of nature to be more and more subservient to physical and moral good.

THE SUBTEXT

Mill is one of the founding figures of liberalism, now unquestionably one of the great survivors of political theory. His brand is grounded in the utilitarian ethic adopted from Jeremy Bentham, rather than on the appeal to fundamental rights of that other great liberal Englishman, John Locke. Despite different starting points, each arrives at the characteristic set of individual rights and freedoms.

Yet if liberalism offers equality before the law, at the same time it accords individuals secondary status: to that law, and the institutions and authorities embodying it. The free-market vision of society is rooted in fear, the central justification behind the state, at least in Thomas Hobbes' and John Locke's brand of 'democracy'. In Hobbes' case, fear of death or of exploitation, in Locke's, and many contemporary capitalist societies, fear of loss of their material possessions. Liberalism does not even suggest any positive purpose for human existence; perhaps thinking individuals should find it for themselves.

The French and American revolutions were epoch-making in that they seemed to correct a sense of inferiority that feudal society engendered and required, replacing it instead with something approaching a sense of dignity and common humanity. Afterwards, for the first time, the state formally recognised the importance of all its citizens, bestowing upon them important powers and rights. Whilst Thomas Hobbes, John Locke and the architects of the American Declaration of Independence held that rights were largely a means of protecting the individual from the rapacious desires of their neighbours, the rights also appeared to include more positive freedoms to create and develop, just the sort of freedoms which lay behind the economic expansion spearheaded by the Protestant entrepreneurs who created the European Industrial Revolution.

Mill himself writes that 'after the means of subsistence are assured, the next in strength of the personal wants of human beings is liberty'. Yet, liberalism is essentially freedom from rather than freedom to. Freedom from arbitrary laws or taxes, from being made to work against one's will, freedom from being told what to believe, and freedom from being obliged to participate in social activities that cannot be justified by being necessary for the well-being of the community. It is not freedom to work, or to live in a home, or to be healthy – as the ever widening underclasses of the consumer societies can vouch for. Indeed, increasingly it is not even 'freedom from' the first two either, as it is increasingly the underclasses who pay the highest proportion of their meagre incomes in taxes (for example, on purchases of alcohol or cigarettes) or are drummed into 'workfare' employment schemes, whilst the rich operate through tax-exempt corporations.

F. A. Hayek, in *The Road to Serfdom*, his influential book written in the aftermath of the Second World War, specifically warns that 'nothing has done so much harm to the liberal cause as the wooden insistence of some liberals on certain rough rules of thumb, above all the principles of *laissez-faire*'. In this they imagine that they follow Mill, whereas in fact, he says, the correct attitude of the liberal towards society should be more like that of a good gardener towards their plants – tend them carefully and try to create the conditions in which they can flourish.

KEY IDEAS

Mill takes the principle of maximising the general happiness and sets it in a framework of individual rights and freedoms. At the same time, he claims to create the social conditions in which talent, creativity and culture can thrive. Conversely when the state interferes:

- it is invariably a worse judge of both policy and of practicality than the individual;
- it normally makes matters worse; and
- it rapidly becomes bureaucratic and inefficient.

The tragedy is, as Mill acknowledged, that without any limitations at all on their freedoms, people will still tend to use them simply to injure and harm one another.

KEY TEXT

J. S. Mill's *The Principles of Political Economy* (1848)

 Timeline:
From Famine to Free Education

1851
One million people have died in the Irish potato famine.

1854
Baron Haussmann begins constructing the characteristic wide sweeps of the Parisian boulevards – for the convenience of troops and as a means of deterring rioters.

1855
Dr Snow's cholera map shows that the cause of an outbreak in Victorian London was the Broad Street drinking pump.

1859
Charles Darwin's *Origin of Species* is published, accidentally changing the way people see social obligations as well as the way they perceive the natural world. *On Liberty*, by John Stuart Mill, is published.

1861
As part of a process of Russian modernisation, all serfs are made freemen.

1862
An early machine gun invented by Gatling is soon followed by the new TNT explosives (1863), the harpoon gun (1864), the 'Winchester' repeating rifle, and the torpedo (1866). Finally, in 1867, Nobel discovers the power of dynamite. After this, Nobel decides armaments have developed too far, and funds the peace prize named after himself.

1865
The American Civil War ends with the surrender of the Confederates. A year later, the Civil Rights Act sets slaves free.

1870
The British introduce (compulsory) free education for all.

13
Durkheim's Strange Science

It is in the nineteenth century that knowledge becomes an industry: a social and public enterprise with a workforce of researchers and scholars, grouped by subject into divisions, communicating with one another by thesis and article, judging work by common standards. Knowledge is churned out in a kind of progression. It accumulates in books and libraries. It becomes an institution.

THE CONTEXT

A small part of the new 'knowledge institution' was immediately given over to sociology, or the academic study of society. And the door formally opens on the new science in the year 1842 with the publication of the *Cours de Philosophie Positive*, by Auguste Comte (1798–1857), a middle-class French intellectual whom John Stuart Mill would later accuse of devising a 'despotism of society over the individual'. Others, however, would trace both the origins of sociology and the despotism to Jeremy Bentham's efforts to ground the authority of the law on the principle of maximising the happiness of the greatest number.

Whatever the truth of that, it is with Comte, who had been inspired by his study of medieval Catholic scholars into attempting to produce a new 'religion of humanity' and a blueprint for a new social order, that the science of society really takes off.

In the *Cours*, Comte, like René Descartes and many philosophers since, starts from a position of deep admiration for both the precision and the authority of the natural sciences, epitomised (at least in the public mind) by the advances in physics and chemistry. His 'positivist' idea is that the methods of natural science are the only way to understand human nature, both in individuals and collectively, and hence the only way to find out how to organise society. And Comte wants to apply these 'scientific', quantitative methods to society itself, dissecting it to discover the laws and the principles governing it. Of these, he later judged his most important discovery to be a 'Law of Human Progress' (well, it sounds important), according to which all societies pass through three stages: the *theological*; the *metaphysical*; and the scientific or *positive*.

The defining feature of each stage is the mental attitude of the people. During the theological stage, people seek to discover the 'essential nature of things' and the ultimate cause of existence, interpreted as God. Philosophers, Comte thought, were stuck at this stage, perpetually but fruitlessly pursuing these sorts of question. Most people, however, were at the next, the metaphysical stage, which involves increasing use of abstract theory, although there is still a sense of the underlying essence of things, epitomised by broadly ethical notions of value. The final stage comes only when enough people put aside the illusions of opinion (echoes of Plato) and confine themselves to logical deduction from observed phenomena. This is the so-called scientific (or positive) stage. 'Now each of us is aware, if he looks back on his own history, that he was a theologian in his childhood, a metaphysician in his youth and a natural philosopher in his manhood', Comte rather unconvincingly declares.

The stages are also supposed to correspond to periods of human history. The first relates to the prehistorical and medieval world, whilst the metaphysical stage is compared to the sixteenth, seventeenth and eighteenth centuries, a time when monarchies and military despots gave way to political ideals such as democracy and human rights, including, most importantly for social life, property rights. The last stage in history will be a scientific, technological age, when all activity is rationally planned and moral rules have become universal.

This, at least, is Comte's vision. It is as this final stage beckons that the science of society comes into its own, with its task of both explaining and determining social phenomena and the history of mankind.

Comte himself was an idealist who wrote of 'love' as the guiding principle and of bringing 'feeling, reason and activity into permanent harmony'. It was left to Emile Durkheim and Max Weber, and also to some extent John Stuart Mill, to examine the mechanisms of social life. Durkheim (1859–1917) in particular attempted to show how a new social consensus could provide the values of community and social order, values that had, he felt, characterised the pre-industrial era, and could now combat the increasing disorder stemming from rapid industrialisation. To do this, he collected statistical evidence on suicides, on the labour force, on religion and on education. But Durkheim, as did Weber, then built upon his empirical base a more profound, metaphysical theory of social life.

THE TEXTS

Emile Durkheim

Durkheim, unlike Marx, tried to achieve this new social consensus without losing the benefits of individual emancipation and freedom that technology is perennially supposed to make possible. His solution is centred around what he calls 'the collective consciousness' and the notion of 'social facts'. These last are 'ways of acting, thinking and feeling, [that are] external to the individual' – such as the customs and institutional practices, moral rules and laws of any society. Although these rules 'exist' in the minds of individuals, Durkheim says their true form can be found only when considering the behaviour of 'the whole' – that is of society itself. In this, not for the last time, there are echoes of Plato and Socrates 2,000 years before. Like Plato, Durkheim considers society to be essentially a moral phenomenon, created within a framework of overarching eternal values. And, like Plato, he rejects individualism and introspection as assumed and proposed by thinkers such as Thomas Hobbes and Adam Smith, with their attempts to create generalities out of particulars and to build social structures out of human atoms. Instead, turning their models upside down, he makes society primary – the cause and not the effect.

Durkheim rejects Hobbes' vision of the world in the 'state of nature', saying that 'when competition places isolated and estranged individuals in opposition, it can only separate them more'. If there is a lot of space at their disposal, he adds, 'they will flee; if they cannot go beyond certain boundaries, they will differentiate themselves, so as to become still more independent. No case can be cited where relations of pure hostility are transformed.'

If society were based, for example, on calculations of interest and social contracts, then the key social relationship would be the economic one, 'stripped of all regulation and resulting from the entirely free initiative of the parties'. Society would simply be the situation 'where individuals exchanged the products of their labour, without any action properly social coming to regulate this exchange'.

But Durkheim thinks this is not actually how society functions. 'Is this the character of societies whose unity is produced by the division of labour?' he asks rhetorically. And he continues, answering himself: 'If this were so, we could with justice doubt their stability. For if [self-] interest relates men, it is never for more than some few moments.'

Taking up Hobbes' challenge (as well as adopting his language) Durkheim goes on:

Where interest is the only ruling force, each individual finds himself in a state of war with every other since nothing comes to mollify the egos and any truce in this eternal antagonism would not be of long duration. There is nothing less constant than interest. Today, it unites me to you: tomorrow, it will make me your enemy.

So we have to look elsewhere for explanation of the 'organic' solidarity of society. Durkheim concludes that since 'the greater part of our relations with others is of a contractual nature', then if it were necessary 'each time to begin the struggles anew', only a fragile kind of social relation could result, 'only a precarious solidarity'. Durkheim chooses instead what he sees as Comte's 'organic' approach, in which everything is related to a whole.

In the same way as an animal colony, for example a beehive, 'whose members embody a continuity of tissue from one individual', every aggregate of individuals who are in continuous contact form a society. The division of labour cannot occur prior to this. Individuals must be linked through material facts, but also by 'moral links' between them. Hence, Durkheim concludes,

the claim sometimes advanced that in the division of labour lies the fundamental fact of all social life is wrong. Work is not divided among independent and already differentiated individuals who by uniting and associating bring together different aptitudes. For it would be a miracle if differences thus born through chance circumstance could unite so perfectly as to form a coherent whole. Far from preceding collective life, they derive from it. They can be produced only in the midst of a society, and under the pressure of social sentiments and social needs. That is what makes them essentially harmonious.

Societies are built up out of shared beliefs and sentiments, and the division of labour emerges from the structure created. Durkheim returns to Comte, to remind the reader that, in Comte's words, 'cooperation, far from having produced society, necessarily supposes, as preamble, its spontaneous existence'. What bring people together are practical forces such as living in the same land, sharing the same ancestors and gods, having the same traditions. Rousseau, Hobbes, and even the utilitarians, are all guilty of disregarding the important social truth, that society predates the individual. 'Collective life is not born from individual life, but it is, on the contrary, the second which is born from the first ... Cooperation is ... the primary fact of moral and social life.'

Compare human beings with animals. Animals are almost completely under the yoke of their physical environments. Human beings, however, are almost free of their environment, but dependent on social causes. Animals have their societies too, but they must be very simple and restricted, and their collective life is very limited. With human societies, there are more individuals living together, common life is richer and more varied: 'social causes substitute themselves for organic causes. The organism is spiritualised.'

As societies become more vast, and particularly, more condensed, a psychic life of a new sort appears. Individual diversities, at first lost and confused amidst the mass of social likenesses, become disengaged, become conspicuous, and multiply. A multitude of things which used to remain outside consciences because they did not affect the collective being became objects of representations. Whereas individuals used to act only by involving one another, except in cases where their conduct was determined by physical needs, each of them becomes a source of spontaneous activity. Particular personalities become constituted and take conscience of themselves.

People exist within and depend on only three 'types of milieu': the organism, the external world, and society.

If one leaves aside the accidental variations of hereditary, – and their role in human progress is certainly not very considerable – the organism is not automatically modified; it is necessary that it be impelled by some external cause. As for the external world, since the beginning of history it has remained sensibly the same, at least if one does not take account of novelties which are of social origin. Consequently, there is only society which has changed enough to be able to explain the parallel changes in individual nature.

Thus, Durkheim introduces the new science of 'socio-psychology'. (Elsewhere he speaks of sociology too as the 'science of ethics'.) As pointed out by Rousseau and Smith in the eighteenth century, and by modern economists like G. K. Galbraith subsequently, the role of necessity actually plays a very small part in economics – much more is explained by reference to psychology. Social facts are not the result of psychic facts, but the latter are in large part an effect of the former. For example, Durkheim disputes claims that in the parent–child relationship we see the logical expression of 'human sentiments inherent in every conscience', insisting that to say this is to reverse the true order of the facts. 'On the contrary, it is the social organisation of the relations of kinship which has determined the respective sentiments of parents and children.' The sentiments would have been completely different if the social structure had been different, and the proof of this (Durkheim triumphantly concludes) is that paternal love is unknown in 'a great many societies'.

In fact, Durkheim explains, 'everything that is found in the conscience, has come from society'. Although society 'may be nothing without individuals', each of them is much more a product of society than a creator of it.

Are there any exceptions to this? Great leaders, for example? Durkheim recalls that in Melanesia and Polynesia, for example, it is said that an influential man has *mana*, and that his influence is due to this quality. However, really, Durkheim says, it is evident that his authority is solely due to the 'importance attributed to him by public opinion'. (Like modern-day 'media personalities', they are just 'famous for being famous'.) The special status and powers of great leaders, as imagined by Max Weber and Friedrich Nietzsche, for example, is an illusion.

And Durkheim considers our very awareness, our 'consciousness', to be a social rather than an individual phenomenon. He argues that there are two types of *symbol* which create societies and cement the individual human beings into the social whole. These are collective representations, such as national flags and other shared symbols, and moral codes, such as notions of basic rights, and even unwritten, generally accepted, beliefs such as the idea that young children should be given toys to play with or that swimming in rivers should be free. Together, these written and unwritten rules create a 'collective consciousness'. This consciousness is part of the psychological make-up of each individual in society, and is also the origin of formal moral codes. Many things follow from this interpretation. For example, stealing from your neighbour is wrong not because of the affront to the neighbour, but because of the affront to the collective consciousness itself. And Durkheim draws from this, more generally, the conclusion that self-interest, or even consideration of the interests of the majority (the goal assumed by utilitarianism), is incapable of producing moral behaviour. Instead, the 'collective consciousness' functions as a kind of watchdog for its own well-being, as well as expressing a position based on certain principles.

Durkheim goes on:

It has often been remarked that civilisation has a tendency to become more rational and more logical. The cause is now evident. That alone is rational which is universal. What baffles understanding is the particular and the concrete ... the nearer the common conscience is to particular things, the more it bears their imprint, the more unintelligible it is.

In essence, the key to social life is symbolism. It is the way that individuals communicate most effectively, and their social values are preserved and embodied in the sacred symbols. Social life

in all its aspects and in every period of its history, is made possible only by a vast symbolism. The national emblems and figurative representations with which we are more especially concerned in our present study are one form of this, but there are many others.

Although Durkheim does not specifically make this point, we might observe here that language itself consists essentially of symbols. But Durkheim does make a novel distinction between types of possible society. This is between 'simple' ones, where the population is small and dispersed within its limited territory, and 'complex' ones, with more members, closely packed, interacting and interdependent. The former are held together by traditions that operate uniformly on the various members, who are like little atoms – undifferentiated in themselves and interchangeable. The individuals in 'simple' societies share a powerful sense of shared purpose and function. This results in a type of social cohesion Durkheim calls 'mechanical'.

The other way of organising society, which Durkheim calls 'organic', is more complex. It involves a range of parallel institutions and traditions, with individuals falling into increasingly distinct sub-groupings, each with its own traditions and 'social norms'. Within each grouping, individuals can become specialised and fulfil a particular function in the social whole. The division of labour, which Marx sought to abolish (as creating inequality), is seen by Durkheim as a desirable aspect of this evolution.

Regulation of the two societies is different too. In the simple, mechanical social structure, punishment's sole purpose and function is to defend the collective from the danger presented by a rogue element, and so is swift and severe. In the organic society, there is more of an emphasis on repairing the malfunctioning part – and so the law is likely to emphasise undoing the wrong done, and preventing further damage, rather than simply rooting out the disease. This is partly because the cohesion of organic society is fundamentally one of interdependence, so even a malfunctioning part is valued.

And there is a particular disease of complex societies that Durkheim identifies and gives a name to, *anomie*. This is the sense of futility and alienation that leads individuals to take their lives, for example, but, also perhaps, to attack their fellow citizens. Durkheim suggests this is caused by a failure to replace the 'mechanical' cohesion of the simple society with new social bonds.

Durkheim's method for investigation was to try to find tangible instances of these admittedly immaterial social facts, through sophisticated analysis and interpretation of official statistics. These he found in careful trawls through official documents: population statistics, official descriptions of the nature of the workforce and professional groupings – even in the minutiae of the judicial codes. His most celebrated study (for want of a better word) is of the number of people committing suicide. For Durkheim, suicide was not just an individual activity (tragedy) but an action directly linked to and reflecting a general breakdown in social cohesion.

In *Suicide: A Study of Ideology*, Durkheim uses the discovery that self-destruction is more prevalent amongst certain religious groups (Protestants) than others (such as Catholics) to argue that this is because the 'collective consciousness' is stronger in the Catholic communities. In a modern society, *anomie* (with its associated feelings of alienation from the whole, and individual futility) is such a threat that Durkheim says that 'professionals' (academics, teachers, medical workers – even politicians) need to be 'united and organised in a single body'. Taking the idea further, in the *Division of Labour*, Durkheim suggests that professional groupings or unions should act almost as an extended family, taking an interest in all aspects of their members' well-being.

We can find a contemporary parallel in Japan. Since the Second World War, the Japanese *zaibatsu*, or large corporations (such as Mitsubishi), have tended to act in this quasi-paternal way, with children joining the same corporation as their parents, having been educated in one of its schools, attending one of its training colleges if necessary, and then working for it all their lives. In addition, Japanese workers will probably spend any free time or holidays at the *zaibatsu*'s leisure facilities, and any job changes will be within the organisation. In return, the corporation expects lifelong loyalty from the workers, and a sense of shared aims and aspirations. It also recognises a lifelong responsibility to provide both for its workers and their families.

The desirable aspect of all this is that workers feel very much part of a group, and gain a sense of security and shared purpose. For the *zaibatsu* this enables them to achieve high standards of industrial performance, with workers' ideas a key part of improving efficiency, and any investment in training being protected by employee loyalty. This is less likely to be the case in the west, with its notion of 'high-flyers' changing jobs and companies at will. Western companies, maximising both workforce and market 'flexibility', tend to operate on short-term investment strategies, demanding that any investment in both physical and human 'capital' show a quick return. The Japanese industrial model allows investment to be protected long enough for long-term gains to become worthwhile.

Even so, there is a downside to the approach. By substituting collective decisions for individual desires and ambitions, the paternalistic *zaibatsu* can contribute to an extreme cult of service like that which characterised the Japanese war machine, and today, contrary to Durkheim's expectations, still leads to many 'unsuccessful' Japanese individuals taking their own lives, feeling that they have failed to live up to the standards of the 'collective consciousness'.

Max Weber

Another of Durkheim's fellow 'knowledge workers', with a more prodigious output than most, was Max Weber (1864–1920). Like Durkheim, he made a study of the different characteristics of the various Christian groupings. He too claimed to have discovered important differences between Protestants and Catholics, with implications for social reality. In fact, Weber built on his own statistical analysis of Protestantism an almost existential model of society in which social science, being rooted in values, was ultimately subjective.

Weber's particular insight, set out in his best known work, *The Protestant Ethic and the Spirit of Capitalism*, was that the Industrial Revolution in Europe was linked to a rejection of traditional and elaborate Catholic religious practice, and a Protestant ideology which emphasised the virtue of a lifetime spent working hard with no greater aim than serving God. The second stage of this realisation was a view of material goods which held them to be important only in that they reflected God's approval of one's efforts. For the new breed of capitalist, Weber thought, this made the success of the entrepreneur something worth striving for. It also, conveniently, justified reducing the number of workers to the absolute bare minimum required for successful production.

In particular, Weber argued that the development of capitalism occurred in Holland and England because they were Protestant powers, and that the economic discoveries associated with the time flowed from this pre-existing fact, rather than vice versa – a view that harmonises with Durkheim's approach, by putting the social before the economic.

Not that Weber is necessarily in favour of this. In *The Origin of Modern Capitalism*, Weber argues that 'in the east it was essentially ritualistic considerations, including caste and clan organisations, which prevented the development of a deliberate economic policy' and thus that capitalism could only develop once the political administration – the bureaucracy – was created, as in the British parliamentary system.

And, in contrast to Durkheim, Weber again makes the individual's perception of the world the key to understanding society. *The Protestant Ethic and the Spirit of Capitalism*, his study of attitudes to work, published in the early years of the twentieth century, attempts to show how individual perceptions are tied up with economic practice. Weber's works on social science in general, such as the *Methodology of Social Sciences*, and the uncompleted *Wirtschaft und Gesellschaft* (Part 1 eventually translated as *Social and Economic Organisation*) contain three new ideas which became highly influential. (At least, that is, in sociological circles ...)

Weber's career was largely spent in several professorial positions in respectable German universities, churning out his heavy-handed theories, although he was actually employed too, for a period, as a bureaucrat himself – as a hospital administrator during the First World War. He defines 'sociology' (in typically turgid style) as the science of the analysis of the social causes of social effects. As a science, it must be 'value free', a notion that was important for Weber and led to an intense and prolonged academic debate within Germany. Of course, Weber realised, values are often present in individual perceptions, and his investigation of the relationship of Christianity, in its Protestant form, and capitalism, exemplifies the central role values play in social life.

Paradoxically, perhaps, Weberian sociology is value-laden in itself. Weber insists, almost as an axiom of his theories, that rationality is good. In fact, like the ancient Greeks, Weber assumes dangerously that an action with a rational purpose must be good – and that, *mutatis mutandis*, as the magician might say producing an implausible rabbit, if an action is not good, it cannot be rational. Any activity without conscious intent is mere 'behaviour'. Digestion is merely behaviour, but stealing apples is social action, Weber says. Actually, the distinction is not really very clear – feeling hungry is not social action, but it might be all that propels someone to steal some apples, without really thinking about it.

THE SUBTEXT

The first novelty of Weberian sociology concerns the organisation of modern societies (those that Weber calls 'bureaucratic'), rationality and explanations of human behaviour; and his theory of 'ideal types', these last being a kind of theoretical model, rather than a value judgement. If the language is confusing and long-winded, Weber's three ideas, to make matters worse, begin to blur into one another, and may even be fundamentally ambiguous and confused. In particular, bureaucracy and rationality are inextricably linked.

Bureaucracies, Weber thinks, naturally promote a 'rationalist' way of life, just as rationality itself is inclined to prefer government according to rules, rather than mere authority. Weber himself, as a German, was particularly influenced by the new highly organised state under Bismarck – although he was also concerned at the threats it posed to individual liberties and differences. Weber wanted to see the bureaucracy taking over the running of itself, monopolising the use of violence through the police and army, but also allowing for certain legal rights for citizens, if necessary against the state, thereby still facilitating the growth of business and capital.

The second social strategy for Weber, as for Durkheim, stems from his conviction that it is not enough to explain activity in terms of causes and mechanisms – there must be a purpose. Furthermore, in society at large, Weber thinks, the purpose is normally an economic one. There may be other types of social cause – artistic, moral, religious or environmental – but in order to be rational, they must:

- 'accord with the canons of logic, the procedures of science or of successful economic behaviour'; or
- 'constitute a way of achieving certain ends, when the means chosen to achieve them accord with factual and theoretical knowledge'.

Otherwise, if the ends are motivated (contaminated) by values – religious, moral or aesthetic – or if values influence or determine the means employed, then the behaviour is 'value-rational' (which is not as good). This is illustrated by the case of the principled parent who refuses to borrow money and so is unable to feed the family properly.

Sometimes the ends may be decided by tradition, which is a kind of value. This is typically the key factor in history, Weber says, describing how in traditional Chinese society, if you sold your house and moved out but later became homeless, you could return to your old home and expect to be taken back in, for the new owner would not risk offending the 'spirits' by refusing to help another. Thus, Weber argues, tradition hinders economic progress. Then again, sometimes behaviour is affected by emotions and passions; this is 'affectual action', and that, too, is opposed to rational behaviour.

It is *zweckrational*, or goal-rational, behaviour which is most logical, similar perhaps also to the more simple-minded models of market economists or utilitarians. For example, if someone wishes to buy a gold watch, they may start doing overtime at work to save money for the purchase. Capitalism depends on rationality in two ways: for the movement of free and property-less workers in response to the demands of the free market; and for the freedom of those with capital to invest – such as entrepreneurs – to choose where to do so, based on maximising profit.

In the *Origin of Modern Capitalism* (1920), one of a series of lectures given at the end of his life, Weber puts it thus: 'Very different is the rational state in which alone modern capitalism can flourish – its basis is an expert officialdom and rational law.'

Actions which result from the way people feel are non-rational, as are certain sorts of actions, like that of the generous Chinese homeowner, motivated solely by a sense of needing to conform to existing practice and authority – the behaviour of the extreme traditionalist. When individuals, with their various notions of rationality, interact, it can be predicted that they will do so in one of just two ways. They will work cooperatively with one another, either for reasons of tradition and other not wholly *zweckrational* reasons, or from a more calculated assessment of their self-interest. The former is typical of family and nationalist bonds, and the latter is found in 'associations' such as those that modern industrial society may create.

So Weber aims to produce out of these various types of rationality, and the three types of society, a formal system for describing and even calculating behaviour. But his theory also has a 'normative' outcome – it acts as a political recipe. Weber argues that unless society is ordered by a strong authority, rational judgments will be limited to pragmatism. He proposes instead that this authority needs to be respected, almost worshipped.

Weber, like his fellow German, Friedrich Nietzsche, provided a philosophical foundation for the later Nazi edifice. Nietzsche enthusiastically describes his 'Superman' exploiting and tyrannising the masses, but Weber still expects the structure of his society to be essentially democratic (through the system of appointments to posts and roles).

He is led to suppose both a need for the 'cultivated man', the cultivated individual who is opposed to the specialist, to staff the bureaucracy, and also a role for something, perhaps akin to both religion and the cult of the individual, that he calls *charisma*. Charisma is a word taken from theology, meaning to have divine grace, something supernatural bestowed upon individuals. According to Weber, society requires a charismatic figure or entity. God is the original charismatic figure, but the people, the folk, the march of history are other examples.

Soon after, indeed, the Fascists would create Weber's ideal of the bureaucracy under the charismatic leader. And, as he had said, 'the masses submit because of their belief in the extraordinary quality of the specific person – the magical sorcerer, the prophet, the leader of hunting and booty expeditions, the warrior chieftain' – a leader not bound to 'general norms, either traditional or rational'.

Actually, Weber, unlike Durkheim, even allows these leaders to change the direction of history, making it impossible to predict (and thereby somewhat undermining the rationality of his whole intellectual edifice). Complex, and full of paradoxes, competing elements of 'social reality' are allowed to subvert the monolithic bureaucratic forces of Weberian modern society.

KEY IDEAS

The 'positivist approach' can give a different, general picture of life and society. Statistical methods are the tools for those today seeking to organise, design and control societies – and their power can be seen in the increasingly sophisticated manipulation of markets by governments, media, and business, perhaps in turn all manipulated by the huge transnational corporations of the modern global economy. Rather than the idealised individuals imagined by Rousseau and some liberal theorists, social science reveals that behaviour can also be explained by seeing people as just atomic parts of the machine that is society.

- Individual morality and indeed consciousness are created from social life and the collective consciousness.
- Social life is created out of a vast symbolism.
- Cooperation is the key to progress.

KEY TEXTS

If much of the new sociology is jargon-ridden and unreadable, these works rise a little above the rest:

Emile Durkheim's *Social Rituals and Sacred Objects* (1912) and *Precontractual Solidarity* (1893)
Max Weber's *The Protestant Ethic and the Spirit of Capitalism* (1930)

Timeline:
From Typewriters to
Wireless Communication

1871
Otto von Bismarck, prime minister of Prussia, marches through a seething Paris as the culmination of his campaign of German unification and expansion.

1874
The first typewriters arrive.

1877
The railway strike heralds a (confrontational) new era in industrial relations for the United States.

1879
Thomas Edison discovers that tungsten in a vacuum glows brightly for a long time, and the first electric light is created.

1882
Standard Oil now has 95 per cent of all refinery capacity in the United States. It will not be until 1911 that the government acts to break up the monopoly.

1884
The Berlin Conference sets out the ground rules for the European 'scramble for Africa' that will trigger the process of turning spheres of influence into full-blown colonies.

1889
The Eiffel Tower opens – by far the tallest building ever built.

1896
The Lumière brothers introduce films to the public, including the famous 'train arriving at a station', which causes panic wherever it

is shown. The first comic strip (by Rudolph Dicks) is printed in the United States.

1899

For the first time, people are able to communicate instantaneously – the 'wireless' is used to send messages between London and Paris. The modern age has truly arrived.

14

The Philosophical Dance with Fascism

Fascism is essentially the doctrine that elevates that part of the human psyche concerned with control over others – power – to a creed. Conservatism, socialism and even liberalism are none of them immune from the siren call of the fascist ideology, with its deceptive egotistical promise of fulfilment.

THE CONTEXT

It seems unfair to associate any one philosophical tradition, let alone any one country, with fascism, yet that is what has happened with Germany, a country which has brought so many cultural and scientific gifts to the world, yet whose name has become historically synonymous with world war and the politics of fascism. In fact, it *is* unfair, not least because fascism is actually an Italian ideology, echoed in Spain, paralleled in Japan; and Hitler himself was an Austrian. Indeed others, such as Karl Popper in the twentieth century, often concentrating more on the superficial aspects than on the philosophical underpinnings, have seen Plato as the original fascist, with the *Republic* providing a paradigm of totalitarianism. But this would be a misreading – both of Plato, and of the fascist ideology. Rarely has a creed been so swiftly and totally severed from its intellectual base.

Fascism, as an ideology, is not particularly repugnant. It is idealistic and, if its practical incarnations are appalling, it is always open to its adherents to say, as the supporters of communism do of the experiment of the Soviet Union, that 'true' fascism has not yet been seen. Nazism bears the same sort of relationship to fascism as Stalinism does to communism, that is to say, a historical rather than a logical one. Nor does fascism have much to do with the present-day holders of the name, who are motivated by a mixture of hatreds and resentments – racism, homophobia, xenophobia, crowned with an emphasis on conflict and 'recognition' – but Nazism certainly does.

Yet conflict and the desire for recognition are the hallmarks of both fascism and Nazism, and both philosophical themes are to be found prominently in German thought, notably in the writings of Hegel. That philosophy professor's dream of a Prussian state run along strictly logical and rational lines does indeed share some characteristics with Plato's, as does his emphasis on the 'universe of mind' existing somewhere apart from the 'universe of nature'. Unlike Plato, though, Hegel mixed together the two universes, creating a very toxic brew.

Georg Wilhelm Hegel (1770–1831) was born in Stuttgart, the son of a minor civil servant, in a rather traditional, conservative, family. The family was also Protestant and Georg was sent to Tübingen seminary, studying there alongside the future poet Friedrich Hölderlin and Friedrich Schelling, his slightly younger fellow philosopher. After this he became a schoolteacher, and all his important work stems from this period, not in fact from his time as a university professor. But his key idea came to him earlier still, when the three German students together witnessed the unfolding of the French revolution and the rise of Napoleon afterwards. It was now that Hegel thought he saw in Napoleon the incarnation of the World-Spirit (the *telos*). The story goes that, with the completed manuscript of *Die Phänomenologie des Geistes (The Phenomenology of Spirit)* lying on his desk,

on the night of October 13, 1806, I saw outside of my study the camp-fires of Napoleon's occupation forces ... Next day, I saw *die Weltseele* (The World Spirit) on horseback marching through the city of Jena.

Or so he wrote in a letter to one of his friends. *The Phenomenology of Spirit* is the book where Hegel offers his 'dialectical' account of the development of consciousness which starts, as the Marxists noted, with individual sensation, proceeds through social concerns expressed in ethics and politics, before culminating one day in pure consciousness of the 'World-Spirit'. For Hegel, as later for both the Marxists and the fascists alike, individual 'freedom' is transcended by people recognising that their essence lies in serving the state. This is the goal of history. And so Hegel, like many political theorists, starts his philosophy with the history of the world.

Drawing heavily on eastern philosophy for many of his ideas, he begins his history with a critical survey of Indian, Persian and Chinese thinkers, claiming that in those societies only the ruler himself had any freedom to think rationally, and that therefore their philosophers were suspect. Only in ancient Greece, according to Hegel, could individuals begin to be rational, albeit they still carried too much intellectual baggage from their religious and social traditions.

Hegel says that it is the Protestant Reformation that suddenly allows each individual the ability to 'find their own salvation', so that a 'glorious mental dawn' occurs. It is then that 'the consciousness of freedom', which is the driving force of history, makes possible the first truly rational communities, such as that exemplified, Hegel suggests, by the Prussian monarchy of his own time. (A system proving its rationality by providing Hegel's professorial salary and position, as Schopenhauer later scoffed.)

THE TEXTS

Hegel's new rational society aims to combine both individual desires – for wealth, for power, for justice – with the social values of the community: a kind of early 'third way' politics. But Hegel's solution also involves reclassifying all desires that are not compatible with the requirements of the social whole as 'irrational', hence not what the individual really wants. Instead, the collective will, the *Geist* (similar, it would seem, to Durkheim's later 'collective consciousness' – though Durkheim's creation does not need any physical form, and Hegel's does) is given complete power and authority. This is what makes Hegel the founding father of the two totalitarian doctrines: fascism and communism.

Lying behind this totalitarian concept of society is a view of the universe not as a collection of fundamental particles, whether atoms or souls, but as a whole, an organic unity. 'The True is the Whole', Hegel writes in *The Phenomenology of Spirit*. It is an illusion to think of anything as separate from anything else, and, in as much as we do so, our thinking is flawed. Actually, even 'the whole', which replaces all these imagined separate objects, is not essentially one substance, but many, just as an organism, such as the human body, is made up of different parts with their own characteristics and functions. Even that most basic distinction, between space and time, results in us misguidedly splitting up the world and thereby losing touch with reality. (This is also what Einstein was concerned to announce in his theories of the 'space–time continuum' and relativity.) Hegel calls reality – this 'whole' – 'the Absolute', and it is his contention that all that is true of the world can be formally deduced from consideration of the Absolute through logic.

But Hegel's notion of logic is different from the usual one. For example, consider a statement like 'the universe is spherical'. For Hegel, this is 'self-contradictory'. It is self-contradictory because the universe is supposed to be infinite, and something cannot be infinite if it is bounded. However, unless the universe is bounded, then it cannot be said to be spherical or indeed to have any shape at all. (While he thought all this certain, mathematicians would disagree.)

This approach illustrates the *dialectic*. The dialectic is a process – here one of reasoning, but it could equally well be of political or economic systems, as it was famously later taken to be by Marx – which proceeds from one view, the thesis, to pose another opposing view – the antithesis. These then combine to produce a synthesis, dissolving the original view, and destroying themselves. However, the synthesis now becomes the new thesis, which in turn is found to be unsatisfactory, so that the process repeats itself.

In the *Science of Logic*, Hegel begins by considering the notion of 'being' as in the proposition 'the Absolute is Pure Being'. But Pure Being without any qualities is nothing, so the Absolute is also not-being or Nothing – the thesis has evoked its own contradiction. The synthesis of this contradiction – the two notions of Pure Being and Nothing – is *Becoming*. (This again is a notion which Hegel has lifted from Eastern philosophy.) And again, the synthesis in turn is still unsatisfactory, so the process continues. Each stage of the dialectic contains elements of the previous stages, so that by the end of the process everything is included, and it is this that is the Absolute.

The progress of abstract categories in the *Logic* is paralleled, Hegel believes, by the progress of societies. History shows us one form of social organisation giving way to another, yet always shuffling forwards towards a kind of 'social absolute'. Again, none of this theory is particularly original to Hegel; the key ideas are there in both oriental and Greek philosophy, and Hegel was well versed in these.

What is more original is that for Hegel, the origin of society is in the first *conflict* between two humans, a 'bloody battle' in which each seeks to make the other recognise them as master, and accept the role of 'slave'. (The conflict between male and female is explained similarly.) In Hegelianism, it is the fear of death that forces part of mankind to submit to the other, and society is perpetually thereafter divided into the two classes: of slaves and masters. It is not material need that propels one class to oppress the other, but a peculiarly human lust for power – the power of the one over another. For many, this risks death, but that is indeed the way towards 'freedom'.

In fact, Hegel modestly claimed his *Phenomenology of Mind* as achieving the final stage in humanity's evolution, by making mankind fully conscious of true freedom. But it *was* still a strange form of freedom – the freedom of following the laws of a monarch or totalitarian state – with Hegel firmly opposed to 'anti-freedom', which was being able to do what you like. He writes:

The history of the world is the discipline of the uncontrolled natural will, bringing it into obedience to a universal principle and conferring subjective freedom ... The German Spirit is the spirit of the new world. Its aim is the realisation of absolute truth as the unlimited self-determination of freedom – that freedom which has its own absolute form as its purpose.

Individuals, for Hegel, have little intrinsic worth, because value resides only in the whole. He identifies Christianity as both the most socially significant religion, and the worst one, because it embodies the political structures of liberal democracy. Christianity suggests that all people are equal, in that they each have a soul of equal worth, and that they are free, in that they are able to choose to live according to the law of God. But Hegel thinks that because it says that God created Man, rather than Man creating God, and because it only offers equality in heaven, Christianity is a *slave ideology*.

Hegel goes on to imply that liberal democracy is also a 'slave ideology' as it offers universal recognition of people's importance, by elevating the Christian edict to 'treat your neighbour as yourself' to a practical legal and political stance.

In his *Encyclopaedia*, Hegel writes:

The aggregate of private persons is often spoken of as the nation. But such an aggregate is a rabble, not a people; and with regard to it, it is the one aim of the state that a nation should not come into existence ... as such an aggregate. Such condition of a nation is a condition of lawlessness, demoralisation, brutishness. In it, the nation would only be a shapeless wild blind force, like that of a stormy, elemental sea, which however is not self-destructive, as the nation – a spiritual element – should be.

The people of the nation are united in facing their common enemies. The heroic state can only emerge through youth, activity, war. 'War has in it the deep meaning that by it the ethical health of the nation is preserved and their finite aims uprooted.' 'War protects the people from the corruption which an everlasting peace would bring upon it.'

Like Machiavelli, Hegel advises that 'to be independent of public opinion is the first condition for achieving anything great'. Instead, Hegel speaks of the 'World Historical Personality' who is able to interpret the sprit of the times and act accordingly.

In public opinion, all is false and true, but to discover the truth in it is the business of the Great Man. The Great Man of this time is he who expresses the will of his time; who tells his time what it wills; and who carries it out.

Hegel's *Volkgeist* ('spirit of the people') philosophy led to Marx and Engels – the neo-Hegelians – adapting and adopting the notion of the dialectic and writing the *Communist Manifesto*; as well as to another 'neo-Hegelian', Giovanni Gentile (in collaboration with Mussolini), writing the *Dottrina del fascismo*. Both doctrines adopt the Hegelian notion of individual self-consciousness being embodied in the state. Both philosophies led to the untold sufferings of millions of ordinary and extraordinary people: victims of ideologues propelled by Hegelian notions of 'the march of history' and with lofty contempt for the sufferings of individuals in the face of it. Both fascism and communism elevated to practical policy an abstract theory that would have been better left to go musty in the common rooms and library of Berlin University.

Indeed, as Hegel's writing, even by the standards of German philosophy, was particularly dry and indigestible, inaccessible to ordinary readers and unlikely to have had any repercussions in the world outside academia, that is most likely what would have happened had it not been for the much more exciting writings of Schopenhauer himself, and later Nietzsche, both of whom owed Hegel more of an intellectual debt than they liked to admit.

At university, Schopenhauer studied medicine, but became interested in philosophy, in particular, Plato, Kant and the ancient Hindu *Upanishads* – a poetical work proclaiming the essential unity of all existence. Together these were the three ingredients of Schopenhauer's proto-existentialist (for want of a real word) work: *The World as Will and Representation*.

The vanity of existence is revealed in the whole form existence assumes: in the infiniteness of time and space contrasted with the finiteness of the individual in both; in the fleeing present as the sole form in which actuality exists; in the contingency and relativity of all things; in continual becoming without being; in continual desire without satisfaction; in the continual frustration in which life consists. (*On the Vanity of Existence*)

Schopenhauer's main idea, developed early, was that beyond the everyday world of experience is a better world in which the human mind pierces appearance to perceive reality. There is *Vorstellung* (representation) and *Wille* (will), which is, he argues, what the world is, in itself. Schopenhauer is a more subtle, profound and, in places, compassionate thinker than Hegel. And whatever the philosophers of his time thought of him, he did later have one influential admirer. One who combined both traditions, and became the prophet of the philosophy of power.

Friedrich Nietzsche's first reading of Schopenhauer's *The World as Will and Representation* came to him, he says, as a revelation – one which he adapted to his own ends. Born in the 'Decade of Revolutions', in 1844 (in the Prussian town of Röcken) Nietzsche sees human beings, and indeed all of life, as engaged in a struggle, a struggle to increase their power. As to alternative theories, for example those of Mill and the utilitarians, as he puts it succinctly in *Twilight of the Idols*, 'Man does not strive after happiness; only the Englishman does that.'

Nietzsche was a philosopher–poet who wrote of Supermen and battles, of 'the will to power', and of magnificent destinies. Yet Nietzsche, the historical man, was a rather less dashing figure, physically unattractive and prone to ill health, headaches and chronic short sight, along with intestinal problems, all together ensuring that he knew little of those two great human pleasures: good food and sleep. It seems likely that he knew little of the third pleasure, either, as there was little romance in his life, despite a claimed 'voracious sexual appetite' and his eventually contracting syphilis. At least, that was what Freud alleged, saying he had contracted it in a Genoese male brothel, explaining Nietzsche's obsession with his own ego as homosexual and narcissistic. (Nietzsche himself did describe a visit to a brothel which took place in 1865, but claimed to have come away without touching anything 'but a piano', from which he would have been most unlucky to have contracted syphilis.) His own self-diagnosis rather feebly blames instead the weather for making him a 'narrow, withdrawn, grumpy specialist' instead of a significant, brave 'spirit'. Then again, he says the sickness 'liberated me slowly', by forcing him to give up his 'bookwormishness'.

At the age of 40, Nietzsche declared himself to be the 'first immoralist' ('proud to possess this word which sets me off against the whole of humanity'), and announced his intention to 'revalue' all values, starting with the unmasking of Christianity (a task already, as we have seen, undertaken by Hegel) before finishing up by, literally, making 'good' 'bad'. Nietzsche prescribes his own version of morality – the anti-morality. Where conventional teaching, epitomised by Christianity, but also so strongly advanced by Socrates, would have it that people should be good, and through being good will come happiness, Nietzsche argues that this 'slave morality' is born out of guilt, weakness and resentment. Good is only a shadow form of the absence of this resentment, whereas in 'master morality', good is primary, being equivalent to 'nobility' and 'strength' (and bad is the derived form, 'low' and 'common', the failure to achieve this). But his task was attempted too late and was never completed. Instead *Ecce Homo*, 'Behold the Man', a semi-blasphemous title in itself, has to stand as his definitive work, for in the spring of 1889 he descended into a twilight world of his own, never emerging from madness.

The end of *Ecce Homo* is supposed to be an ode to his own excellence, but it is more nearly an anthem to the later German fascist creed.

The concept 'God' invented as the antithetical concept in life – everything harmful, noxious, slanderous, the whole mortal enmity against life brought into one terrible unity! The concept 'the Beyond', 'real world' invented so as to deprive of value the *only* world which exists – so as to leave over no goal, no reason, no task for our earthly reality! The concept 'soul', 'spirit', finally even 'immortal soul', invented so as to despise the body, so as to make it sick – 'holy' – so as to bring to all the things in life which deserve serious attention, the questions of nutriment, residence, cleanliness, weather, a horrifying frivolity! ... Finally, it is the most fateful, in the concept of the *good* man common cause made with everything weak, sick, ill-constituted, suffering from itself, all that *which ought to perish* – the law of *selection* crossed, an ideal made of opposition to the proud and well-constituted, to the affirmative man, to the man certain of the future and guaranteeing the future.

It is here that the Nazi policies of eugenics and race found their voice, sitting comfortably alongside Hegel's earlier attempts to recommend the breeding of Prussian characteristics. The fact that Nietzsche's terminal illness was brought on by the sight of a coachman beating his horse in a cruel manner, a spectacle prompting the first immoralist to intervene out of – of all things! – pity, is one of the small ironies of history.

But why did Nietzsche hate Christianity so? Nietzsche's father had been a Lutheran minister, and his mother was the daughter of another. The things are likely connected. Again, his father went mad eventually, and so did Nietzsche, from 1889. Perhaps it is the incipient sense of insanity that makes his writings so distinctive. After his father's death, the young Nietzsche was brought up in Naumburg by his mother, her sisters and, from his father's side, his grandmother and two of her sisters. The experience did not agree with him. Alongside his dislike of the meek, forgiving, caring Christian, Nietzsche's philosophy is characterised by a deep contempt for womankind. The other half of the species are seen as incapable of 'greatness', and his writing is sprinkled liberally with snide references often of no particular relevance to the philosophical issues under discussion.

Who knows? Perhaps I am the first psychologist of the eternal-womanly. They all love me – an old story: excepting the *abortive* women, the 'emancipated' who lack the stuff for children. Happily, I am not prepared to be torn to pieces: the complete woman tears to pieces when she loves ... I know these amiable *maenads* ... Ah, what a dangerous, creeping, subterranean little beast of prey it is! And so pleasant with it! ... A little woman chasing after her revenge would over-run fate itself. The woman is unspeakably more wicked than the man, also cleverer; goodness in a woman is already a form of *degeneration*.

Strangely enough, despite Freud's theory, Nietzsche spent much time happily with both his sister Elisabeth, who later wrote up his notes, and thereby earned the blame of subsequent philosophers for everything 'bad' in his philosophy and the credit for nothing meretricious, as well as with his mother; and indeed wooing 'Lou', a lady friend, with whom he posed in a photograph with a cart, Lou holding a whip, and Nietzsche and friend acting as the horses. Some might look for evidence of sexual confusions in the fact that the young Nietzsche had been sent (like Schopenhauer) to a respectable German boarding school at an impressionable age. It was there that he immediately stood out by writing a precocious essay in praise of Hölderlin, a then uncelebrated German poet whose work also had the mark of insanity. This scarcely reassured his teachers, who already (wrongly) considered the young Nietzsche to be physically suspect by virtue of his father's illness, but Nietzsche eventually did go to university where he studied theology and philosophy. His eccentric style impressed others so much that at the scandalously young age of 24 he was made a professor without ever so much as having had to write a 'serious' essay. Leipzig conferred a doctorate without thesis or examination, and Nietzsche was free thereafter to concentrate on his bizarre but original work.

Typical of this was what emerged after Nietzsche looked at ancient Greek society. Instead of idolising it as a cultured and rational theatre, source of enlightened ideas and virtues, as other philosophers did, under Nietzsche it becomes a dreadful place, full of the screams and sounds of drunken excess from Dionysian orgies, culminating eventually in (magnificent) tragedy, full of unspeakable horror. Nietzsche liked the idea of such orgies. Developing his theme in *Of the Use and Disadvantage of History for Life* (1874), he wrote (as already noted) that the goal of humanity is not in some supposed general strategy or process, such as the maximisation of happiness, but is rather in the activities of its 'highest specimens'. These are men who 'transcend history', and are bound by no laws other than that of their own pleasure. 'The man who would not belong in the mass needs only to cease being comfortable with himself; he should follow his conscience which shouts at him: 'Be yourself!' You are not really all you do, think, and desire now' (*Schopenhauer as Educator*, 1874).

Like Hegel, Nietzsche applies his theory of power to history, and makes some illuminating new interpretations, all based on power psychology. The Superman – *Übermensch* – (sometimes implausibly translated as the 'Overman', which sounds like some sort of waterproof shoe) is for Nietzsche the logical outcome of his theory, an individual enjoying his (and it must be *his*) power to the full, untrammelled by notions of justice or pity. In 1884, Nietzsche wrote, in *Der Wille zur Macht*, 'One must learn from war to associate death with the interests for which one fights – that makes us proud; [and to] learn to sacrifice many and to take one's cause seriously enough not to spare human lives.' Uplifting thoughts like this led Hitler to include snippets of Nietzsche in the army packs for his storm troopers.

In fact, Hitler read Nietzsche avidly, seeing in the philosopher some sort of fellow spirit, and Nietzsche's philosophy was adopted and quoted by the Nazis as in some sense embodying Nazi values. It is the discussion of the 'master–slave' relationship that is of most historical resonance. But many of Nietzsche's rhetorical flourishes, such as the despising of the weak, the sick and the handicapped, also fed easily and conveniently into the policies of the Nazi state – even if, as was indubitably also the case, Nietzsche himself had no time for theories of racial supremacy and actually admired the Jews for having crucified the Christian prophet. In fact, Nietzsche even rails regularly against his fellow countrymen: 'As far as Germany extends, it ruins culture ... the Germans are incapable of any conception of Greatness'; 'the Germans have no idea whatever how common they are; but that is the superlative of commonness – they are not even ashamed of being German'.

The Nazi propagandists got around this apparent contradiction by explaining that his writing was merely a criticism of Germany before the Third Reich. And Hitler too regularly derides his fellow countrymen in *Mein Kampf*. More importantly, Nietzsche's anti-morality certainly elevated war to the status of being an end in itself. 'Among the decisive preconditions for a Dionysian task is the hardness of the hammer, joy even in destruction.' In the concluding chapter of *Ecce Homo*, 'Why I Am Destiny', Nietzsche says in a passage which appears both gleefully and uncannily to anticipate the Holocaust:

I know my fate. One day, there will be associated with my name the recollection of something frightful – of a crisis like no other before on earth, of the profoundest collision of conscience, of a decision evoked against everything that until then had been believed in, demanded, sanctified. I am not a man, I am dynamite.

Hitler certainly saw himself as a kind of 'philosophical despot and artist tyrant' as imagined by the philosopher. In one of his works, Nietzsche explains how such despots will

mould men as an artist would ... to achieve that universal energy of greatness, to mould the future man by breeding and, at the same time, by destroying millions of bungled humans, we will not be deterred by the suffering we create, the equal of which has never been seen!

There has been some debate about the influence of his sister Elisabeth and his friend Peter Gass, who edited his books, in misrepresenting his philosophy, inserting, it is said, the 'Nazi' elements.

But even in the notebooks he carried around with him and in which he made notes for his eventual books, his ideas are clear: the need to unshackle the great men from the constraints of morality; the philosopher's role in creating society. In the notebook for Autumn 1887, he writes:

The progressive diminishment of man is what drives one to think about the breeding of a stronger race, a race whose surplus would lie precisely in those wares where the diminished species was becoming weak and weaker (will, responsibility, self-assurance, the capacity to set itself goals).

He continues:

The necessity of a chasm opening, of distance, of an order of rank is thus given: not the necessity of slowing down the process ... As soon as it is achieved, this levelled species requires justification: that justification is the service of the higher, sovereign type which stands upon it and can only rise to its own task from that position ... Not merely a master race, whose task would be limited to governing, but a race with its own sphere of life, with a surplus of force for beauty, value, culture, manners, right up to the highest intellectual realm: an affirming race which can grant itself every great luxury ... strong enough not to need the tyranny of the virtue-imperative, rich enough not to need thrift and pedantry, beyond good and evil.

In words strikingly similar to Hitler later, he offers some of the most promising curbs and remedies for 'modernity':

1. universal military service, with real wars and no more joking
2. national bigotry (simplifying, focusing; admittedly sometimes also squeezing dry and exhausting with overwork)
3. improved nutrition (meat)
4. increasingly clean and healthy dwellings
5. domination of physiology over theology, moralism, economics and politics
6. military severity in demanding and dealing with 'what one is expected to do' (no more 'praising' ...)

In the notebook for Autumn 1887, otherwise preoccupied with lamenting the abolition of slavery and the propaganda of treating people as 'equal', Nietzsche speaks of his struggle against Rousseau and his notion of natural man as good. It is a philosophy born, Nietzsche declares fiercely, 'out of a hatred of aristocratic culture'. In the notebook for Spring 1888, he adds some more advice 'On the asceticism of the Strong', which runs:

First stage: to endure atrocities; to commit atrocities.
Second, more difficult, stage: to endure baseness; to commit basenesses: including, as a preliminary exercise: to become ludicrous, make oneself ludicrous.

– to provoke contempt and nevertheless sustain distance by means of an (unfathomable) smile from above
– to take upon oneself a number of degrading crimes, e.g. stealing money, so as to test one's sense of balance.
... not to be afraid of the five bad things: cowardice, ill-repute, vice, lying, woman.

Nietzsche's writings are not really terribly good literature – but the philosophers think they are. And they are not really terribly good philosophy – but the literary critics think they are. Both are impressed by his rejection of 'rationality' (Socrates' 'great mistake') and by his 'deliberate contradictions'. In this way, he has been able to retain a largely undeserved reputation for profundity and originality.

Philosophically, Nietzsche's point is that there is no meaning to life except that which individuals can create for themselves. The only way out of this futility and meaninglessness for the individual is through action and creation – and the purest form of these is through the exercise of power. In practice, the Nazi state promised individuals a chance to have power over others, and to enjoy it, untrammelled, as Nietzsche said, by 'notions of justice or pity'.

Nietzsche's legacy is not so much a philosophical justification for anti-morality, as a philosophical precedent for it. He offers legitimacy to those seeking to explain why fundamental offences against common morality are not important. The chain of ideas that led from Hegel through Schopenhauer to Nietzsche was now ready to be given a concrete incarnation in Italy.

ITALIAN FASCISM

Fascism, although widely bandied about as a term for any regime that people disapprove of, is correctly identified as the ideology of the Italian Fascists in the first half of the twentieth century under Benito Mussolini. And Mussolini actually started his career as a socialist, gradually developing extreme syndicalist notions centred around an all-powerful state. The manifesto of his party can be said to be *La dottrina del fascismo*, written by Mussolini and the former liberal Giovanni Gentile, a respected 'neo-Hegelian' philosopher.

In a sense, Hitler's Nazis were barely 'fascists' – in the same way that they were barely 'socialists', national or otherwise. Mussolini and Gentile's doctrine was rather more subtle and persuasive.

Gentile gave fascism an idealistic and spiritual aspect. Where liberalism and socialism sought to benefit each individual, fascism sought to benefit the nation. As President Kennedy put it once, people were not to ask what the state could do for them, but only ask what they could do for the state. The well-being of the nation provided a high moral purpose for each individual, a purpose that took precedence over the squabbles of workers and unions on the one hand, and of capitalists and libertarians on the other. The original fascists felt that the philosophies both of socialism and of individualism served only to divide the nation and weaken it. Hence, instead of trade unions and private enterprise, fascists created a single unifying force, capable of ensuring that companies and workers alike worked in the interests of the state. This force was to be the Fascist party, united behind a charismatic leader. The Fascists created Weber's ideal of the bureaucracy under the charismatic leader.

But Gentile's language in describing the benefits of this approach went further too. Fascism, he wrote, echoing Hegel, would restore the patriotic morality of 'service, sacrifice and indeed death'.

The elements of the Fascist state are set out in an official government publication written by Benito Mussolini and Gentile, *The Doctrine of Fascism* (1932) in which it is explained that 'many of the practical expressions of Fascism, such as party organization, system of education, and discipline can only be understood when considered in relation to its general attitude toward life'. And the document continues:

A spiritual attitude. Fascism sees in the world not only those superficial, material aspects in which man appears as an individual, standing by himself, self-centered, subject to natural law, which instinctively urges him toward a life of selfish momentary pleasure; it sees not only the individual but the nation and the country; individuals and generations bound together by a moral law, with common traditions and a mission which suppressing the instinct for life closed in a brief circle of pleasure, builds up a higher life, founded on duty, a life free from the limitations of time and space, in which the individual, by self-sacrifice, the renunciation of self-interest, by death itself, can achieve that purely spiritual existence in which his value as a man consists.

Like Hegel, the fascist:

conceives of life as a struggle in which it behooves a man to win for himself a really worthy place, first of all by fitting himself (physically, morally, intellectually) to become the implement required for winning it. As for the individual, so for the nation, and so for mankind. Hence the high value of culture in all its forms (artistic, religious, scientific) and the outstanding importance of education. Hence also the essential value of work, by which man subjugates nature and creates the human world (economic, political, ethical, and intellectual).

The idea that fascists, let alone the Nazis, had no ethical sense is misleading. Both philosophies insist on their superior ethics. Mussolini explains:

This positive conception of life is obviously an ethical one. It invests the whole field of reality as well as the human activities which master it. No action is exempt from moral judgment; no activity can be despoiled of the value which a moral purpose confers on all things. Therefore life, as conceived of by the Fascist, is serious, austere, and religious; all its manifestations are poised in a world sustained by moral forces and subject to spiritual responsibilities. The Fascist disdains an 'easy' life.

Again following Hegel, the 'Anti-individualistic, the Fascist conception of life stresses the importance of the State and accepts the individual only in so far as his interests coincide with those of the State'. The state stands for the 'conscience and the universal will of man as a historic entity'. Mussolini and Gentile say specifically it is 'opposed to classical liberalism', which they interpret in dialectical fashion as 'a reaction to absolutism' that has now 'exhausted its historical function'. Instead the new Fascist state is 'the expression of the conscience and will of the people'. Liberalism, they finish, denied the state in the name of the individual; Fascism reasserts it:

Fascism stands for liberty, and for the only liberty worth having, the liberty of the State and of the individual within the State. The Fascist conception of the State is all-embracing; outside of it no human or spiritual values can exist, much less have value.

It follows from this that the fascist is

opposed to trade unionism as a class weapon. But when brought within the orbit of the State, Fascism recognizes the real needs which gave rise to socialism and trade unionism, giving them due weight in the guild or corporative system in which divergent interests are coordinated and harmonized in the unity of the State.

Fascism is also opposed to 'that form of democracy which equates a nation to the majority, lowering it to the level of the largest number'. It blames liberalism for the First World War, saying that never has any religion claimed so cruel a sacrifice. Instead of liberalism, Fascism 'denies the materialistic conception of happiness as a possibility, and abandons it to the economists of the mid-eighteenth century'. 'This means that Fascism denies the equation: well-being = happiness, which sees in men mere animals, content when they can feed and fatten, thus reducing them to a vegetative existence pure and simple.'

In place of liberal democracy is put 'the will of the mass, of the whole group ethnically molded by natural and historical conditions into a nation, advancing, as one conscience and one will, along the self same line of development and spiritual formation'. However,

the Italian doctrine then stresses, this is 'Not a race, nor a geographi-
cally defined region, but a people, historically perpetuating itself; a
multitude unified by an idea and imbued with the will to live, the
will to power, self-consciousness, personality.'

THE SUBTEXT

Fascism was not just an economic theory, or a quasi-legal structure of
rights, but much more – a way to live and a way to attain fulfilment.
It was not enough to do what the Fascist government said – the Fascist
citizen also had to *want* to do it, and to believe in doing it. That is
why one of the most potent images of the Fascist state is of massive
parades lined with enthusiastically waving crowds.

Mussolini added to this his own notion of fascism as an 'action
theory' – and the highest form of action was violence. It was only
through violence that individual Fascists could truly fulfil themselves
and it was only through wars that the Fascist state could maintain its
ideological purity. When Mussolini used violence to seize power in
Italy in 1922, the process was part of the new way of governing – not
just a necessary prerequisite. In many people's eyes, the courage of the
Fascists in fighting for power conferred nobility on the movement and
cleansed it of the impurities of the shambling democratic state. (Hitler
intended his failed Munich 'Putsch' to be the same sort of thing.)

Like Hitler, but certainly not like Nietzsche, Mussolini also stressed
nationalism. For Mussolini, Bismarck was a great figure, who had
succeeded in binding together the various elements of Germany into
a powerful nation, and he also admired Machiavelli for what he saw
as Machiavelli's endorsement of power, especially military power
– ignoring or missing the earlier Italian's emphasis on justice.

However, Mussolini's nationalism should not be confused with the
German brand, which identified nationality with 'race'. Crucially, for
Mussolini, it was the role of the state to create a people out of what in
reality would be a mix of very different races. Instead Hitler created
a chilling system of bureaucratic rules and structures, all aiming to
make logical a doctrine of racial purity created out of irrational hatred
and prejudice. Yet Mussolini himself, the father of Fascism, even
wrote at one point explicitly that *a people is not a race*; instead it is a
group united by an idea perpetuating itself. However, over the period
of the Second World War, Italian Fascism too adopted the anti-Semitic
policies of the Nazis, and even if these were never implemented
with any enthusiasm by the Italians, increasing German pressure

for action, together with Nazi officers gradually taking control of the region, led to much the same end.

Likewise, although Mussolini built up a fairly efficient party machine, and installed party members in key jobs, it was left to Hitler on the right, and Stalin on the left, to really create the conditions of fear and total control that the fascist philosophy suggested. Mussolini banned strikes and nationalised key industries, but Italy's economic performance remained stuck at the same levels. The claim that Mussolini at least 'made the trains run on time' is probably the greatest thing that can be said of his fascist society, and this claim is largely apocryphal.

For, indeed, Italy proved infertile soil for its new seed. The most extreme symbol of Italian Fascism – the Abyssinian exploit, in which the Italian army annexed their former colony – was barely achieved, shocking though it was as an example of a sophisticated modern army attacking simple villagers with planes and bombs. (Nowadays, such wickedness is a commonplace. Even the most liberal democrats scarcely hesitate to order the use of such force.) It was also evident to all that the Fascists had little more than self-aggrandisement and defiance of the League of Nations as their aims.

The Italian people had as much appreciation of grand displays as anyone, but they also had a well-developed distrust and cynicism about the motives of their leaders, and the Fascists were no exception. Unlike the German SS, the Italian army was made up of conscripts who were disinclined to fight for a political party, and perhaps also reluctant to abandon their humanity for an ideology. Ordinary Italians largely refused to go down the path of atrocity that others were to explore so eagerly.

KEY IDEAS

For Fascism,

- all life is a striving after *power*, with human beings important only as the means to the ends of the exercise of this power;
- the state should be organised rationally, with individuals complying with and fitting in to its requirements.

If we recall, with Smith, that 'wealth, as Mr Hobbes says, is power', and that money is power in tangible, exchangeable form, then there are parallels between the more radical doctrines of materialism and fascism. It can be argued that the philosophical appeal of life as the pursuit of power goes deeper than just a historical stage, apparently now passed through.

KEY TEXTS

Nietzsche's *Ecce Homo* (1908)
Benito Mussolini's *The Doctrine of Fascism* (1932)

Timeline:
The Modern Era:
From Fordism to Fascism

1903
Henry Ford sets up an automobile company, and the first Model T cars follow five years later. The first coast-to-coast crossing of the United States by car takes just 65 days. Meanwhile, in Britain, Emmeline Pankhurst sets up a Women's Social and Political Union to demand the vote.

1906
The Trades Disputes Act in Britain allows unions to organise strike action without being liable for damages in the civil courts, thus evening up the balance between employers and employed.

1907
Free meals and medical care for school children, and pensions for the retired, are introduced in Britain. The state has assumed responsibility for looking after its citizens.

1909
Sweden introduces votes for all adults, male and female, but campaigns by the suffragettes in Britain for the same rights are unsuccessful, and the leaders of the movement are imprisoned in 1913.

1915
Poison gas is used for the first time, during the First World War. Hitler is one of the first soldiers to suffer the effects. A year later, the Battle of the Somme results in over 1 million casualties.

1917
In October, the Bolsheviks overthrow Russia's provisional government and Lenin becomes Chief Commissar. Within months, the revolutionary Bolshevik government in Russia nationalises all large-scale industries.

1919

Benito Mussolini establishes the Italian Fascists. Out of the ruins of the First World War have emerged two great ideological forces – fascism and communism.

15
Hitler's Doctrine of Hate

National Socialism, or Nazism as it is normally known, is not discussed much these days. It is, to put it mildly, rather a discredited doctrine. But here is a peculiar thing. The principles of National Socialism live on in political circles in many of the world's governments today. Patriotism, military strength, building a strong nation, suspicion and dislike of 'the other', loathing of communism, manipulation of public opinion, ruthless indifference to the effects of their foreign policy – all of these are still common currency.

In Mein Kampf, *Hitler, surely the first tyrant to be democratically elected on a* programme *of tyranny, outlines a sophisticated method for controlling and directing public opinion, starting from a shrewd understanding of the other, darker side of human nature.*

THE CONTEXT

History, it is said, needs at least 50 years' perspective before it can make its judgments. Yet, over 60 years since his suicide, it is often easier to dismiss Hitler as a 'madman', and leave his philosophy, as unashamedly and precisely set out in *Mein Kampf*, unread. After all, to do otherwise is to raise up the spectres of the tragedy that was Nazism, to hear again the thud of the fists and boots of Nazi 'storm troopers', crushing, as Hitler frequently gloats, the heads of those who organised against him. Why bother with the long passages of rabid, one might well say pathological anti-Semitism, railing against what he describes as the worldwide Jewish conspiracy of Marxism. Yet Hitler's influence is by no means so easily dismissed. Take, for instance, Nazism's three main practical recommendations:

- destruction of trade unions as protectors of the whole class of workers
- devotion of the nation's resources to the development of military power as an instrument of national policy and measure of national pride
- single-minded centralisation of power in one central government headed by a supposedly charismatic figure.

These have all become the 'modern' consensus. If today (since the collapse of apartheid South Africa) few countries formally prefer one racial group over all the others, it is a commonplace that countries project their 'national interest' at the expense of everyone else. Even Hitler's aim, which he proposed to the Allies as a way of solving 'the Jewish problem', of driving the Jewish people out of Europe to a separate state, has been followed. The tragedy of the founding of a 'Jewish state' anywhere, let alone in Palestine, is that it had of necessity to be built upon racial and religious discrimination, and be designed to split people apart.

More subtle legacies of the Nazi philosophy abound as well. There is the elevation of propaganda as a way of manipulating opinion and controlling the population; the calculated use of rites and the creation of traditions to create a charismatic aura around the leader of the government; central government control of education; creation of an all-powerful police and secretive security apparatus. In terms of ideology, even before the dust had settled from the destruction of the Second World War, the United States had opened up a new front on 'communism', thereby carrying on Hitler's obsession. Scarcely remarkable, then, to note that surveys today show that most US citizens believe that the Russians were the enemy against whom the war was fought – not the key ally that turned the tide against Nazism. All that is left to bridge the contradiction with the supposed war aims are frequent government pronouncements on their dedication to the causes of 'liberty', 'democracy' and 'freedom'. But *Mein Kampf* too is full to the brim of these great words, along with pious references to serving the will of the people, or even more ludicrously, 'the Lord', and decorated with paeans to beauty, nobility and goodness.

Mein Kampf is such an obnoxious document that perhaps the most remarkable thing about it is that people were prepared to support Hitler, the Nazi party and their programme. This surely says something profound if unwelcome about human nature. Hitler had considerable support amongst the general population, particularly women. This last factor has been often neglected. Women, who had only gained the right to vote, along with guarantees of equality, in the 'democratic revolution' of 1918, handed Hitler, who announced that women were inferior human beings and advocated the most extreme social discrimination, victory at the polls in 1932.

The conventional view is that what gave the Nazis so much support was their image as a determined force of order and reconstruction at a time when all traditional structures – be they economic or social

– seemed to break down. Yet, of course, the NSDAP (National Socialist German Workers' Party) and the *SturmAbteilung* (SA, or 'Protection Division') in particular did their utmost to exacerbate the chaos from which they promised to deliver Germany. The reality was that the 'establishment', the old elites and the bosses of the centre-right parties, like Lloyd George, agreed with many Nazi goals even though they had misgivings about the NSDAP's violence and radicalism or sniffed at its 'plebeian' character.

This is why the so-called democratic parties were prepared to tolerate Hitler's violent coup attempt, which failed due to the loyalty of the army and police to the official government. When a terrifying column of 3,000 Nazis, brandishing their usual batons, led by Hitler, Göring and Ludendorff, marched toward the War Ministry in the centre of Munich, they were stopped there by a contingent of about a hundred armed policemen. Hitler demanded that they surrender, but they refused to and when the Nazis tried to press through they opened fire. A few minutes later, 16 Nazis and three policemen were dead. Göring was shot in the groin and Hitler himself was injured after falling over. Afterwards, Hitler, contrary to the 'death or glory' image of himself in *Mein Kampf*, then crawled along the pavement to avoid being seen by the police before dashing to a waiting car, leaving his comrades behind. The rest of the Nazis scattered or were arrested.

Hitler spent the next few days hiding in a friend's attic. He expected to be shot by the authorities. On the third night, the police arrived and he was arrested and taken to the prison at Landsberg, where his spirits lifted somewhat after he was told he was going to get a public trial. The Republic had been saved by the courageous action of its guardians, but now here is a curious thing. The authorities allowed him to be 'tried' by two Nazi-sympathisers, who let him use the court case as a propaganda opportunity and launch long rambling denunciations of the government that had so narrowly managed to stave off his insurrection. His closing statement was widely admired: 'for it is not you, gentlemen, who pass judgement on us. That judgement is spoken by the eternal court of history.'

Newspapers quoted Hitler at length. For the first time, the German people as a whole had a chance to get acquainted with this man and his thinking. And many liked what they heard. In due course the judges admonished rather than punished Hitler for his capital crime, which had cost the lives of the three policemen, imposing a five-year sentence, reduced by parole to six months, to be served in the old fortress at Landsberg. It was here, in a spacious private apartment with a fine view, filled with his own furniture and gifts, that Hitler received visitors (whenever he liked) and dictated the text of *Mein Kampf* to his own private secretary, Rudolph Hess.

It was this celebrity 'imprisonment', that propelled the Nazis from regional impotency to becoming Germany's largest political party. And even when Hitler submitted a bill to the Reichstag that granted the government the right to decree laws without any parliamentary control for the following four years (the Enabling Act), the centre-right parties overcame any misgivings and approved the bill.

In reality, they became the gravediggers of the last remainders of German democracy and of their own parties. On 23 March, when the bill was passed with the necessary two-thirds majority, only the SPD deputies, surrounded by SA guards and Nazi flags, voted against it, and their leader made a courageous speech (echoing Machiavelli too) arguing that the Nazis had power on their side but not justice.

THE TEXT

Unlike *Capital*, to which Hitler compares his work, *Mein Kampf* (which translates as 'My Struggle') is surprisingly readable. Hitler would, I am sure, have made a successful newspaper columnist or 'spin doctor', if not really much of an author. He claims to have 'dictated' it while in prison following his unsuccessful 1923 'Putsch', and it reads in many places more like entries in a personal diary than a philosophical analysis. But then Hitler was, of course, an egomaniac.

It opens with an engaging, even amusing, account of his arrival in Vienna, the grand capital of Austria, from the small school in the provinces.

I had set out with a pile of drawings, convinced that it would be child's play to pass the examination. At the *Realschule* I had been by far the best in my class at drawing, and since then my ability had developed amazingly; my own satisfaction caused me to take a joyful pride in hoping for the best ...

Yet sometimes a drop of bitterness put in its appearance: my talent for painting seemed to be excelled by my talent for drawing, especially in almost all fields of architecture. At the same time my interest in architecture as such increased steadily, and this development was accelerated after a two weeks' trip to Vienna which I took when not yet sixteen. The purpose of my trip was to study the picture gallery in the Court Museum, but I had eyes for scarcely anything but the Museum itself. From morning until late at night, I ran from one object of interest to another, but it was always the buildings which held my primary interest. For hours I could stand in front of the Opera, for hours I could gaze at the Parliament; the whole Ring Boulevard seemed to me like an enchantment out of *The Thousand-and-One-Nights*.

This is the personable, the charming Mr Hitler that so impressed western statesman. Like a modern-day president appearing as special guest on a chat show, Hitler is a leader who knows how to tell little personal stories. However, Hitler does not intend his account to be amusing. He is unaware of any irony. When the Director of the Art School tells him that he might do better to try and study architecture, he assumes this is recognition of another great talent of his, rather than as a polite way of getting rid of him. (Hitler, after all, could hardly enrol to study architecture, as he lacked the preliminary qualifications, whereas he was eligible to enter art school.)

Impossible or no, a few lines later, Hitler returns to Vienna, declaring that his 'old defiance had come back' and his goal was now clear and definite: 'I wanted to become an architect, and obstacles do not exist to be surrendered to, but only to be broken.' Although not, it would seem, obstacles to becoming an artist. In this small way, the teenage Hitler reveals himself to be a blusterer capable of deceiving himself with his own rhetoric. Alas, this character trait would have rather more serious consequences later.

Of course, Hitler did not become an architect either. Instead, he ambled leisurely around Vienna like a little aristocrat, dissipating the family inheritance until it eventually ran out. After that, he was dependent on charities offering food and shelter for the poor, the kind of social services for 'down and outs' that he despised, and any money he could earn shovelling snow or painting street scenes. Hitler does not admit any of this in *Mein Kampf,* other than in vague references to how he was 'hardened' by poverty. He does not mention that he sold his paintings in small shops often owned and run by 'the Jews'. Instead, here is how Hitler describes 'meeting his first Jew' in the street in Vienna:

Once, as I was strolling through the Inner City, I suddenly encountered an apparition in a black caftan and black hair locks. Is this a Jew? was my first thought. For, to be sure, they had not looked like that in Linz. I observed the man furtively and cautiously, but the longer I stared at this foreign face, scrutinising feature for feature, the more my first question assumed a new form: Is this a German?

... As always in such cases, I now began to try to relieve my doubts by books. For a few hellers I bought the first anti-Semitic pamphlets of my life.

Unfortunately, they all proceeded from the supposition that in principle the reader knew or even understood the Jewish question to a certain degree. Besides, the tone for the most part was such that doubts again arose in me, due in part to the dull and amazingly unscientific arguments favouring the thesis.

In a neat piece of values reversal, Hitler says he 'relapsed for weeks at a time, once even for months', unsure of whether to hate these people – or not.

The whole thing seemed to me so monstrous, the accusations so boundless, that, tormented by the fear of doing injustice, I again became anxious and uncertain.

Hitler credits the Zionists with a key role in solidifying his racial views, saying that 'whatever doubts I may still have nourished were finally dispelled by the attitude of a portion of the Jews themselves'. Hitler does not like Zionists either, of course, although significantly alone out of the Jewish groups they continued to be allowed to function under the Nazis. He considers it 'one of the most ingenious tricks that was ever devised', to make this state sail under the flag of 'religion', thereby, he implausibly adds, 'assuring it of the tolerance which the Aryan is always ready to accord a religious creed'. The reality is very different, he continues (still not referring to the tolerance of the Aryan race to minorities either). But then the Nazis could be very pragmatic and even set up a special system whereby rich 'Jews' could buy papers officially confirming their German origins. (The philosopher Wittgenstein used this system to buy such papers for his sisters.)

But back to Hitler on the Zionists. He says that, in a short time, 'this apparent struggle between Zionistic and liberal Jews disgusted me; for it was false through and through, founded on lies and scarcely in keeping with the moral elevation and purity always claimed by this people'. Hitler immediately juxtaposes these ideas of 'moral elevation and purity' with some of his crudest racialist language, part of what he elsewhere describes as 'talking the language of the streets'.

The cleanliness of this people, moral and otherwise, I must say, is a point in itself. By their very exterior you could tell that these were no lovers of water, and, to your distress, you often knew it with your eyes closed. Later I often grew sick to my stomach from the smell of these caftan-wearers. Added to this, there was their unclean dress and their generally unheroic appearance.

Mind you, this is still just a personal dislike. Hitler has yet to establish the political significance. This he speedily attempts.

In a short time I was made more thoughtful than ever by my slowly rising insight into the type of activity carried on by the Jews in certain fields. Was there any form of filth or profligacy, particularly in cultural life, without at least one Jew involved in it? If you cut even cautiously into such an abscess, you found, like a maggot in a rotting body, often dazzled by the sudden light – a – kike!

Now, encouraged as ever by his own spleen, Hitler excitedly continues to describe his 'findings':

I now began to examine carefully the names of all the creators of unclean products in public artistic life. The result was less and less favourable for my previous attitude toward the Jews. Regardless how my sentiment might resist, my reason was forced to draw its conclusions. The fact [was] that nine tenths of all literary filth, artistic trash, and theatrical idiocy can be set to the account of a people.

Similarly, the 'deeper he probed' into the arts, the more the object of his 'former admiration' shrivelled. He complains that the

style became more and more unbearable; I could not help rejecting the content as inwardly shallow and banal; the objectivity of exposition now seemed to me more akin to lies than honest truth; and the writers were – Jews. A thousand things which I had hardly seen before now struck my notice, and others, which had previously given me food for thought, I now learned to grasp and understand.

Nonetheless, this is all still superficial observation. The great insight came when, as Hitler puts it, he 'recognised the Jew as the leader of Social Democracy'. On this day, 'the scales dropped from my eyes. A long soul struggle had reached its conclusion.' This is the 'struggle' of the title, *Mein Kampf*, and it illustrates why the persecution of the Jews dominated Hitler's political programme, even at the expense of his military aims.

Yet it is a profound error to focus on Hitler's hatred of the 'Jews' in order to untangle his philosophy and its subtle influence and appeal. In fact, Hitler was not really attacking that group of religiously observant 'Jews' that would have been immediately identifiable, but specifically creating a kind of monster 'race', some of whom are observant Jews – and hence easily identifiable – and some of whom are not. The 'Jews' are everywhere, especially among the ranks of the 'social democrats' and the leaders of the trade unions, in journalism and in art. In fact, everyone Hitler dislikes is called a 'Jew'.

Nazism is a philosophy with only one plank – prejudice. It was successful because racial prejudice, however outrageous, however irrational, is never very deeply buried in the human psyche. Hitler launched his early tirades, as he would his later wars, against many other categories of 'inferior humans' too. There were the Slavs who had taken the land that rightly belonged to the German people (and of whom in due course many tens of millions would perish); there were the 'negroes' that he accuses of having begun to threaten Europe's bloodlines 'via France' (that's two race cards played at once!); and even what he calls the 'yellow races', such as the Japanese. If, a few years later, Hitler would rely on the Japanese alliance for his strategy of war, in *Mein Kampf* he calls such a tactic 'almost unpardonable', on account of his racial theories. Indeed, even his future allies the Italians are clearly to be avoided – Hitler refers to their blood as 'hopelessly adulterated' – especially in the south. Hitler explains the significance to the German public with a crude parody of evolutionary theory:

Any crossing of two beings not at exactly the same level produces a medium between the level of the two parents. This means: the offspring will probably stand higher than the racially lower parent, but not as high as the higher one. Consequently, it will later succumb in the struggle against the higher level. Such mating is contrary to the will of Nature for a higher breeding of all life. The precondition for this does not lie in associating superior and inferior, but in the total victory of the former. The stronger must dominate and not blend with the weaker, thus sacrificing his own greatness.

He goes on:

A stronger race will drive out the weak, for the vital urge in its ultimate form will, time and again, burst all the absurd fetters of the so-called humanity of individuals, in order to replace it by the humanity of Nature which destroys the weak to give his place to the strong.

Hitler's political philosophy revolves around this unhappy caricature of Darwinism. He imagines an ideal people, the 'Aryan race', and credits them with a historical mission. '*All the human culture, all the results of art, science, and technology that we see before us today, are almost exclusively the creative product of the Aryan.*' Hitler tells us that during his 'worker' period he read widely, but does not say what. However, the language is reminiscent of Hegel, not to mention Heidegger, today one of the most highly respected western philosophers, who was an enthusiastic member of the Nazi party and likewise considered the Germans to have a historic role in the history of the world and the development of 'culture'. Here is what Hitler says though, in one of his characteristic, ridiculous pieces of populism:

All the human culture, all the results of art, science, and technology that we see before us today, are almost exclusively the creative product of the Aryan. This very fact admits of the not unfounded inference that he alone was the founder of all higher humanity, therefore representing the prototype of all that we understand by the word 'man'. He is the Prometheus of mankind from whose bright forehead the divine spark of genius has sprung at all times, forever kindling anew that fire of knowledge which illumined the night of silent mysteries and thus caused man to climb the path to mastery over the other beings of this earth. Exclude him – and perhaps after a few thousand years darkness will again descend on the earth, human culture will pass, and the world turn to a desert.

Even though Hitler's super-race excludes most of his listeners, this sort of philosophy was attractive to many in his audience. If that seems strange, it is only like the well-noted paradox today whereby it is possible to advocate the channelling of wealth towards a privileged few, and be applauded enthusiastically by the plebeian majority who will gain nothing, indeed may have to pay, yet prefer to imagine themselves as one of the elite.

And surely, the rewards dangled before the public for supporting Hitler and his Nazi programme were rather meagre. Hitler adopts a contemptuous tone towards 'the Germans' and regularly castigates their supposed weakness and failings. He warns the 'imperfect' ones that they will not even be allowed to have children, only to undertake military service and expect to die for their country. And in the meantime, of course, they must work harder. Is it here that lies the secret of the success of Nazism, as evidenced by the rapid growth of the movement? Or is it rather in the negative invocation of the power of hate? A chance to hate 'an enemy within' society – the cause of poverty, of strife and sickness. The enemy that Hitler calls 'social democracy'. The enemy that consists of the 'reds', the trade unionists, the pornographers, the handicapped, the deviant artists and so on. It is such a long and confusing list of enemies that it is no wonder that Hitler invents a simple version. All of the bad things in German society, indeed in the world, are the fault of what he calls 'the Jews'.

Curiously, Hitler admits that when he started, back in 1918, 'there was nothing like an organised anti-Semitic feeling', adding:

I can still remember the difficulties we encountered the moment we mentioned the Jew. We were either confronted with dumb-struck faces or else a lively and hefty antagonism. The efforts we made at the time to point out the real enemy to the public seemed to be doomed to failure.

Only very slowly did 'a kind of anti-Semitism' being to 'slowly take root', he remarks proudly. Crucial to this was the spread of his quasi-philosophical theory that, as Hitler puts it: 'All great cultures of the past perished only because the originally creative race died out from blood poisoning.' War follows logically from this. 'Nature knows no political boundaries. First, she puts living creatures on this globe and watches the free play of forces. She then confers the master's right on her favourite child, the strongest in courage and industry.' Like Nietzsche and Hegel, Hitler promises a better world, to be achieved through future conflicts.

No one can doubt that this world will some day be exposed to the severest struggles for the existence of mankind. In the end, only the urge for self-preservation can conquer. Beneath it so-called humanity, the expression of a mixture of stupidity, cowardice, and know-it-all conceit, will melt like snow in the March sun. Mankind has grown great in eternal struggle, and only in eternal peace does it perish.

Hitler saw the First World War in theological terms as a struggle between good and evil, sprinkling his account with religious references: 'And then the first mighty lightning flash struck the earth; the storm was unleashed and with the thunder of Heaven there mingled the roar of the World War batteries.' In lines that were doubtless delivered with much shouting and gesturing, he adds:

the struggle of the year 1914 was not forced on the masses – no, by the living God – it was desired by the whole people … A fight for freedom had begun, mightier than the earth had ever seen; for once Destiny had begun its course, the conviction dawned on even the broad masses that this time not the fate of Serbia or Austria was involved, but whether the German nation was *to be or not to be!*

Hitler's philosophising was, rather ironically (he says), triggered during a compulsory course on 'civic thinking', for demobbed soldiers. The 'central theoretical breakthrough' occurred to him as he listened to one Gottfried Feder lecture on the topic of interest rates, of all things. As Hitler records pompously:

I knew at once that this was a theoretical truth which would inevitably be of immense importance for the future of the German people ... the development of Germany was much too clear in my eyes for me not to know that the hardest battle would have to be fought, not against hostile nations, but against international capital.

The next step in Hitler's political development was again prompted by the activities of the existing regime. Hitler relates how he was told to investigate a small group called the German Workers' Party and how, after the meeting, one of the members handed him its manifesto and encouraged him to become a member. In this curious little story, apparently, lie the origins of the Nazi party.

Since I regularly woke up before five o'clock in the morning, I had gotten in the habit of putting a few left-overs or crusts of bread on the floor for the mice which amused themselves in my little room, and watching the droll little beasts chasing around after these choice morsels. I had known so much poverty in my life that I was well able to imagine the hunger, and hence also the pleasure, of the little creatures.

... At about five o'clock in the morning after this meeting, I thus lay awake in my cot, watching the chase and bustle. Since I could no longer fall asleep, I suddenly remembered the past evening and my mind fell on the booklet which the worker had given me. I began to read. It was a little pamphlet in which the author, this same worker, described how he had returned to national thinking out of the Babel of Marxist and trade-unionist phrases; hence also the title: 'My Political Awakening'. Once I had begun, I read the little book through with interest; for it reflected a process similar to the one which I myself had gone through twelve years before. Involuntarily I saw my own development come to life before my eyes. In the course of the day I reflected a few times on the matter and was finally about to put it aside when, less than a week later, much to my surprise, I received a postcard saying that I had been accepted in the German Workers' Party; I was requested to express myself on the subject and for this purpose to attend a committee meeting of this party on the following Wednesday.

So far, it is all a little like the experience of Jostein Gaarder's young philosopher in that recent bestseller, *Sophie's World*, who also received curious letters. But Hitler's new friend is part of an organisation. And so:

Every month, and later every two weeks, we tried to hold a 'meeting.' The invitations to it were written on the typewriter or sometimes by hand on slips of paper and the first few times were distributed, or handed out, by us personally.

Each one of us turned to the circle of his friends, and tried to induce someone or other to attend one of these affairs. The result was miserable.

I still remember how I myself in this first period once distributed about eighty of these slips of paper, and how in the evening we sat waiting for the masses who were expected to appear. An hour late, the 'chairman' finally had to open the 'meeting.' We were again seven men, the old seven. We changed over to having the invitation slips written on a machine and mimeographed in a Munich stationery store. The result at the next meeting was a few more listeners. Thus the number rose slowly from eleven to thirteen, finally to seventeen, to twenty-three, to thirty-four listeners.

Assuredly, these were small beginnings. Hard to believe from such would come a movement that would cost nearly a billion people their lives. For indubitably, Hitler was a pioneer of the power of the pamphlet, the political speech, the mass meeting – in two words, of the art of propaganda. In about October 1919, he says, a second, larger meeting took place in the *Eberlbraukeller*. 'Topic: Brest–Litovsk and Versailles. Four gentlemen appeared as speakers. I myself spoke for almost an hour and the success was greater than at the first rally. The audience had risen to more than one hundred and thirty.' And he adds a new detail. An attempted disturbance had at once been 'nipped in the bud' by his comrades. 'The disturbers flew down the stairs with gashed heads.'

As Hitler puts it, the 'future of a movement is conditioned by the fanaticism, yes, the intolerance, with which its adherents uphold it as the sole correct movement, and push it past other formations of a similar sort'. And so it was now time to formalise the movement. First of all, the 'twenty-five points' of the manifesto. These included: the union of all Germans in a greater German Reich, the rejection of the Treaty of Versailles, the demand for additional territories for the German people (*Lebensraum*), citizenship determined by race (with no citizenship for Jews), all income not earned by work to be confiscated, creation of a national education system, religious freedom 'except for religions which endangered the German race' – and so on. How did these points go down with those early audiences? Rather like the programme for a potential president at an American Republican Party Convention.

From minute to minute the interruptions were increasingly drowned out by shouts of applause. And when I finally submitted the twenty-five theses, point for point, to the masses and asked them personally to pronounce judgement on them, one after another was accepted with steadily mounting joy, unanimously and again unanimously, and when the last thesis had found its way to the heart of the masses, there stood before me a hall full of people united by a new conviction, a new faith, a new will.

Hitler's alternative theory of the state follows soon after. He rejects the conventional philosophical view that the state is primarily an economic institution, which can be governed according to economic requirements, saying firmly that 'the state has nothing at all to do with any definite economic conception or development'. Instead, there is a mysterious higher purpose: 'the achievement of the aim which has been allotted to this species by Providence'.

He contrasts three theories of the state, of which his racially defined vision is to be preferred. The first is briskly summed up as one in which 'those who hold that the State is a more or less voluntary association of men who have agreed to set up and obey a ruling authority', and a 'positively dog-like adoration of so-called state authority'. This is because, he adds,

in the minds of these people the means is substituted for the end, by a sort of sleight-of-hand movement. The State no longer exists for the purpose of serving men but men exist for the purpose of adoring the authority of the State ... The State must see that public peace and order are preserved and, in their turn, order and peace must make the existence of the State possible.

Hitler contradicts himself here, as elsewhere, because he also makes much play of the Nazi virtue of *Pflichterfullung*. This he describes as 'fulfilment of duty', which represents the voluntary subjugation of individual interests to the national one. This 'self-sacrificing will to give one's personal labour and if necessary one's own life for others' is most strongly developed in the Aryan', says Hitler, who also rather surprisingly grants that if the Aryan is 'not greatest in his mental qualities as such', he still 'excels in the extent of his willingness to put all his abilities in the service of the community':

In him the instinct of self-preservation has reached the noblest form, since he willingly subordinates his own ego to the life of the community and, if the hour demands, even sacrifices it ... This state of mind, which subordinates the interests of the ego to the conservation of the community, is really the first premise for every truly human culture.

By comparison, among the Jewish people 'the will to self-sacrifice does not go beyond the individual's naked instinct of self-preservation'.

As for 'liberal democracy', it consists of societies in which the authority of the state is no longer the sole and exclusive end for which the state exists. It must also promote the good of its subjects.

Ideas of 'freedom', mostly based on a misunderstanding of the meaning of that word, enter into the concept of the state as it exists in the minds of this group. The form of government is no longer considered inviolable simply because it exists. It must submit to the test of practical efficiency.

The problem with this kind of state (and this worried Plato too) is that it seems to degenerate inevitably into one of the other possibilities. For Hitler at least, to political problems there are biological solutions: there is the quite different possibility of the racially defined state. 'What makes a people or, to be more correct, a race, is not language but blood'. The 'fundamental principle' of this kind of state is that it is not an end in itself but the means to a biological end.

As if conscious of having strayed into areas of political debate where few would want to follow him, Hitler then returns to messianic invective, warning that if, with the help of his Marxist creed, 'the Jew is victorious over the other peoples of the world', his 'crown will be the funeral wreath of humanity' – and the planet will, 'as it did thousands of years ago, move through the ether devoid of men'. For 'Eternal *Nature inexorably avenges the infringement of her commands'*. Hence, Hitler adds implausibly, he is 'acting in accordance with the will of the Almighty Creator' and 'by defending myself against the Jew, I am fighting for the work of the Lord'.

This kind of quasi-religious appeal is characteristic of Hitler as of all politicians of his kind. The personification of 'evil' in the supposed 'race' of the Jews fits easily with the Christian standpoint of the Jews as the killer of the Messiah. And today many ostensibly secular governments are led by those who likewise refer pointedly to their personal commitment to Christianity and desire to fight evil and wickedness. Such talk is easy and politically effective, if also dangerous.

In language very reminiscent of Professor Hegel, he says:

for the first time a high inner purpose is accredited to the State. In face of the ridiculous phrase that the State should do no more than act as the guardian of public order and tranquillity, so that everybody can peacefully dupe everybody else, it is given a very high mission indeed to preserve and encourage the highest type of humanity which a beneficent Creator has bestowed on this earth. *Out of a dead mechanism which claims to be an end in itself a living organism shall arise which has to serve one purpose exclusively: and that, indeed, a purpose which belongs to a higher order of ideas.*

This new mechanism is Hitler's political theory. He starts by noting that the strength of the 'old state' rested on three pillars: the monarchical form of government, the civil service, and the army.

Popular support is the first element which is necessary for the creation of authority. But an authority resting on that foundation alone is still quite frail, uncertain and vacillating. Hence everyone who finds himself vested with an authority that is based only on popular support must take measures to improve and consolidate the foundations of that authority by the creation of force. Accordingly we must look upon power, that is to say, the capacity to use force, as the second foundation on which all authority is based. This foundation is more stable and secure, but not always stronger, than the first. If popular support and power are united together and can endure for a certain time, then an authority may arise which is based on a still stronger foundation, namely, the authority of tradition. And, finally, if popular support, power, and tradition are united together, then the authority based on them may be looked upon as invincible.

In language that again would not be out of place in Plato's *Republic*, Hitler promises that the People's State will have to consider the physical training of the youth after the school period just as much a public duty as their intellectual training; and this training will have to be carried out through public institutions and will also be a preparation for subsequent service in the army.

After the citizen has completed his military training, two certificates will be handed to him. Rather like the ancient Greeks, one certificate will be his diploma as a citizen of the state, a 'juridical document which will enable him to take part in public affairs'. The other will be an attestation of his physical health, which guarantees his fitness for marriage. Again, this unpleasant view is found in Plato too, and was, at the time Hitler was writing, not unpopular in European and American political circles.

General instruction in all subjects will be obligatory, and specialisation will be left to the choice of the individual. The advantage of this would be that the scholastic programme would be shortened, and thus 'several school hours would be gained which could be utilised for physical training and character training, in will-power, the capacity for making practical judgements, decisions, etc.' Naturally, 'the spirit of nationalism and a feeling for social justice' must be fused into one sentiment in the hearts of the youth. Then a day will come 'when a nation of citizens will arise which will be welded together through a common love and a common pride that shall be invincible and indestructible for ever'. In a nod to the hardship faced by many in his audience, Hitler promises 'a wiser scale of wages and salaries' which, he says, will enable everyone, 'including the humblest workman who fulfils his duties conscientiously', to live an honourable and decent life both as a man and as a citizen. Nonetheless, Hitler maintains grandly, 'we must face the calculators of the materialist Republic with faith in an idealist Reich'.

Mind you, only athletes need further education. 'An ill-kept body is not made a more beautiful sight by the indwelling of a radiant spirit', says Hitler briskly, like a mad PE teacher.

We should not be acting justly if we were to bestow the highest intellectual training on those who are physically deformed and crippled, who lack decision and are weak-willed and cowardly. What has made the Greek ideal of beauty immortal is the wonderful union of a splendid physical beauty with nobility of mind and spirit.

Not a single day should be allowed to pass 'in which the young pupil does not have at least one hour of physical training in the morning and one in the evening', and this should include every kind of sport and gymnastics. But there is one kind of sport which Hitler thinks should be specially encouraged, although 'people who call themselves *völkisch*' consider it brutal and vulgar, and that is boxing.

Unusually, Hitler (who friends and colleagues alike recall as being completely unable to countenance disagreements without flying into a rage) does consider, briefly, a counter-argument here. Boxing is considered brutal, he notes. Why? For there is no other sport 'which equals this in developing the militant spirit, none that demands such a power of rapid decision or which gives the body the flexibility of good steel'. Hurrumpth! It is not the purpose of the People's State to educate a colony of æsthetic pacifists and physical degenerates. Hitler's state does not consider that the human ideal is to be found in the honourable philistine or the maidenly spinster, but in the 'dareful personification of manly force and in women capable of bringing men into the world'.

The interest in sexual politics extends into masturbation. Hitler writes (for once rather delicately) that 'excessive emphasis on purely intellectual instruction and the neglect of physical training also encourage the emergence of sexual ideas at a much too early age'.

Fortunately, he thinks that the youth 'who achieves the hardness of iron by sports and gymnastics succumbs to the need of sexual satisfaction' less than the 'stay-at-home fed exclusively on intellectual fare'. 'We must also do away with the conception that the treatment of the body is the affair of every individual. There is no freedom to sin at the cost of posterity and hence of the race.'

Hitler also, like Mohammed, has his own strong views on other personal matters, such as how people should dress.

It is really lamentable to see how our young people have fallen victims to a fashion mania which perverts the meaning of the old adage that clothes make the man. Especially in regard to young people clothes should take their place in the service of education. The boy who walks about in summer-time wearing long baggy trousers and clad up to the neck is hampered even by his clothes in feeling any inclination towards strenuous physical exercise. Ambition and, to speak quite frankly, even vanity must be appealed to. I do not mean such vanity as leads people to want to wear fine clothes, which not everybody can afford, but rather the vanity which inclines a person towards developing a fine bodily physique. And this is something which everybody can help to do.

The aim of all this is to heighten sexuality and encourage breeding. After all, if the beauty of the body were not completely forced into the background today through our stupid manner of dressing, adds Hitler nastily, 'it would not be possible for thousands of our girls to be led astray by Jewish mongrels, with their repulsive crooked waddle'. Contraception will be made illegal, and 'procreation impossible for syphilitics and those who suffer from tuberculosis or other hereditary diseases, also cripples and imbeciles'.

Of course, some people may not like being told they are unfit to have children. Yet Hitler is optimistic. Why should it not be possible to induce people to make this sacrifice, he continues gaily, if, instead of such a precept, 'they were simply told that they ought to put an end to this truly original sin of racial corruption which is steadily being passed on from one generation to another'? Alas, Hitler complains, some will not understand these things. 'They will ridicule them or shrug their round shoulders and groan out their everlasting excuses: "Of course it is a fine thing, but the pity is that it cannot be carried out."'

Mein Kampf includes lengthy description of practical policies for the new state, notably eugenics, indoctrination and propaganda. The cleansing of culture in general must be extended to all fields.

Theatre, art, literature, cinema, press, posters, and window displays must be cleansed of all manifestations of our rotting world and placed in the service of a moral, political, and cultural idea. Public life must be freed from the stifling perfume of our modern eroticism, just as it must be freed from all unmanly, prudish hypocrisy. In all these things the goal and the road must be determined by concern for the preservation of the health of our people in body and soul. The right of personal freedom recedes before the duty to preserve the race.

And so, Hitler returns, at last, to his original career of painting. It is not so much 'Impressionism', or the various new movements in France, but 'Art Bolshevism' which is the enemy here, being the cultural form and spiritual expression of Bolshevism as a whole. Anyone seeing this 'will be confronted by the morbid excrescences of insane and degenerate men, with which, since the turn of the century, we have become familiar under the collective concepts of cubism and Dadaism, as the official and recognised art'.

As to architecture, Hitler's other potential career, 'All public buildings and monuments in the cities should dominate the city picture, and be symbols of the whole epoch', designed along Nazi lines, 'to reflect, not the wealth of an individual owner, but the greatness and wealth of the community'.

In these areas, it must never be forgotten, he explains, it is the individual that is important. But so too, he says, it is in politics. The best constitution and the best form of government is 'that which makes it quite natural for the best brains to reach a position of dominant importance and influence in the community'. The state must be meritocratic in outlook as 'not only does the organisation possess no right to prevent men of brains from rising above the multitude but, on the contrary, it must use its organising powers to enable and promote that ascension as far as it possibly can'.

Marxism, in sad contrast, attempts to eliminate the dominant significance of personality in every sphere of human life. In so saying, curiously, Hitler presages the view that communism (by failing to permit individuals to flourish) suppresses and constricts activity in society, leading to its gradual collapse. This view has become much more plausible since the collapse of the Soviet Union, but was by no means evident at the time Hitler was writing. Indeed, communist societies continued to outperform comparable 'individualistic' ones (in economic terms) up until the 1960s.

In fact, Hitler observes, politics comes down to individuals, not grand coalitions. And it is here, in the area of manipulating public opinion, that *Mein Kampf* becomes a distinctive if rather poisonous contribution to political theory.

What won over millions of workpeople to the Marxist cause was not the *ex cathedra* style of the Marxist writers but the formidable propagandist work done by tens of thousands of indefatigable agitators, commencing with the leading fiery agitator down to the smallest official in the syndicate, the trusted delegate and the platform orator. Furthermore, there were the hundreds of thousands of meetings where these orators, standing on tables in smoky taverns, hammered their ideas into the heads of the masses, thus acquiring an admirable psychological knowledge of the human material they had to deal with. And in this way they were enabled to select the best weapons for their assault on the citadel of public opinion. In addition to all this there were the gigantic mass-demonstrations with processions in which a hundred thousand men took part.

Despite having just denied the power of collective endeavours, Hitler promptly then recognises its power.

Mass demonstrations on the grand scale not only reinforce the will of the individual but they draw him still closer to the movement and help to create an *esprit de corps*. The man who appears first as the representative of a new doctrine in his place of business or in his factory is bound to feel himself embarrassed and has need of that reinforcement which comes from the consciousness that he is a member of a great community. And only a mass demonstration can impress upon him the greatness of this community. If, on leaving the shop or mammoth factory, in which he feels very small indeed, he should enter a vast assembly for the first time and see around him thousands and thousands of men who hold the same opinions; if, while still seeking his way, he is gripped by the force of mass-suggestion which comes from the excitement and enthusiasm of three or four thousand other men in whose midst he finds himself; if the manifest success and the consensus of thousands confirm the truth and justice of the new teaching and for the first time raise doubt in his mind as to the truth of the opinions held by himself up to now – then *he submits himself to the fascination of what we call mass-suggestion*. The will, the yearning and indeed the strength of thousands of people are in each individual. A man who enters such a meeting in doubt and hesitation leaves it inwardly fortified; he has become a member of a community.

This is Hitler's *forte*: propaganda and mass-suggestion.

The art of propaganda lies in understanding the emotional ideas of the great masses and finding, through a psychologically correct form, the way to the attention and thence to the heart of the broad masses ... The receptivity of the great masses is very limited, their intelligence is small, but their power of forgetting is enormous. In consequence of these facts, all effective propaganda must be limited to a very few points and must harp on these in slogans until the last member of the public understands what you want him to understand by your slogan. As soon as you sacrifice this slogan and try to be many-sided, the effect will piddle away, for the crowd can neither digest nor retain the material offered. In this way the result is weakened and in the end entirely cancelled out.

Propaganda is not 'creative', because its purpose is not to 'provide interesting distraction for blasé young gentlemen, but to convince, and what I mean is to convince the masses'. And as the masses are 'slow-moving', they always require a certain time before they are ready even to notice a thing, 'and only after the simplest ideas are repeated thousands of times will the masses finally remember them'.

Propaganda is not and cannot be the necessity in itself, since its function, like the poster, consists in attracting the attention of the crowd, and not in educating those who are already educated or who are striving after education and knowledge, its effect for the most part must be *aimed at the emotions and only to a very limited degree at the so-called intellect* ... All propaganda must be popular and its intellectual level must be adjusted to the most limited intelligence among those it is addressed to. Consequently, the greater the mass it is intended to reach, the lower its purely intellectual level will have to be.

Hitler says he learnt the black arts of propaganda from the English.

Here, too, the example of enemy war propaganda was typical; limited to a few points, devised exclusively for the masses, carried on with indefatigable persistence. Once the basic ideas and methods of execution were recognised as correct, they were applied throughout the whole War without the slightest change. At first the claims of the propaganda were so impudent that people thought it insane; later, it got on people's nerves; and in the end, it was believed. After four and a half years, a revolution broke out in Germany; and its slogans originated in the enemy's war propaganda.

Hitler, now truly into his role of a pioneer 'spin doctor', analyses in some detail the role of propaganda, the press and its readers. These last fall into three groups: those who believe everything they read; those who have ceased to believe anything; and those who critically examine what they read, and judge accordingly. Naturally, the first group is the largest.

For the members of this third group, it must be admitted, the nonsense that newspaper scribblers can put down is not very dangerous or even very important. Most of them in the course of their lives have learned to regard every journalist as a rascal on principle, who tells the truth only once in a blue moon. Unfortunately, however, the importance of these splendid people lies only in their intelligence and not in their number – a misfortune at a time when wisdom is nothing and the majority is everything! Today, when the ballot of the masses decides, the chief weight lies with the most numerous group, and this is the first: the mob of the simple or credulous.

THE SUBTEXT

It is not politically important that *Mein Kampf* is inaccurate and even ridiculous on many matters of fact. Hitler begins by following Rousseau's strategy, by setting aside the facts as they will not affect the question. For example, the 'betrayal' of Germany in the First World War, much bemoaned by Hitler, was in fact an invention of the German Army, which had been defeated, and whose own leaders had initiated the surrender talks. Hitler's discourse instead is of 'the traitors of 1918' responsible for the so called 'stab in the back', which left the Army undefeated on the battlefield but undermined by political treachery at home. Unfortunately, the Allies were happy to allow the German Army to avoid any public admission of defeat, preferring instead to concentrate on territorial concessions and setting unrealistic demands for 'reparations'. Thus it was that in the 1920s, as Europe generally plunged into economic chaos, the German people were literally being starved in order to pay off the reparations bill of $33 billion to the French and British governments. This created not only runaway inflation but that infamous 'fertile climate for extremists' in Germany.

Instead of facts, *Mein Kampf* is made up of pages upon irrelevant pages dealing with the Fuehrer's early years, views on clothing, descriptions of the appearance of Jews, et cetera, et cetera. This is because *Mein Kampf* is a new kind of politicial philosophy – it is a work not of rational argument but of irrational or emotive appeals – of propaganda.

And even if there are still revisionist historians who say otherwise, everyone else knows where Hitler's propaganda ends: in the neat, white-tiled shower rooms of the death camps. No government since has applied that technique to dealing with unwanted populations. Even so, genocides and mass killings have punctuated the twentieth century, and look set to continue in the twenty-first. And in part this is because, in another sense, Hitler's experiment continues today, as governments adopt the methods and tactics that the Nazis so successfully used to consolidate their power in the early twentieth century.

Indeed, even if the death camps came at the end of Hitler's period in government, as it were, the Nazi doctrine which anticipated them was embraced by many in the western democracies as a fine thing.

The British prime minister, Lloyd George, wrote on visiting Mr Hitler that :

I have now seen the famous German leader and also something of the great change he has effected. Whatever one may think of his methods – and they are certainly not those of a parliamentary country – there can be no doubt that he has achieved a marvellous transformation in the spirit of the people, in their attitude towards each other, and in their social and economic outlook.

The British government was not unduly concerned that in *Mein Kampf* Hitler had suggested killing ethnic minorities, 'reds', and the handicapped: quite the opposite. Lloyd George, whom Hitler praises in the book for being a great propagandist, says only:

There is for the first time since the war a general sense of security. The people are more cheerful. There is a greater sense of general gaiety of spirit throughout the land. It is a happier Germany ... *I have never met a happier people than the Germans and Hitler is one of the greatest men.* (Extract from the report published in the *Daily Express*, London, 17 September 1936)

KEY IDEAS

At the heart of Nazism is an appeal to orthodoxy, and to aristocracy.

- There should be a return to traditional role hierarchies and passive, indeed feudal, respect for inequalities of both power and wealth.
- The flourishing of the talented (Aryan) individual is the proper concern of the state, not the (racially impure) masses.
- Most people are slow and stupid and for that reason leaders are both entitled, and required, to manipulate opinion.

The society created by Hitler, born out of manipulation of democracy, was inegalitarian, militaristic and utterly lacking in a sense of common humanity. Alas, today, his political philosophy has resurfaced in many countries, many times, under many new names.

KEY TEXT

Hitler's *Mein Kampf* (1923)

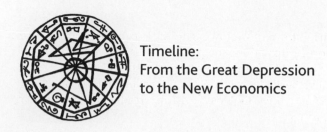

Timeline:
From the Great Depression
to the New Economics

1924

In the Soviet Union, Lenin dies and is succeeded by Stalin, who establishes a personal dictatorship. In Italy, the Fascists are successful in the elections and, from 1925, also establish a dictatorship.

1925

Experimental television pictures are transmitted by John Logie Baird in Britain.

1927

The Shanghai massacres of communists by the Nationalist government take place in China. Chiang Kai Shek rules as a dictator.

1929

The Wall Street Crash. The world economy plunges into depression. From Glasgow, unemployed marchers make their way to London.

1930

The Nazis are now the second largest party in the German parliament.

1931

Collapse of 3,000 German banks as unemployment rises to nearly 6 million.

1932

Fascist parties are founded in Britain and Spain. The Nazis are now the largest party in the German parliament. Aldous Huxley's *Brave New World* is published. The slump reaches its nadir in the US, there is a 'Great Hunger March' in London, and in India the British put Gandhi in prison.

1933
The Nazis use their new powers to set up a one-party state. Concentration camps are opened for enemies of the party. When the German president, Hindenberg, dies the following year, Adolf Hitler becomes sole leader – Fuehrer – of Germany. The 'Long March' begins in China, saving Mao's peasant army, ready one day to defeat Japanese fascism.

1935
Nazis start systematically targeting Jews. The Italians invade an independent country, Abyssinia, demonstrating the impotence of the League of Nations.

1936
Germany, Italy and Japan reach strategic agreements.

1938
First anti-Semitic laws in Italy. Germany annexes Austria.

1939
Spain joins the fascist community. Germany annexes Czechoslovakia, and then Poland, precipitating the Second World War.

1941
Germany sets up the first extermination camps.

1942
Two technological breakthroughs in the United States – the first nuclear reactor and the first 'modern' computer.

1944
The Bretton Woods Conference creates two international institutions, the International Monetary Fund and the World Bank, to determine the shape of the post-war world.

1945
Violent end to Italian, German and finally Japanese fascist movements. Perhaps 35 million people have died in the fighting (most of them on the Eastern Front), and at least another 10 million have been murdered in the concentration camps. In China, a new People's Republic is being set up under Chairman Mao.

16
Mao's Little Red Book

The most popular political pamphlet of them all is Mao's little Red Book. It has been helped by being more or less compulsory for millions of people. And not only to buy, but to read and memorise. But, in fact, it is quite a good read: short, pithy and to the point. For more than two generations, the effects and implications of this pocket-sized collection of Mao's philosophising shaped the world's most populous nation. But Maoism's influence goes far beyond China's borders.

THE CONTEXT

The Chinese Marxists under Mao had two primary goals: to save China from the foreign enemies who had overrun it, and to make the country strong and rich in the future. Both of these were to be achieved through programmes of technological modernisation and public education. Being essentially pragmatic in outlook, they selected from any of the range of Marxist and Chinese philosophies those elements that they felt could be used most effectively in the pursuit of these aims. Maoism became a mixture of Marx and Engels' writings, Lenin and Trotsky's subsequent interpretations, and the two distinctive Chinese philosophies of Confucianism and Taoism.

In Confucianism, the primary function of government, apart from details such as raising taxes, is education. All officials, from the emperor and the mandarins down, have a sacred duty of educating the masses, particularly in a moral sense. Li Dazhao, one of the early Chinese communists, influenced the development of Marxism in China away from historical determinism, by allowing countries to 'telescope' their progress from an agrarian society to communism, by education, that is through a consciousness of the class struggle. This doctrine was also incorporated into Maoism as the policy of 'permanent revolution'.

Another element in Confucianism is the desire to create a 'one-minded' society. So also Maoism. The people should all think the same on any important matter. Mao himself included egalitarianism as such a 'one-minded' goal. The challenge of this orthodoxy by

Liu Shaoqu contributed to the destructive conflict of the Cultural Revolution, Mao's flailing attempt to reassert his philosophical dominance and political supremacy. Following Mao's death in 1976, and Deng Xiaoping's succession, egalitarianism was abandoned in place of something closer to the western conservative notion of 'trickle-down' – some people must get rich first, creating wealth that later benefits the others.

In the west, surprisingly few consider Maoism a distinct philosophy and fewer still have looked at what the little Red Book actually said. But the story of human society in many ways begins in China, and the text continues to guide and direct the leaders of the world's most populous nation.

THE TEXT

Strictly speaking, the text in question is entitled *Quotations from Chairman Mao Tse-Tung* (nowadays usually spelt 'Zedong'). However, as even in party circles in China itself no one actually uses this unwieldy title – it is mostly just called the 'Red Book' – I have used either this or the affectionate sounding soubriquet 'little Red Book' instead. Though in China itself, it should be noted, the book inspired a great deal more than just affection. For many years it had almost the status of a bible or holy book, carried around for reference at all times, and even touched for good fortune, or for protection at moments of strife.

The little Red Book starts with Marxism, or, at least, with what is perceived to be 'the science of dialectical materialism' behind the varied and inconsistent writings of Marx and Engels. It speaks in revolutionary phrases, short statements designed to be learnt and recited (and for decades in all China's schools and colleges and work places they were). And the Red Book starts, as does the Chinese state, as do all good Marxists, with the Communist Party. It proclaims straight away, with no concessions to the browsing reader:

If there is to be revolution, there must be a revolutionary party. Without a revolutionary party, without a party built on the Marxist–Leninist revolutionary theory and in the Marxist–Leninist revolutionary style, it is impossible to lead the working class and the broad masses of the people to defeat imperialism and its running dogs.

The Red Book recognises that it will be 'an arduous task' to ensure a better life for the several hundred million people of China and to build up an 'economically and culturally backward country' into a prosperous and powerful one with a high level of culture. So, like both Confucius and Plato 3,000 years before, Mao starts with education. And, Mao thinks, there is one good thing about China:

Apart from their other characteristics, the outstanding thing about China's 600 million people is that they are 'poor and blank'. This may seem a bad thing, but in reality it is a good thing. Poverty gives rise to the desire for change, the desire for action and the desire for revolution. On a blank sheet of paper free from any mark, the freshest and most beautiful characters can be written, the freshest and most beautiful pictures can be painted.

Education here means 'Marxist education'. But what is Marxist education? The key is 'revolutionary theory', combined with knowledge of history and a 'profound grasp of the practical movement'. Together, these are *rectification* – a 24-carat Marxist word – which means the whole Party studying Marxism. Rectification is 'putting yourself right', and practising self-criticism, to ensure that political action and social policy remain correct. In order to shoulder the task of constructing the new communist society competently and work better alongside 'all non-Party people who are actuated by high ideals and determined to institute reforms', communists need to conduct 'rectification movements', both now and in the future, and constantly rid themselves of wrong thinking.

So the 'Cultural Revolution' of the 1950s was not entirely an anomaly. Maoism, again like Platonism and Confucianism, was always obsessed with protecting the republic and maintaining the purity of the revolution in the face of the manifest tendency for material contamination and dilution. If Plato worried about the influence of bad poetry, and wanted only approved plays performed, in Red China education revolved only around the approved political poetry of party slogans such as: 'What is work? Work is struggle'; 'There are difficulties and problems for us to overcome and solve. We go there to work and struggle to overcome these difficulties'; and 'A good comrade is one who is more eager to go where the difficulties are greater.'

Or around uplifting political stories such as the ancient fable of 'The Foolish Old Man Who Removed the Mountains'. This tells of a greybeard who lived in northern China long, long ago. His house faced south and beyond his doorway stood the two great peaks, Taihang and Wangwu, obstructing the way. He called his sons, and hoe in hand, began to dig up the mountains with great determination.

The moral is (teacher would add) that today, the two big mountains oppressing the Chinese people are imperialism, and feudalism, and they too can be slowly dug away.

So, revolutionary theory and history are straightforward to teach. But what of the 'practical movement'? Mao's two most famous essays, 'On Practice' and 'On Contradiction', both from 1937, are concerned with this. Both reflect the guerrilla roots of Maoism – the strategy is a democratic one of building up support in the countryside ready to overthrow the Japanese. But the policy also reflects a theoretical belief about the nature of knowledge. Knowledge starts with sense-perception, is distilled into ideas and theory, and then tested through practice. Essentially, the 'practical movement' is learning through experience, through experiment even. As the Red Book goes on, 'Only through the practice of the people, that is, through experience, can we verify whether a policy is correct or wrong and determine to what extent it is correct or wrong.'

The Red Book emphasises the need for Party workers to indulge in this sort of 'investigation and study', rather than end up behaving like 'a blindfolded man catching sparrows', or 'a blind man groping for fish' – or even to 'indulge in verbiage' and rest content with a 'smattering of knowledge'. Better instead that everyone engaged in practical work investigate conditions at the lower levels. 'No investigation, no right to speak.' Although there are many people who, 'the moment they alight from the official carriage', will make a hullabaloo, spout opinions, criticise this and condemn that, in fact, 'ten out of ten of them will meet with failure'. For such views or criticisms, not being based on thorough investigation, are 'nothing but ignorant twaddle'. Countless times, Mao recalls, the Party suffered at the hands of these imperial envoys, who rushed here, there and everywhere. Stalin was right to say that 'theory becomes purposeless if it is not connected with revolutionary practice'. For, to 'investigate a problem is indeed to solve it', the Red Book advises.

It explains that the 'only way to know conditions is to make social investigations, to investigate the conditions of each social class in real life'. The best method is to concentrate on a few cities and villages according to a plan, designed from the fundamental viewpoint of Marxism, i.e. the method of class analysis, and make a number of thorough investigations. (Which have some of the same aspects as today's citizens' panels in the United States.)

A fact-finding meeting need not be large; from three to five or seven or eight people is enough. Ample time must be allowed and an outline for the investigation must be prepared; furthermore, one must personally ask questions, take notes and have discussions with those at the meeting. One certainly cannot make an investigation, or do it well, without zeal, a determination to direct one's eyes downward and a thirst for knowledge, and without shedding the ugly mantle of pretentiousness and becoming a willing pupil.

This applies equally to any political system concentrating power. With victory, certain moods may grow within the rulers, such as

arrogance, the airs of a self-styled hero, inertia and unwillingness to make progress, love of pleasure and distaste for continued hard living. With victory, the people will be grateful to us and the bourgeoisie will come forward to flatter us. It has been proved that the enemy cannot conquer us by force of arms. However, the flattery of the bourgeoisie may conquer the weak-willed in our ranks. There may be some Communists, who were not conquered by enemies with guns and were worthy of the name of heroes for standing up to these enemies, but who cannot withstand sugar-coated bullets.

Democracy was taken very seriously in pre-revolutionary China, more so, in some respects, than in western democracies. 'Our duty is to hold ourselves responsible to the people. Every word, every act and every policy must conform to the people's interests, and if mistakes occur, they must be corrected – that is what being responsible to the people means.' What of the smaller concerns of the people? 'We should pay close attention to the well-being of the masses, from the problems of land and labour to those of fuel, rice, cooking oil and salt.' All such problems concerning 'the well-being of the masses' are to be placed on the agenda. 'We should discuss them, adopt and carry out decisions and check up on the results. We should help the masses to realise that we represent their interests, that our lives are intimately bound up with theirs.' Certainly, later, communists should help people to proceed from these things to an understanding of the higher tasks, the tasks of the revolutionary war, spreading the revolution and so on, but communists should also pay attention to detail. In short, Mao recognises that education and democracy are inseparable.

What though of freedom? Social science is one of the key weapons in the fight for mankind's freedom.

For the purpose of attaining freedom in society, man must use social science to understand and change society and carry out social revolution. It is man's social being that determines his thinking. Once the correct ideas characteristic of the advanced class are grasped by the masses, these ideas turn into a material force which changes society and changes the world.

Secondly, both ideas and the practical work of the Party come necessarily 'from the masses, to the masses'. This means: take the ideas of the masses (scattered and unsystematic ideas) and 'concentrate them' (that is, through study turn them into concentrated and systematic ideas), then go back to the masses and propagate and explain these ideas 'until the masses embrace them as their own, hold fast to them and translate them into action'. Finally, remember to test the correctness of the ideas in practice. Then once again concentrate ideas from the masses and once again go to the masses so that the ideas are persevered in and carried through. 'And so on, over and over again in an endless spiral, with the ideas becoming more correct, more vital and richer each time.' This is truly the science of society.

For communists, in the appraisal of their work, it is one-sided to regard everything either as all positive or as all negative. Recognising this 'fundamental aspect' should bring humility (even in a one-party system).

To regard everything as positive is to see only the good and not the bad, and to tolerate only praise and no criticism. To talk as though our work is good in every respect is at variance with the facts. It is not true that everything is good; there are still shortcomings and mistakes. But neither is it true that everything is bad, and that, too, is at variance with the facts. Here analysis is necessary.

We must not be like the 'frog in the well'. In a speech at the Chinese Communist Party's National Conference on Propaganda Work (12 March 1957), Mao had declared that:

In approaching a problem a Marxist should see the whole as well as the parts. A frog in a well says, 'The sky is no bigger than the mouth of the well.' That is untrue, for the sky is not just the size of the mouth of the well. If it said, 'A part of the sky is the size of the mouth of a well' that would be true, for it tallies with the facts.

Such 'holism' even brings Mao to muddy the holy water of Marxist materialism:

While we recognise that in the general development of history the material determines the mental and social being determines social consciousness, we also – and indeed must – recognise the reaction of mental on material things, of social consciousness on social being and of the superstructure on the economic base.

Of course, Mao hastens to add, this does not go against materialism; on the contrary, 'it avoids mechanical materialism and firmly upholds dialectical materialism'.

So the Red Book tells communists that, if they remember nothing else, they should always remember one key truth: it was the class struggles of the peasants, the peasant uprisings and peasant wars that were the engine driving historical development in Chinese feudal society. 'Classes struggle, some classes triumph, others are eliminated. Such is history, such is the history of civilisation for thousands of years.'

And inspirational messages for revolutionaries from talks given by Mao are given under headings like: 'People of the World, Unite and Defeat the US Aggressors and All Their Lackeys'. These pledge support for oppressed groups abroad, notably the American blacks.

It is up to us to organise the people. As for the reactionaries in China, it is up to us to organise the people to overthrow them. Everything reactionary is the same; if you don't hit it, it won't fall. It is like sweeping the floor; where the broom does not reach, the dust never vanishes of itself.

In Mao's immortal phrase,

A revolution is not a dinner party, or writing an essay, or painting a picture, or doing embroidery; it cannot be so refined, so leisurely and gentle, so temperate, kind, courteous, restrained and magnanimous. A revolution is an insurrection, an act of violence by which one class overthrows another.

But, in practice, often it is hard to tell who is who, who is your friend and who is your enemy. So for this reason, in general, polarisation is a good thing, helping to pinpoint the enemy. In a speech in the Red Book dating back to the early years of the revolution, Mao surveys Red China and sees socialist transformation completed in the system of ownership, and the 'large-scale, turbulent class struggles of the masses' in the main come to an end, but he sees too 'remnants of the overthrown landlord and comprador classes', a bourgeoisie still hanging on, and the 'remoulding of the petty bourgeoisie' only just started. In short, the class struggle is by no means over. Realistically, then, Mao predicts that 'bourgeois and petty-bourgeois ideology', anti-Marxist ideology, will continue to exist for a long time. There needs to be a strategy to deal with the pernicious effects of what Mao calls 'liberalism', and others, even in his own Party, call 'humanism'.

Liberalism is extremely harmful in a revolutionary collective. It is a corrosive which eats away unity, undermines cohesion, causes apathy and creates dissension. It robs the revolutionary ranks of compact organisation and strict discipline, prevents policies from being carried through and alienates the Party organisations from the masses which the Party leads. It is an extremely bad tendency.

People who are liberals in China look upon the principles of Marxism as abstract dogma. They approve of Marxism, but are not prepared to practise it, or to practise it in full; they are not prepared to replace their liberalism by Marxism. These people have their Marxism, but they have their liberalism as well – they talk Marxism but practise liberalism; they apply Marxism to others but liberalism to themselves. 'They keep both kinds of goods in stock and find a use for each.'

One of the problems with these liberals is their version of 'freedom' and 'democracy'. Isn't Maoism democratic enough? The Red Book acknowledges that it denies some freedoms, but allows others.

Within the ranks of the people, we cannot do without freedom, nor can we do without discipline; we cannot do without democracy, nor can we do without centralism. This unity of democracy and centralism, of freedom and discipline, constitutes our democratic centralism. Under this system, the people enjoy broad democracy and freedom, but at the same time they have to keep within the bounds of socialist discipline.

For party members, this freedom has a particular form:

1. the individual is subordinate to the organisation;
2. the minority is subordinate to the majority;
3. the lower level is subordinate to the higher level; and
4. the entire membership is subordinate to the Central Committee.

In fact, the Party is a hierarchy, just as Confucius recommended. Non-members are either completely free or completely subordinate, depending on your point of view.

At no time and in no circumstances should a Communist place his personal interests first; he should subordinate them to the interests of the nation and of the masses. Hence, selfishness, slacking, corruption, seeking the limelight, and so on, are most contemptible, while selflessness, working with all one's energy, whole-hearted devotion to public duty, and quiet hard work will command respect.

(You can see why capitalism became more popular.)

Communists should set an example. Indeed, 'We Communists are like seeds and the people are like the soil. Wherever we go, we must unite with the people, take root and blossom among them.' Communists must listen attentively to the views of people outside the Party and let them have their say. If what they say is right, they ought to welcome it, and learn from the people. If it is wrong, 'we should let them finish what they are saying and then patiently explain things to them'.

Still on the horticultural theme, Mao goes on: 'All erroneous ideas, all poisonous weeds, all ghosts and monsters, must be subjected to criticism; in no circumstances should they be allowed to spread unchecked.' But the criticism should be fully reasoned, analytical and convincing, and 'not rough, bureaucratic, metaphysical or dogmatic'.

Communists can however rely on the fact that, as Marx had demonstrated (on paper) a century before, their victory 'is an objective law independent of man's will'. Even if the reactionaries try to hold back the 'wheel of history', sooner or later revolution will take place and it will triumph. It is a simple matter of the operation of economic forces. After all, the changeover from individual to socialist, collective ownership in agriculture and handicrafts and from capitalist to socialist ownership in private industry and commerce is 'bound to bring about a tremendous liberation of the productive forces'. (Collectivisation in particular actually caused massive famines in China, as it had in the Soviet Union beforehand.)

But land reform was politically essential; it was the key to all other reforms. 'The political authority of the landlords is the backbone of all the other systems of authority. With that overturned, the clan authority, the religious authority and the authority of the husband all begin to totter.' Mao here is explicitly linking economic progress to women's emancipation. In fact, Maoism was always extremely progressive with regard to women, whom Mao described as 'holding up half the sky':

A man in China is usually subjected to the domination of three systems of authority [political authority, clan authority and religious authority] ... As for women, in addition to being dominated by these three systems of authority, they are also dominated by the men (the authority of the husband). These four authorities – political, clan, religious and masculine – are the embodiment of the whole feudal–patriarchal system and ideology, and are the four thick ropes binding the Chinese people, particularly the peasants.

It makes economic sense to embrace equality of the sexes, Mao points out. 'China's women are a vast reserve of labour power. This reserve should be tapped in the struggle to build a great socialist society.' And men and women 'must receive equal pay for equal work in production'.

In the west, there is a popular perception that the conventional patriarchal family is the defining model of the family, and hence of the state too. Yet it is not necessarily so. Plato, as we have seen, thought children should be brought up collectively, and should not even know who their father was, whilst Rousseau specifically argued against the nuclear family as reducing individual freedom and encouraging laziness. In contemporary western societies, there is great concern at the breakdown of 'the family' (actually just the nuclear family: there is little concern at the earlier breakdown of the extended networks of relatives and in-laws) and its often problematic replacement by the one-parent family.

But the world's most populous nation has successfully experimented with the weakening of paternal authority, without weakening social cohesion. In fact, Mao thought the two things were opposed in a communist state.

Nonetheless, the old patriarchal model outlived Mao. Many Chinese women, particularly in rural areas, remain second-class citizens, with limited autonomy and economic rights (as are many western women, let alone those in Middle Eastern and developing countries). Some Marxists would say this was inevitable in attempting to make political changes prior to economic ones.

Mao himself predicts that even after both the countrywide victory of the Chinese revolution and the solution of the land problem, two basic 'contradictions' would still exist in China, threatening to undermine the revolution. The first would be the 'internal contradiction', that is, between the working class and the bourgeoisie. The second would be the external one, that is, between China and the 'imperialist' countries. As far as the internal contradiction goes, Mao, like Plato (and the Soviet Union) was unrelenting towards anyone identified as a class enemy – or 'liberal'. A ' people's democratic dictatorship' using censorship to control thought patterns is advocated enthusiastically, in the interests of the well-being of the state as a whole.

For instance, to arrest, try and sentence certain counter-revolutionaries, and to deprive landlords and bureaucrat–capitalists of their right to vote and their freedom of speech for a specified period of time – all this comes within the scope of our dictatorship.

The second function of the dictatorship is to protect the country from 'subversion' and possible aggression by external enemies, to resolve the 'external contradiction'. The aim of this dictatorship is 'to protect all our people so that they can devote themselves to peaceful labour and build China into a socialist country with a modern industry, agriculture, science and culture'.

But post-Mao, China is flirting with competition, entrepreneurship and profit, all of which it tries to include in the definition of 'socialism'. Yet the question remains whether this is possible or whether in fact the forces of the 'free market' once unleashed will bring the whole edifice of socialism crashing down. As the third millennium – China's fifth millennium – begins, voices are increasingly predicting the end of the Maoist experiment, and that Chinese communism will merge seamlessly into western-style capitalism. But such predictions were being made even at the communist state's founding. This is why the Red Book warns that if:

the landlords, rich peasants, counter-revolutionaries, bad elements and monsters were all allowed to crawl out, while our cadres were to shut their eyes to all this ... were to collaborate with the enemy and were corrupted, divided and demoralised by him, if our cadres were thus pulled out or the enemy were able to sneak in, ... then it would not take long, perhaps only several years or a decade, or several decades at most, before a counter-revolutionary restoration on a national scale inevitably occurred, the Marxist–Leninist party would undoubtedly become a revisionist party or a fascist party, and the whole of China would change its colour.

To forestall this, the 'people's democratic dictatorship', from its inception, must use two methods. Towards internal enemies, it must use the method of dictatorship, that is, 'for as long a period of time as is necessary', such citizens cannot take part in political activities and are compelled 'to obey the law of the People's Government and to engage in labour and, through labour, transform themselves into new men'. Towards the rest of the people, on the other hand, it uses not compulsion but 'democracy', that is, political activities and persuasion through education. Of course, there is a contradiction here (the people are both the enemy and the partners), resolved, it would appear, by the whim of the rulers.

Art and culture are part of this process of education and persuasion. The Red Book explains:

in the world today all culture, all literature and art belong to definite classes and are geared to definite political lines. There is in fact no such thing as art for art's sake, art that stands above classes or art that is detached from or independent of politics. Proletarian literature and art are part of the whole proletarian revolutionary cause; they are, as Lenin said, cogs and wheels in the whole revolutionary machine.

The literary and art workers must gradually move over to the side of the workers, peasants and soldiers, to the side of the proletariat, through the process of going into their very midst and into the thick of practical struggles and through the process of studying Marxism and society. 'Only in this way can we have a literature and art that are truly for the workers, peasants and soldiers, a truly proletarian literature and art.'

There is a political criterion and there is an artistic criterion, and they are related. Even if politics 'cannot be equated with art, nor can a general world outlook be equated with a method of artistic creation and criticism'.

In another well-known passage, Mao outlines the cultural policy:

What we demand is the unity of politics and art, the unity of content and form, the unity of revolutionary political content and the highest possible perfection of artistic form. Works of art which lack artistic quality have no force, however progressive they are politically. Therefore, we oppose both the tendency to produce works of art with a wrong political viewpoint and the tendency towards the 'poster and slogan style' which is correct in political viewpoint but lacking in artistic power. On questions of literature and art we must carry on a struggle on two fronts ... Letting a hundred flowers blossom and a hundred schools of thought contend is the policy for promoting the progress of the arts and sciences and a flourishing socialist culture in our land.

Different forms and styles in art should develop freely and different schools in science should be allowed to 'contend' freely. Mao even warns that it will be harmful to the growth of art and science if administrative measures are used to impose one particular style of art or school of thought and to ban another. Questions of right and wrong in the arts and science should instead be settled through free discussion in artistic and scientific circles and through practical work in these fields. They should not be settled in summary fashion. Indeed, 'An army without culture is a dull-witted army, and a dull-witted army cannot defeat the enemy.'

This brings us to the Red Army. Orthodox Marxist theory made the army the chief component of state power. Whoever wants to seize and retain state power needed to have a strong army. In Plato's *Republic*, the auxiliaries or army took very much second place in the social hierarchy to the policy group – the Guardians, or philosophers. In China, the army continues to be held in higher esteem even than the party. In part, this is because the army is also 'the Guardian'. In part it is because, like Plato's auxiliaries, it is kept to a clearly defined role and (ideally) encroaches neither on the material interests of the people, nor on the political interests of the Party, whilst playing a role in both. During the building of the new People's Republic, the army led the way in 'socialist production' and agriculture, eagerly shouldering additional burdens.

Even so, the richest source of power to wage war lies in the masses of the people. It was mainly because of the unorganised state of the Chinese masses that Japan dared to bully China, the Red Book says. When this defect was remedied, then the Japanese aggressor, 'like a mad bull crashing into a ring of flames', was surrounded by hundreds of millions of Chinese people standing upright; 'the mere sound of their voices struck terror into him, and he was burned to death'.

History shows that wars are divided into two kinds, just and unjust. All wars that are progressive are just, and all wars that impede progress are unjust. We Communists oppose all unjust wars that impede progress, but we do not oppose progressive, just wars. Not only do we Communists not oppose just wars, we actively participate in them.

War, 'the highest form of struggle for resolving contradictions', is needed when these have developed to a certain stage. Whether between classes, nations, states or political groups, this war has existed ever since the emergence of private property and of classes (as Hobbes put it too). In one of Mao's celebrated aphorisms, 'Every Communist must grasp the truth, "Political power grows out of the barrel of a gun".' Revolutionary war is an antitoxin which 'not only eliminates the enemy's poison but also purges us of our own filth'. Every just, revolutionary war is endowed with tremendous power, which can transform many things or clear the way for their transformation. This is because although weapons are an important factor in war, the decisive one is people. The contest of strength is not only a contest of military and economic power, but also a contest of human power and morale.

However, Maoists advocate not so much the 'omnipotence of war' as the omnipotence of revolutionary war. War itself is a 'monster of mutual slaughter among men', and would eventually be eliminated by the progress of human society. But there is only one way to eliminate it surely: more war. By opposing counter-revolutionary war with revolutionary war, counter-revolutionary class war with revolutionary class war ... then, 'when human society advances to the point where classes and states are eliminated, there will be no more wars, counter-revolutionary or revolutionary, unjust or just; that will be the era of perpetual peace for mankind'.

In practical terms, this view of war as evil, as opposed to the fascist and 'romantic' notions of war as 'joy in destruction', the purest form of action, means communists must 'endeavour to establish normal diplomatic relations, on the basis of mutual respect for territorial integrity and sovereignty and of equality and mutual benefit, with all countries willing to live together with us in peace'.

People all over the world are now discussing whether or not a third world war will break out. On this question, too, we must be mentally prepared and do some analysis. We stand firmly for peace and against war. But if the imperialists insist on unleashing another war, we should not be afraid of it. The First World War was followed by the birth of the Soviet Union with a population of 200 million. The Second World War was followed by the emergence of the socialist camp with a combined population of 900 million. If the imperialists insist on launching a third world war, it is certain that several hundred million more will turn to socialism, and then there will not be much room left on earth for the imperialists.

But aggressive military power is not necessary. One day it is also likely that the 'whole structure of imperialism will utterly collapse'. It is inevitable as all reactionaries, like their bombs, are 'paper tigers'. In appearance they are terrifying, but in reality they are not so powerful. 'From a long-term point of view, it is not the reactionaries but the people who are really powerful.'

In past history, before they won state power and for some time afterwards, the slave-owning class, the feudal landlord class and the bourgeoisie were vigorous, revolutionary and progressive; they were real tigers. But over time, as their opposites – the slave class, the peasant class and the proletariat – grew in strength, struggled against them and became more and more formidable, these ruling classes changed step by step into the reverse. They changed into reactionaries, into backward people, into paper tigers. And eventually they, in turn, were overthrown, by the people.

The 'reactionary, backward, decaying classes' retain this dual nature even in their 'last life-and-death struggles against the people'. On the one hand, they were real tigers; they ate people, ate people by the millions and tens of millions. Destroying the rule of imperialism, feudalism and bureaucrat capitalism in China took the people more than a hundred years and cost them tens of millions of lives before the victory in 1949. These were indeed fearsome, living tigers, iron tigers, real tigers. 'But in the end they changed into paper tigers, dead tigers, bean-curd tigers.' As for Taiwan, the Lebanon and all the other military bases of the United States on foreign soil, these are

just so many nooses round the neck of US imperialism. The nooses have been fashioned by the Americans themselves and by nobody else, and it is they themselves who have put these nooses round their own necks, offering the ends of the ropes to the Chinese people, the peoples of the Arab countries and all the peoples of the world who love peace and oppose aggression. The longer the US aggressors remain in those places, the tighter the nooses round their necks will become.

For imperialism cannot last long, as it always does evil things. 'It persists in grooming and supporting reactionaries in all countries who are against the people, it has forcibly seized many colonies and semi-colonies and many military bases, and it threatens the peace with atomic war.' Thus, forced by imperialism to do so, the vast majority of the people of the world either are rising up or will soon rise up in struggle against it.

By riding roughshod over everything, the Red Book warns presciently, the United States must make itself the enemy of the people of the world and end up increasingly isolated. Mao is equally prescient when he looks ahead to the turn of the millennium. Writing in 1956, he predicts an industrial Utopia and a new powerful China.

It is only forty-five years since the Revolution of 1911, but the face of China has completely changed. In another forty-five years, that is, in the year 2001, or the beginning of the twenty-first century, China will have undergone an even greater change. She will have become a powerful socialist industrial country. And that is as it should be. China is a land with an area of 9,600,000 square kilometres and a population of 600 million people, and she ought to have made a greater contribution to humanity. Her contribution over a long period has been far too small.

Yet the Chinese *should* be modest – not only now, but 45 years hence as well. 'We should always be modest. In our international relations, we Chinese people should get rid of great-nation chauvinism resolutely, thoroughly, wholly and completely.'

China still follows the 'modest' policy. It is deeply engrained in Chinese values and long pre-dates Mao. The extent to which Mao himself managed to do this is debatable, but certainly for many of the early years he maintained a virtuous model of simplicity and abstinence. He was famous for only having clothes with patches, and when clothes could no longer be patched, for cutting them up to make the patches themselves.

In a review of economic policy worthy of Adam Smith, 'Building our Country through Diligence and Frugality', the little Red Book advises: 'Diligence and thrift should be practised in running factories, shops and all state-owned, co-operative and other enterprises. The principle of diligence and frugality should be observed in everything. It is one of the basic principles of socialist economics.'

Yet, towards the end of the Red Book, Mao sighs that 'it seems as if Marxism, once all the rage, is currently not so much in fashion'. His solution then was that communists needed to redouble their ideological and political work. Both students and intellectuals would have to study harder. In addition to their specialised subjects, they would have to progress ideologically and politically, through studying Marxism, current events and politics. For not 'to have a correct political orientation is like having no soul'.

There is only one way forward. What Maoism has to offer to the young people, in particular, is a tempting recipe entitled:

SELF-RELIANCE AND ARDUOUS STRUGGLE

THE SUBTEXT

Mao Zedong, for all his later obsessions, delusions, excesses and cruelties, left a legacy of commitment to the rights of the rural poor and to women, and set new minimum standards for education and health across the 'developing' world. By addressing himself to the uneducated, agrarian poor, Mao also changed the perception of class struggle and society in both communist and non-communist societies. And certainly, without Maoism, the Japanese fascist party would have remained transcendent in Asia, whatever reverses in Europe the fascists might have suffered.

As to Mao's place in history, Quan Yanchi, Mao's personal bodyguard for many years, relates a curious incident that took place in the mid 1950s. It arose after Mao was overheard by his personal physician reading poetry to himself. The doctor asked the name of the writer and was told it was Cao Cao, an ancient ruler of China. Because Cao Cao was generally despised as 'a bad man with a hideous face', the doctor expressed surprise. This caused Mao to become very agitated, and he rushed to correct what he felt to be an unfair assessment of a historical figure. In fact, he launched upon a vehement defence of the unloved ancient, saying he had unified the most important region of China, clipped the wings of the powerful, encouraged the peasants to open up more land and boosted production, all the while strengthening the rule of law and counselling frugality. Cao Cao achieved all this, said Mao, whilst the country was recovering from the ravages of war. 'Wouldn't you call that great?' Mao challenged his doctor. Yet the 'men of letters', with their 'orthodox views', had destroyed Cao Cao's name and reputation. Perhaps, then, the same is true for Mao.

KEY IDEAS

Mao declares that 'the history of mankind is one of continuous development from the realm of necessity to the realm of freedom'. This is an old story, seen in Marx and Hegel and earlier philosophers. But Mao changes the emphasis significantly. The process is never-ending; as in any society in which classes exist, class struggle is inevitable. Even in the long-awaited classless society, the struggle 'between the new and the old and between truth and falsehood' will never end. In the 'fields of struggle for production and scientific experiment' progress is continuous and nature undergoes constant change. Things never remain at the same level.

- Education and democracy are inseparable.
- In politics, indeed in all areas of life, nothing is either all positive or all negative.

Where western theorists see a linear progression, with single causes leading to single effects, Mao sees complexity and relationships: the eastern conception of the great interplay of positive and negative, yin and yang, added to a western notion of simple cause and effect. Maoism hints at a 'third way' between communism and capitalism, which is what the Chinese government today is still seeking to explore. On their success or failure hinges more than the Chinese political system.

KEY TEXT

Mao's *Quotations from Chairman Mao Tse-Tung* (the 'Red Book') (1945)

Timeline:
From Atom Bombs to
the Triumph of Capitalism

1945
The 'Enola Gay', the affectionately named US Air Force bomber, drops 'Little Boy' on Hiroshima, bringing about the largest single mass killing in human history – and the unconditional surrender of the Japanese.

1948
The United Nations adopts the Universal Declaration of Human Rights. The World Health Organisation is set up. NATO is founded to defend the west. COMECON is set up by the USSR and Eastern European satellite states.

1949
Mao finally drives the rump of the Nationalist armies, led by Chiang Kai Shek, off the mainland to Taiwan and announces the new People's Republic.

1950
The Korean War starts, to end in US humiliation, mainly due to China's support for the Koreans.

1952
The first contraceptive pills are produced. This heralds a time of social and sexual liberalisation.

1954
The US Supreme Court rules that racial segregation in schools is unconstitutional. A year later, the black inhabitants of Montgomery boycott the segregated city buses, winning further concessions.

1955

The Warsaw Pact is established to replace COMECON, in the year of the death of Stalin. For four decades the world will be divided between two distinct blocs of influence.

1957

The European Common Market is established, but the United Kingdom is not part of it, busy instead detonating its own H-bomb on Christmas Island. The Russian sputnik alarms the United States into a 'space race'.

1958

Mao's 'Great Leap Forward' proves disastrous as agrarian reform leads to famine. Ten years later the Cultural Revolution, an equally disastrous 'back to basics' campaign, results in anarchy and random murder.

1959

Fidel Castro overthrows the Batista government in Cuba and sets about reforming the sugar plantations. Two years later a US invasion at the Bay of Pigs is a fiasco, but John F. Kennedy manages to win the showdown of the missile crisis the following year.

1961

Yuri Gagarin becomes the first man in space.

1969

Neil Armstrong is the first man on the moon. Buzz Aldrin is the second. The Soviet Union is not even in sight. The west has won the race – and not just for the moon.

Epilogue:
The End of History?

Is society proceeding slowly but surely towards a final Utopia – or towards an equally final cataclysm? Or are we following only a random and unpredictable process of change? Could slavery, mass famine, even human sacrifice, be part of the future as well as the past?

Most of the political philosophers seem to discern a pattern to history, and usually a positive one, generally putting great store by the apparently consistent and cumulative effects of technology. After all, once invented, few things are uninvented, at least, few things which find a profitable market. Yet, if political society is about the well-being of the people, the progress seems to be less clear. The poverty and despair of past epochs seem to change form, never to disappear. Indeed, Rousseau's noble savage may well have been a happier fellow than today's suburban clock watcher or mortgaged wage slave, let alone the unemployed or imprisoned.

It is true, if rather politically suspect, to say that in *material* terms there has been some kind of steady progression, if not progress, in the quality of human lives in almost every region of the world. Even in the eighteenth century, Adam Smith marvelled at the standard of living of the typical European worker, as compared to the property-less serfs and villeins of earlier times. How much more so should we marvel at the access to goods and indeed services – health, education – that pass almost unremarked today. This is the justification for political society in the liberal democracies that have spread over the globe. Yet the material progress is uneven, and access to it remains largely determined by birth. The wealth gap between the richest and the poorest – both societies and citizens – is increasing by leaps and bounds.

In the 20 years after 1960, the richest fifth of the world's societies increased their share of the overall cake from most of it to nearly all of it – from 70 per cent to 82 per cent. For the poorest 50 or so countries (with a fifth of the world's population) that left just 1.5 per cent of world income. In the following 20 years, the trend has, if anything, accelerated.

In all liberal democracies, despite Mill's warnings, power is still largely inherited. You even have what is at best the absurdity, and at worst the obscenity of 'political families', like the po-faced Bushes, the ill-fated Kennedys and the shiny Clintons in the United States, or the enduring tradition in the United Kingdom of political con-stituencies being handed on by retiring legislators to relatives or protégés. Then there are the media families, where the showbiz personality of one generation is the son or daughter of a showbiz parent, and the celebrated authors whose parents (it turns out) are also media icons with well-connected agents. Not to forget, of course, the commonplace but not at all 'liberal' passing on of ever more gigantic industrial and commercial empires, some of them the size of small nations. It was this principle of inheritance that Mill himself specifically condemned as particularly unjustifiable – yet it has become the unchallenged cornerstone of modern capitalism. Similarly, while classical liberalism insists on the equality of the sexes, the International Labour Organisation calculates that two-thirds of women's work is unpaid – and that on top of this, women work one-sixth harder than men. In much of the world, from wealthy Switzerland to westernised states like Saudi Arabia, women are denied basic voting rights and economic rights to work, to health care and education.

And if, in the 25 years since the first man on the moon, global life expectancy did indeed rise (from 53 to 62 years; and infant mortality rates fell, from 110 per thousand children born, to 73 per thousand, even if regions such as sub-Saharan Africa defied the trend, suffering dramatically deteriorating conditions), behind the overall and real improvement is a corresponding reality of the continuing direct relationship between health and wealth. In the richest countries life expectancy is now 78 years, in the poorest, 43 years – and the gap is widening.

Then within countries there are equivalent contrasts. In rich, white Australia, life expectancy now is fully 30 years longer for the 'settlers' than it is for the indigenous Australians, expelled to squalid camps on the fringes of a hi-tech, consumer society. In Brazil, the affluence of the new 'middle classes' (which challenges Marxist theory) still has to be set against the illness, crime and poverty of some 120 million people – out of a total population of 153 million. Even in the richest countries, like the United States, a large 'underclass' remains in the shadow of unprecedented material prosperity. These are underclasses living in conditions of poverty, sickness – even of massacres – that

seem completely incompatible with the veneer of modern sophistication. As a result, at the start of the third millennium there are now
more people in the world than ever before – it is estimated at 100
million – who are actually disabled as a result of extreme poverty or
avoidable disease. Not for them the opportunities of laissez-faire.

Liberalism also says that people are equal in the eyes of the law.
Yet it was only in 1957 that the US Civil Rights Act moved to enforce
desegregation, outlawing 'separate but equal' facilities for non-white
Americans. Nor did the Act truly herald a new approach to this disease
of society. So it is that, at the end of the twentieth century, American
blacks were still three times more likely to be living in poverty than
their white fellow citizens. Average income for a non-white family
was less than two-thirds that of a white family. A similar story can be
read in those long-established liberal democracies, Australia, Canada
and New Zealand.

If, at one level, Israel is liberal, democratic and successful, at
another level, apartheid lives on as Palestinians are institutionally
denied basic rights, such as rights to work, to travel and even to live
in certain areas. In recently democratic Russia, with its 'constitution'
and its Parliament elected by universal suffrage, in reality there is not
even the right not to vote – those failing to support the new president
have to be prepared to risk being physically attacked or sacked for
their independence. Liberal democracy in many countries does not
preclude torture, state assassination of opponents, or wholesale
destruction of homes and property – even as the west celebrates
such countries as members of the same club.

In recent years, the comfortable assumptions of liberal democracy
have been challenged on the political level, not just by the resurgence
of nationalism and racism, in countries like Serbia and Russia, but also
(and this is even more incomprehensible to those who see the world
in terms of an inexorable philosophical progression) the resurgence of
medieval dogmas and resolutely irrational belief systems, exemplified
by the interpretations of Islam of conservative oligarchies such as
Saudi Arabia, Egypt and Iran. In these states, the masses, far from
resenting their political disenfranchisement, seem to have examined
the political model of the industrial democracies, with its promises,
as the American Declaration of Independence puts it, of inalienable
rights and a lifetime in the free pursuit of wealth, and preferred
instead to opt for a kind of new vassal status, subject to numerous
restrictions imposed by unchallengeable authorities.

But then, from another perspective, liberalism creates a weak society of grasping individuals, interested only in the satisfaction of their desires, the achievement of a comfortable, bourgeois lifestyle, lacking any sense of pride or dignity, living either a life of ultimately meaningless self-indulgence – or resenting the absence of such. If there is a fundamental contradiction in liberalism, it is that it celebrates individualism whilst, at the same time, it appeals to public spiritedness, self-sacrifice and consideration for others. Yet if, as Adam Smith assures us, we may rely on the self-interest of the butcher, baker and candlestick maker for the prompt delivery of meat, bread and candles, it is equally sure that the same calculations will not discourage them from tipping their rubbish in the local brook, let alone persuade them to keep up their deliveries if we're out of work and can't pay.

The 'neo-conservative' academic Francis Fukuyama (but there is not so very much 'neo' about his theory) predicted in his popular monograph, *The End of History* (1993) that the tide towards liberal democracy was inevitable and unstoppable. He carefully tabulated all the newly overthrown dictatorships and praised the spread of the new American-sponsored enlightenment. Yet nothing is ever so simple, and particularly not when talking about human society. Not for nothing did Karl Popper dedicate his 1957 book, *The Poverty of Historicism*, to 'the countless men and women of all creeds or nations or races who fell victims to the fascist and communist belief in Inexorable Laws of Historical Destiny'. Popper considered such attempts to be the result of misguided efforts to apply the techniques of science to society, instead of merely noting the effects of certain historical changes in social policy, in the manner of Machiavelli, Rousseau, and many others. Popper, being an Austrian, and writing in the aftermath of the Nazi *Anschluss* of his country, is particularly aware of the tendency of democracies to slide towards totalitarianism. This, he thinks, can be explained by the idealism of the Platonists: by advocating the rule of the wise, the just or simply the best, they invite tyranny. In *The Poverty of Historicism*, he argues that an 'open society' concentrates on constructing neutral institutions instead, allowing for the peaceful displacement of any political grouping which becomes too attached to power.

As to the historicists, Popper considers it simply not possible for us to 'observe or describe a whole piece of the world, or a whole piece of nature'. In fact, not even the smallest whole piece may be so described, since all description is necessarily selective. It may even be said that 'wholes ... can never be the object of any activity, scientific or otherwise'. John Stuart Mill flatly put it: one problem with deconstructing history by using rules is that the task is so complex that it cannot 'possibly be computed by human faculties'. The historicists overlook this, and operate with trends as if they were in fact laws; for example, believing in the inexorability of *progress*. *The Poverty of Historicism* concludes:

Modern historicists, however, seem to be unaware of the antiquity of their doctrine. They believe – and what else could their deification of modernism permit? – that their own brand of historicism is the latest and boldest achievement of the human mind, an achievement so staggeringly novel that only a few people are sufficiently advanced to grasp it.

Many political philosophers, indeed many politicians, believe that they have unravelled one of the oldest problems of speculative metaphysics, the problem our study started with, identified by Heraclitus and Parmenides – the problem of change. They believe that their advance is due to their living in a uniquely important period of history – one in which change has accelerated, revealing for the first time the revolutionary truth. But the reality is that the more everything changes, the more everything remains the same.

References and Sources
for Further Reading

As political philosophy is a broad discipline, with connections to psychology, social studies, community studies, history of ideas, economics and so on, any reading list is extremely limiting. However, the following may serve as starting suggestions.

GENERAL

Brenda Almond, *Exploring Ethics*, Blackwell, Oxford, 1998

R. Beiner, *What's the Matter with Liberalism?* University of California Press, Berkeley, 1990

Trevor Blackwell and Jeremy Seabrook, *The Revolt Against Change: Towards a Conserving Radicalism*, Vintage, London, 1993

Tom Burden, *Social Policy and Welfare*, Pluto Press, London, 1998

David Edwards, *The Compassionate Revolution*, Green Books, Totnes, 1998

Robert Eccleshall and others, *Political Ideologies: An Introduction*, Routledge, London, 1994

Francis Fukuyama, *The End of History*, Penguin, London, 1993

A. Gutmann, *Liberal Equality*, Cambridge University Press, Cambridge, 1980

F. A. Hayek, *The Constitution of Liberty*, Routledge, London, 1960

Karl Mannheim, *Ideology and Utopia: an Introduction to the Sociology of Knowledge*, Routledge, London, 1952

Robert Nozick, *Anarchy, State and Utopia*, Blackwell, Oxford, 1990

Karl Popper, *The Open Society and its Enemies*, Routledge, London, 1945 (fifth edition 1966)

Karl Popper, *The Poverty of Historicism*, Routledge, London, 1991 (first published 1957)

John Rawls, *A Theory of Justice*, Harvard University Press, Cambridge, Mass., 1971

J. L. Talmon, *The Origins of Totalitarian Democracy*, Mercury Books, London, 1961

John Thompson, *Studies in the Theory of Ideology*, Polity Press, Cambridge, 1984

And finally, there is Martin Cohen, *Philosophical Tales*, Blackwell, Oxford, 2008, which contains intriguing extra details on Confucius, Plato, Aristotle, Locke, Hobbes and others.

PLATO AND ARISTOTLE

Most of the quotes are easily found in any version of Plato's *Republic*. I have used *The Republic of Plato*, translated by Francis MacDonald Cornford,

Oxford University Press, 1941; other translators adopt different styles for the dialogues, and the *Collected Works of Plato* (various editions) is probably the best source for any study of Plato's philosophy. All editions adopt the same system of book and paragraph numbers, to indicate the precise location of discussion, using a traditional system.

For an account of Democritus and early Greek philosophy, see, for example, Jonathan Barnes, *Early Greek Philosophy*, Penguin, 1987, especially from page 277.

The discussion of 'justice' is illustrated with quotations directly from Plato's *Republic*. See, in particular: Book 2, page 373, where a theory as to the origins of society is put forward; Book 8, page 543; Book 7, page 337; Book 2, pages 377 and 378; Book 3, page 417, where the 'training' of the Guardians is described; Book 3, page 410, where 'temperance' is extolled; and Book 4, page 422.

On the 'deviant' states and their consequences, see, for example, Book 8, pages 546, 547 and 550.

For Aristotle's differing account of the essential nature of the state, see: the *Politics*, 1280, Book 3, and the *Nicomachean Ethics*, 1189, Book 4. Finally, the thoughts of Socrates in prison can be tracked down in the account of *The Last Days of Socrates*, edited by Hugh Tredennick in the Penguin Classics series (1972).

Further Reading on Plato and Aristotle

Plato (390–347 BCE), *Complete Works*, edited by J. M. Cooper, Hackett, Indianapolis, 1997 (also available in separate editions)

G. Grube, *Plato's Thought*, Athlone Press, London, 1980, and J. L. Ackrill, *Aristotle the Philosopher*, Oxford University Press, 1981 (both have accessible introductions)

CONFUCIUS

An accessible recent version is *The Original Analects: Sayings of Confucius and His Successors*, by E. Bruce Brooks and A. Takeo Brooks (published by Colombia University Press in 2001), while Arthur Estate's *The Analects of Confucius* is counted as something of a classic version, and was republished by Routledge in 2004.

MOHAMMED

The Project Gutenberg e-book text of the Koran is at http://www.gutenberg.org/etext/2800.

Several interesting books on modern Islam are also published by Pluto Press in its series *Critical Studies on Islam* (editors: Azza Karam and Ziauddin Sardar).

Islam and the Political: Theory, Governance and International Relations (Pluto 2008), by Amr G. E. Sabet, argues that Islam offers a 'serious alternative' to Western systems.

MACHIAVELLI

Machiavelli's works have always been popular, both as literature and as sociological and philosophical and political studies. There are again many translations, drawn largely from a version translated by Father Leslie Walker from Guido Mazzoni and Mario Casella's *Tutte le opere storiche e letterarie di Niccolò Machiavelli*, G. Barbera, Florence, 1929.

The page numbers below refer to these popular editions: the *Discourses*, edited by Bernard Crick, Pelican, 1970 and *Machiavelli's 'The Prince': Text and Commentary*, by Jean-Pierre Barricelli, Barron's Educational Series, New York, 1975.

For the note on Machiavelli's reason for writing books, see *The Prince*, page 29; on the nature of power, see page 102; on Catholicism and the state's relations with the Church, page 103. The infamous 'means justifies the ends' passage is on page 107; on the origins of society on pages 106–7; on justice, page 368; on the need for elections, pages 527, 388; on the need for pragmatism in politics, page 496 of *The Prince* and page 121 of the *Discourses*; on the conflicting interests of prince and people, page 276 of the *Discourses*; on the gullibility of the masses, page 239; on the need to please 'the mob', pages 112, 114, 268 and 477; and on the value of democracy, pages 116, 132, 280 and 347.

Further Reading on Machiavelli

S. de Grazia, *Machiavelli in Hell*, Princeton University Press, Princeton, NJ, 1989

HOBBES

Hobbes' *Leviathan* (original text 1651) is little read but frequently referred to. As a result, like *The Prince*, it is often misquoted.

The references in the text can be found in any standard text, but I have used *Hobbes' Leviathan*, edited by C. B. MacPherson, Pelican, London, 1968.

For Hobbes 'mechanistic' view, see page 81, page 119 and pages 29–30. The 'motions' leading to 'motivations' is discussed on page 150, including the well-known quote on the 'general inclination of mankind' on page 161 and the motivation of fear on page 163. (The 'origin of speech', crucial to social life, is discussed on pages 101–2, and 105–6.)

The 'war' of 'every man against every man' is around pages 185–6, and the nature of justice is discussed on page 188 as well as on pages 199 and 223. Hobbes' view that people are all more or less the same is on page 184, and the 'false belief' the founders of the commonwealth must implant is suggested on page 177.

The 'laws of nature' are introduced on page 188, and the 'contract' itself on page 192. Man's antisocial character is discussed around pages 227–8 and 234, where the 'Leviathan' is offered as a solution.

Technical and practical problems with the social contract are noted on and around pages 239–40, 269, 270, 328 and 348.

Further Reading on Hobbes

R. Peters, *Hobbes*, Penguin, Harmondsworth, 1956

D. Baumgold, *Hobbes' Political Theory*, Cambridge University Press, 1988

LOCKE

The quotes are from John Locke: *The True, Original Extent and End of Civil Government*, originally published in 1651. Page references where given are to the Penguin Everyman edition, *Two Treatises of Government*, edited by Mark Goldie, revised edition, 1993.

Locke's discussion of the 'State of Nature' is from the *Second Treatise*, and can be found especially on page 61, and the 'Law of Self-preservation' can be found on page 149, as well as on page 6; the importance of 'reason' in liberty is described on page 63.

Locke's vision of the thirsty man and the right to quench his thirst is on page 33, while the view of nature as conveniently there to be 'developed' is pursued on pages 39–40.

Locke's view of social security is produced in the *Second Treatise of Civil Government*, Part 1; see pages 42 and 95–6 in particular.

The 'Common Weal' is praised on pages 89, 92, 124 and 131, whilst what to do if this is not the motivation is considered on pages 233 and 241.

The Thomas Paine quotations are as indicated in the text. Readers may also be interested to see Mary Wollstonecraft's *Mary and the Wrongs of Woman* (1798) for a semi-autobiographical critique of political life in the late eighteenth century, as well as *Vindication of the Rights of Man* (1790) and *A Vindication of the Rights of Women* (Dent, London, 1992 – first published 1792) in which, after witnessing the excesses of the French Revolution, she has in mind to expose the limitations of Rousseau's philosophy.

Further Reading on Locke and Liberty

T. Jefferson, *Selections form the Writings of Thomas Jefferson* (edited by M. Prescott), Cambridge University Press, 1984

Thomas Paine, *Common Sense*, Dover Publications, New York, 1997

ROUSSEAU

The quotations in Chapter 8 are from Jean-Jacques Rousseau, *Discourse on Inequality*, edited by Maurice Cranston (Penguin Classics, 1984).

Rousseau's views on 'natural law' can be found on pages 60 and 69–70, where ignorance of man's nature is identified as a problem for social scientists and philosophers.

Hobbes' particular failures are noted on page 98, Locke's on pages 109 and 115, and Locke himself finally 'falls in ruins' on page 166.

Problems with 'social contract theory' are discussed on page 78, while the *noblesse* of the savage is remembered fondly on pages 82 and 145. The good life, being for Rousseau the solitary one, is praised on page 113, and the dangers of subjection to materialism described on pages 119–20 and 150.

314   Political Philosophy

The loss of liberty is condemned on page 37 and denounced again on pages 126 and 128.

The unpleasant fate of 'civil man' is described ominously on page 136.

Further Reading on Rousseau

R. Grimsley, *The Philosophy of Rousseau*, Oxford University Press, 1973

J. Shklar, *Men and Citizens*, Cambridge University Press, 1969

THE AMERICAN CONSTITUTION

There is no need to look hard for these documents. A reliable and accessible web site is ConstitutionFacts.com which includes historical and background information.

However, the site does not have much in the way of analysis. Instead, Pluto Press offers its own special perspective on US democracy in books like *Necessary Illusions: Thought Control in Democratic Societies* (1990) or *The Prosperous Few and the Restless Many* (2003), both by Noam Chomsky.

ADAM SMITH

All references in Chapter 10 are to Adam Smith, *An Inquiry into the Nature and Causes of the Wealth of Nations*, 1776. A convenient edition of this is the Pelican Classics edition of 1970, edited by Andrew Skinner.

As the book is heavily indexed by Smith, further referencing would be superfluous. Suffice to say, the most interesting part of the work is to be found in Book 1, where the origins of money, the division of labour and the nature of profit are dealt with. Book 2 looks at 'accumulation' and the relationship of capital and interest, whilst Book 3 is a series of observations on 'different nations'.

Further Reading on Smith and Economics

D. D. Raphael, *Adam Smith*, Oxford University Press, 1985

D. Hausman (editor) *The Philosophy of Economics: An Anthology*, Cambridge University Press, 1984

MARXISM

The references in Chapter 11 are all from the *Communist Manifesto* of 1848. The Penguin edition of 1967, translated by Samuel Moore, with an introduction by A. J. P. Taylor, is the one I have used below.

Marxism's fundamental proposition is set out on page 46. The 'spectre' haunts page 48, and a Hobbesian 'state of war' is described on page 49, all blamed, on page 51, on 'free trade'.

Capitalism's problems are sketched out on pages 52–4 and the prediction of the 'modern labourer' sinking ever deeper into pauperism is made on pages 60–1.

The warning not to wrangle over details is included on page 65 of the short pamphlet, and the 'programme' for the revolution is set out in bullet form on page 11.

Further Reading on Marx

Out of all the vast Marx catalogue, some of the most useful to look at are: the *Theses on Feuerbach*, on political philosophy in general; Volume 1 of *Capital*, for some Marxist economics; *The German Ideology*; and Engels' *The Condition of the Working Class in England*.

A good general work is *Marx: A Clear Guide*, by Edward Reiss (Pluto Press, London, 1997).

A good general work on Engels is from the Past Masters Series, *Engels*, by Terrell Carver (Oxford University Press, 1981).

Chuschichi Tsuzuki's *Life of Eleanor Marx, 1855–1898* (Clarendon Press, Oxford, 1967), *The Unhappy Marriage of Marxism and Feminism*, edited by Lydia Sargent (Pluto Press, London, 1981), and Hilary Rose's *Love, Power and Gender* (Polity Press, Cambridge, 1994) give different perspectives.

Selected Writings in Sociology and Social Philosophy (Marx), edited by Tom Bottomore and Maximilien Rubel (Penguin, Harmondsworth, 1963), gives the sociological perspective.

Finally, interesting and historically important is Vladimir Ilyich Lenin, *What is to be Done?* International Publishers, New York, 1969.

MILL AND LIBERALISM

Mill's writings are easily available in many editions. I have used the Penguin edition of Books 5 and 6 of *The Principles of Political Economy*.

The discussion of profits falling is on page 77, and of prices on page 88; the 'marvellous' inventions of the time are praised on page 57. The limits of utility are noted on page 307, and of government itself from around 308–11. *Laissez-faire* is examined on page 314, and education is praised on page 318. Women's rights appear on page 324, and the limits of charity conclude Book 5 on page 335.

Further Reading on Mill, Utilitarianism and Rights

Jeremy Bentham, *An Introduction to the Principles of Morals and Legislation*, Athlone Press, London, 1970 (first published 1789)

J. Waldron, *Nonsense Upon Stilts: Bentham, Burke and Marx on the Rights of Man*, Methuen, London, 1987

William Godwin, *An Enquiry Concerning Political Justice*, Penguin, Harmondsworth, 1976 (first published 1884)

THE SCIENCE OF SOCIETY

The quotations in Chapter 13 are from a number of works, as indicated in the main text.

Further Reading on Durkheim and Social Science

Emile Durkheim, *Rules of Sociological Method* (Chicago University Press, 1893) is the attempt to justify social science.

Durkheim's views on symbolism and society can be best seen in *Social Rituals and Sacred Objects* (1912), and his explanation of the social nature of the individual in *Precontractual Solidarity* (1893), both reprinted in *Four Sociological Traditions*, edited by Randall Collins (Oxford University Press, 1985/1994).

K. Thompson, *Emile Durkheim*, Tavistock, New York, 1982: an introduction and overview.

R. H. Tawney, *Religion and the Rise of Capitalism* (Penguin, 1926) on Max Weber: a scholarly if rather stodgy account of Weber's theory. Tawney traces medieval theories of social ethics through to an examination of the historical evidence for the relationship of capitalism and Puritanism.

Max Weber's long-winded theorising is summed up in just one work, the *General Economic History*, a series of lectures delivered late in his life, which, although less celebrated than *The Protestant Ethic and the Spirit of Capitalism*, is a much clearer account.

A very readable account of the role of mass marketing in manipulating the purchasing decisions of individuals can be found in J. K. Galbraith's classic work *The Affluent Society* (Penguin, 1999).

FASCISM

The Nietzsche quotes are from *Ecce Homo*, translated by R. J. Hollingdale (Penguin, London, 1979).

Nietzsche on 'the soul' and God can be found on pages 133–4; on women, on pages 75–6; and on the joy of war, on pages 81 and 111.

Nietzsche attacks the Germans for being common on pages 58 and 124, and describes himself as 'dynamite' on page 126.

A clear and readable account of Schopenhauer is to be found in Christopher Jannaway, *Schopenhauer*, Past Masters Series, Oxford University Press, 1994.

See Benito Mussolini, *The Doctrine of Fascism* (in Michael Oakeshott (editor), *Social and Economic Doctrines of Contemporary Europe*, second edition, New York, 1943) for more on the original fascist vision.

If you want to try some Hegel, a reasonable precaution is NOT to read any of the original works, but to stick to a secondary text, such as Peter Singer's *Hegel* (Oxford, 1983) or Francis Fukuyama's *The End of History* (Penguin, 1993). After all, no one agrees on what Hegel was really saying, so you may as well read an interesting adaptation – as Fukuyama's is.

Further Reading on Hegel and Nietzsche

G. W. F. Hegel, *Elements of the Philosophy of Right*, Cambridge University Press, 1991 (first published 1821)

R. Schact, *Nietzsche*, Routledge, London, 1985. A comprehensive survey of Nietzsche's philosophy.

The extracts from Nietzsche's 'notebooks' are taken from the useful collection, *Nietzsche: Writing from the Late Notebooks*, edited by Rüdiger Bittner, Cambridge University Press, 2003.

NAZISM

Mein Kampf is the authentic voice of Nazism, but to understand it, and its implications for today, is a very different matter.

Two interesting books (both published by Pluto Press) are *Understanding the Nazi Genocide: Marxism after Auschwitz* by Enzo Traverso (1998) and *Fascism, Theory and Practice* by Dave Renton (also 1998).

MAOISM

The quotes are all from the little Red Book, the text of which is available on the Internet, but otherwise only with difficulty in the west.

The book itself, however, is a collection of speeches and essays. In China, there are shops selling just Chairman Mao's thoughts, but here we must be content with a few web sites. Once there, try looking at:

'Revolutionary Forces of the World Unite, Fight Against Imperialist Aggression!' (November 1948) from the Selected Works; and 'On Coalition Government' (24 April 1945) from Selected Works, Volume 2.

The 'muddleheaded revolutionaries' can be found in a speech 'At the Conference of Cadres in the Shansi-Suiyuan Liberated Area', 1 April 1948.

The reality of class struggle is explained in 'Cast Away Illusions, Prepare for Struggle'; and in a speech at the 'Meeting of the Supreme Soviet of the USSR in Celebration of the 40th Anniversary of the Great October Socialist Revolution' (6 November 1957).

The 'poisonous weeds' of free speech are pulled up in a speech at the 'Communist Party's National Conference on Propaganda Work', 12 March 1957.

Democracy as a way of settling disputes is advanced in 'On the Correct Handling of Contradictions among the People', 1957.

The 'dual nature' of everything, and the 'paper tigers' of imperialist America are described in a 'Talk with the American Correspondent, Anna Louise Strong' in August 1946, whilst the importance of winning the battle for minds is stressed again in 'On Protracted War', May 1938.

The (Marxist) history of mankind is described in 'Premier Chou Enlai's Report on the Work of the Government to the First Session of the Third People's Congress of the People's Republic of China' (now that's something like a title), whilst 'On Practice', July 1937, sets out Marxist doctrine generally.

The 'frog in the well' is found in 'On Contradiction', August 1937, and the 'blindfolded man catching sparrows', in 'Rural Surveys', March and April 1941.

Lastly, the dinner party quote comes from an early 'Analysis of the Classes in Society', in 1926.

Further Reading on Chinese Marxism

A. Dirlik, *The Origins of Chinese Marxism*, Oxford University Press, New York, 1989

S. Schram, *The Political Thought of Mao Tse-tung*, Praeger, New York, 1963

Index

entries in **bold** indicate a major topic